THE TRUTH

A Nobody

Content

—◦∞◦—

Why This Book

First of all, the book was written because I was led to write it— not by man, but by God. God put this in my path and allowed me to accept His request and do something about it. This book is not about my promoting who I am. It is not about being successful or proud in any way. This book is to show one thing: that there is a truth, that no matter what circumstances you are in or who you are, there is a truth you can depend on and use to help you.

The reason for A. Nobody is because I am not important to this world in the grand scheme of things. I am neither famous nor rich in wealth. I am not popular or an idol. I am, in a sense, a nobody. If I were to die today, I would not be featured on the news. No one in the limelight of society would stop the presses to acknowledge my life. However, the truth is I am somebody to some very special people called my family. Although I am a nobody to the world, God showed me that I am *somebody* to Him. I will always be unique and like no other, forever and ever. The world vanishes, and the greatest on earth may be nothing in heaven. I am just an instrument being used to say that true peace is attainable in your life. This will only come from one place, through: God, Christ, and the Holy Spirit, all working as one in your life. I didn't write the truth, or design it, or follow it for most of my life.

I do not need my picture or name on this book, for the truth is written by God and Him alone. The money from the proceeds of this book will go to missions to declare to a world that the truth is here, the truth is ready, and the truth is yours, if only you will receive it.

Compared to most of the world, I am rich because I live in the United States. I have my freedom, an education, and a job. In the United States, I am not a very wealthy man; I am in the middle class, and to tell the truth, fleshly speaking, I would love to make millions on this book. I would love to put my name all over it and create fame for myself. That is the very reason my name is not on the book. That is why I am not accepting any money from the sale of the book, because those are not things that are synonymous with truth and Christ. The truth is pure and not created by humans. I am not perfect, and the things in this book I have written are not perfect. But what is perfect is the Scripture in this book, every single letter, word, and sentence, all the truth without flaw. Your job is not to agree with me or anyone else. Instead, your job is to know the truth, acknowledge the truth, and accept the truth. After all, when you don't have truth, all you have is a lie.

In Christ,

A. Nobody

Introduction

———∞∞∞———

Hello, I'm A. Nobody.

Who I am is not important, but what I am going to tell you is. There is only one thing in this world you can depend on every day, at every time, no matter who you are or what your circumstances may be at any given moment. The guarantee? There is such a thing as truth. Truth is something we all strive for and want more of because with it comes knowledge and power. We all want truth, but most of us only want it when it benefits us, or meshes with our plans in life. In fact, we even run from truth at times, especially when we know it is against us or something we have done. However, truth, when embraced, acknowledged, and sought after, will bring peace, patience, power, and prosperity. But when it is denied deceit, dishonor, and depravity always follow, and at the end of it all, as we all must die, this is the reason death occurs through sin. May all the words of this book be based on this truth as opposed to opinions— not *my* truth or *your* truth, but the truth from God, who says He is the Definer, the Giver, and the Essence of truth. As opinions change like the wind, truth will never sway or bend. It is constant for all, no matter what time, condition, or circumstance.

Some people will never read this book, for the truth is denied and rejected when it comes against a lie. However, we all know the truth exists; some just choose not to accept it.

Truth at its beginning is the foundation of all things; God, by definition, is truth.

May these words praise Your name, God, for the love You made, gave through Your Son, Jesus Christ, and give every day through the Holy Spirit to ALL who will receive. This book is dedicated to my grandmother, who showed me that truth is not only real and equal to us all, but is to be lived and not just spoken of.

Truth Defined

If we can define that there is a truth for all, we can then all be in one accord with what is acceptable and what is not in our society, our country, and our world, as well as by God. When this has taken place, it comes down to a choice of whether or not to follow the truth. At the end of it all, as we all must die, your choice will be evident. If this statement is proved accurate, we will all have to at least admit that the same truth exists for us all, and we are all judged by the same measure, by the only One who says He is perfect enough to judge us, God Himself.

Romans 14:11 says:

> For it is written, As I live, saith the Lord, every knee
> shall bow to me, and every tongue shall confess to
> God.

Before we get started, let's take a look at how Merriam-Webster
online defines the word "truth":

Main entry:

Pronunciation: \□trüth\

Function: *noun*

Inflected form(s): *plural* **truths** \□trü<u>th</u>z, □trüths\

Etymology:

> Middle English *trewthe,* from Old English *trēowth* fidelity; akin
> to Old English *trēowe* faithful — more at TRUE

Date: before 12th century

1 a *archaic* : FIDELITY CONSTANCY

  b: sincerity in action, character, and utterance

2 a (1): the state of being the case : FACT (2): the body of real things,
events, and facts : ACTUALITY (3) *often capitalized* : a transcen-
dent fundamental or spiritual reality

  b: a judgment, proposition, or idea that is true or accepted as true
    <*truths* of thermodynamics>

  c: the body of true statements and propositions

3 a: the property (as of a statement) of being in accord with fact or
reality

b *chiefly British* : TRUE 2

c: fidelity to an original or to a standard

4 *capitalized Christian Science* : GOD

— **in truth**

: in accordance with fact : ACTUALLY

CHAPTER 1

Nothing but the Truth, So Help Me God

——∞——

GOD SAYS HE IS TRUTH AND WILL NEVER CHANGE!

I will reference the Holy Bible in this entire book because it claims to be the truth in every way. Then we shall see if it can hold to that fact, for if it is false in one way, it is false in all. Many great Christian writers have said, and still say today, that some things we cannot understand about God and His ways. The reasons for life and the happenings that surround it are to be observed, but not questioned, as God is *God*, and who are we to ask such things. I am here to say that the truth has answers. When a child asks his father for guidance and direction without tempting him and asks in faithfulness, the father is pleased to answer and has the answers to it all.

Luke 11:9-13 states:

> [9]And I say unto you, Ask, and it shall be given you; seek, and ye shall find; knock, and it shall be opened

unto you. [10]For every one that asketh receiveth; and he that seeketh findeth; and to him that knocketh it shall be opened. [11]If a son shall ask bread of any of you that is a father, will he give him a stone? Or if he ask a fish, will he for a fish give him a serpent? [12]Or if he shall ask an egg, will he offer him a scorpion? [13]If ye then, being evil, know how to give good gifts unto your children: how much more shall your heavenly Father give the Holy Spirit to them that ask him?

So, let us go to where God says He began it all. **Genesis 1:1** states, "In the **beginning** God created the heaven and the earth."

When God made the heavens, He said He made them perfectly, including the seraphim, the cherubim, and the angels. This means God made Satan and the angels, including both the fallen and the obedient. Let us first decide (as if we could), before God even made man and woman, did God make a mistake from day one by creating something that would reject Him? If we find that God has mistaken anything in any way at any time, in the past or the future, then we have proved He is not perfect, and therefore we should not believe He is. The Bible says He is in *every* way without fault—and He always will be. Read these two Scriptures:

I am Alpha and **Omega,** the beginning and the ending, saith the Lord, which is, and which was, and which is to come, the Almighty.

Revelation 1:8

Be ye therefore perfect, even as your Father which is in heaven is perfect.

Matthew 5:48

So the question is, Can God's perfection still maintain itself by creating something that rejects Him? If God would have made us without free will, the ability to choose to love Him or to choose anything, for that matter, then would He have really made anything at all? Had God not created us with free will, we would just be objects, puppets whose every move He could and would control. But objects have no choices in life and are programmed to say and do whatever their programmers decide. Even though they may have different directions they can go in, the directions they go in are determined by what is programmed, not by free will, or choice. By God's making us in His own image, His perfection was complete by giving us a will to choose, a will to make our own decisions, especially when it comes to whom we will obey and whom we will follow.

As **Genesis 1:27** states, "So God created man in **his own image**, in the **image** of God created he him; male and female created he them."

With this ability to make our own decisions came our ability to decide whether to obey Him. Just as a child can decide whether to obey (I hope my boys pay special attention here), we can choose whether to obey. This is how we were made perfectly. While He made us all in His own image, He made us unlike anyone else. We are all unique, with many different characteristics. For instance, our fingerprints and our voices identify us and no one else from the past, present, or future. I could write a book completly on the differences in people, but broadly speaking, just look at the differences among races, countries, and men and women alone. He made us perfectly different so we would realize our place as His child, special and like no other.

This uniqueness is stated in Scripture. **Matthew 10:30** says, "But the very **hairs** of **your head** are all numbered."

Though we have many differences, God gave us all so many things alike. Examples are our emotions, such as joy, happiness, sadness, and anger. Also, He gave us all the same design, including eyes, lips, a heart, and a mind. He designed us after Himself, uniquely and exquisitely—and that, my friend, is the perfect creation made by a perfect God!

After He had done these things, God said that it was good. Read **Genesis 1:31**: "And God saw everything that he had made, and, behold, it was very good. And the evening and the morning were the sixth day."

Now, when Satan and a third of the angels rebelled, they were cast away from God, as **Revelation 12:9** and **Isaiah 14:12-21** state.

And the great dragon was cast out, that old serpent, called the Devil, and Satan, which deceiveth the whole world: he was cast out into the earth, and his **angels** were cast out with him.

Revelation 12:9

This did not take away from God's perfection or His perfect creation. It actually shows us that God made us having a choice whether to obey Him. Satan chose not to obey, and by rejecting God and His position, Satan got what he wanted from God: his separation from Him. Satan chose himself above God and all else. Still today, this is the difference between people who have given themselves to Christ, and people who have put themselves before Him. If you have chosen to deny Christ, you have chosen the flesh. If your choice is to accept Christ, then you have received the Spirit.

<u>John 3:6</u> tells us, "That which is **born of the flesh is flesh**; and that which is **born of the Spirit is spirit**."

God also says his desire isnone should perish. This is what **2 Peter 3:9** states:

The Lord is not slack concerning his promise, as some men count slackness; but is longsuffering to us-ward, not willing that any should **perish**, but that all should come to repentance.

Above all, He will grant you your request to be or not to be with Him, obey or not obey Him, want to spend or not spend eternity with Him. As He did with Satan and the other fallen angels, the Bible says He will cast you away from Him, for that will be your request and your desire, not His.

Let's get back to the perfection of His creation. When God made Adam and Eve, he made them perfect, according to <u>Genesis 2:25</u>, which says, "and they were both **naked**, the man and his wife, and were **not ashamed**."

They knew no shame, and they walked with God. God says He made Adam as He made all things, perfectly. But to truly be perfect, as we discussed, we must have the opportunity to choose—to choose what we will love, whom we will obey, and what kingdom we eventually will reside in for all eternity. God will not *make us* love Him or choose His ways, but He has done and will do all He can to draw us to Him.

Many of us can see this easily enough when we look into our own children's eyes. What significance is there if I make my child tell me he loves me? On the other hand, if he comes to me on his own and professes his love and admiration for me, the world will stand still for that. That brings tears of joy and gladness to a father or mother, which will overcome the sting of death itself.

Deuteronomy 11:1 says, "Therefore thou shalt love the lord thy God, keep his charge, and his statutes, and his judgments, and his commandments, always."

God is perfect and the only truth, not because that is my or your opinion, but because He remains constant, never changing. It is because God's Word says He is infallible and perfect in every way. He says He is the I AM, THE TRUTH. God's words have the power to create and cause actions. He said He spoke all things into existence, including the world and the entire universe. **Genesis 1:3** says, "And **God said, Let there** be light: and **there was** light."

When Jesus was in the Garden of Gethsemane, and the soldiers came to take Him away, He spoke the words "I AM," and the mighty soldiers and Pharisees as well as all those who came to take Him fell to the ground at His word.

God's statement is that He is perfect in every way, and His Word is without flaw. Because all around us we find heartache and pain, death and anguish, starvation and destituteness, the sick and the poor, it does not make His design any less perfect. It is what WE did that brought all these things upon us. Adam and Eve had none of these things when they were walking with God in His perfect creation. They brought these things upon themselves and unto the world when they chose to bring rebellion and sin through their disobedience. God gave them everything they needed; they were lacking nothing. But they listened to Satan and decided, as he had decided, that all this was not good enough; they wanted to be gods themselves.

God told them if they chose to disobey Him, they would die, and die they did. Satan told Eve, "Surely you will not die, and you will know good and evil and be as God is." Satan lied to Eve, yet he told her something that ended up being true. He said, "Surely you will not die," and they did not die instantly. As God spoke the real truth, when they ate the fruit, they became mortal in that they would know eventual physical death and immediate spiritual death.

Adam and Eve knew no death before this. They would have lived forever, as God said He intended. Also, Satan said, "You will be as God and know good and evil." Yes, they did now know both sides, but they had no power as God did. You see, Satan is the father of lies and the opposite of truth, yet he will use God's Word and leave something out or add something to it to change its meaning. Satan does this in our lives every day; he uses other people and many other things to take our eyes off the real truth, which is God's Word. He uses perverted priests, broken men of God, social gatherings, and, most of all, rule-based religion to change what God really wants to tell us. The Word of God is the only thing that we can be assured will never fail. His Word will not fail, not because I say this or you say that, but because God said it.

So what did God do when Adam and Eve were deceived and disobeyed? He clothed them, and put them out of the garden and out of His perfect creation. That is why we all suffer today.

At that very moment, all the vileness and atrocities entered the world. That is why we have all these wretched things as part of life—the sickness, the sin, the abuses of all sorts, and so on. But do not despair! The Bible says God made a way for those who would choose Him and obey Him to obtain His perfection. The best part about this is that God cannot be beat or outsmarted. Truth, real truth, 100 percent truth is unchangeable. God said Satan bruised the heel, but the Son would crush the head of Satan, and as Jesus died at the cross, He provided for us the bridge back to God and His perfect creation. God knew in the beginning that this would happen, but God's plan is as infallible as He says. God knew Adam and Eve would make the choice they did, and the consequences followed.

However, God made the way for us all to get back to His garden, and unlike Adam and Eve, we will not be placed there without it being our choice, not knowing good and evil. We who accept Christ and the sacrifice He gave, admitting our sin and putting Him above ourselves will have CHOSEN the good fruit and want to be with Christ. We will enter into the garden of eternity, where there is no sickness, shame, starvation, or wickedness. We can walk with God, knowing He made us and chose us, and we accepted. We will have chosen to receive Him, not denying the truth, and then His home becomes our home. Where He is we will be also. Don't we all long for a home, a place of peace and comfort, a place where our father will be and a family, whom we can love and will love us? Heaven is that place for all who want it! You just need to follow the truth, search for it, and it will find you.

CHAPTER 2

"I Didn't Do It! Why Am I Being Punished?"

—⊶⊷—

If you have kids, I dare say you have heard this one before. So why are we being punished for Adam and Eve's choice? Why are there sick, helpless children starving at this very moment who never did anything to deserve it? Why are some people's lives easier and better than others' (the silver spoon kids)? How does a perfect God allow this to happen? Why doesn't He just fix it all, as well as everything else that is wrong with this world? The answers to these questions can only come from God Himself, so let's ask, and see what He has to say.

Why am I being punished for Adam and Eve's mistake? we ask.

As an example, we can look at the reason a child is punished for his mother's or father's mistakes. As a child, I did nothing to deserve an alcoholic father. I never caused him to drink (at least not in the early years of my childhood). He brought his anguish and his addiction on himself. I deserved a dad like my friends had, one who would be there for me and guide me. I needed a dad who would hold on to me and show me what it means to be a real man. Why was I cheated because of his mistakes? That's just it,even though Adam and Eve brought this unto themselves, it is our problem now. We must now deal with the issues of our parents' mistakes. So how can I change what has already been done by those who are deceased? While I cannot change the fact that my father was an alcoholic, I can choose not to be one myself. Similarly, God says that even though Adam and Eve left us with these problems, He has made us a way back to Him!

Just read **John 3:16**:

For God so loved the world, that he gave his only begotten Son, that whosoever believeth in him should not perish, but have everlasting life.

God made it so one day we could be with Him for eternity, at peace with ourselves and with Him. Did this come at a price, or was it free? This came at the highest price possible—the price of sacrifice, and not just any sacrifice, but the highest Sacrifice. Not just any life, but the life of One who never sinned. Not just any father, but the greatest and highest Father. Not just any sacrifice, but a perfect Sacrifice, His only Son.

There is no greater love than a person's giving his or her life for another, but the ultimate sacrifice would be to give my son, a perfect son's life for another. That is sacrifice. What else could He do? What else could He give you that would be greater than that? When you stand before God one day, and you come up with all the arguments you can conjure up, it will all come down to God's saying He made a way for you, but you refused it. Is there a better way for us to get back to truth? Is there a better plan? I am sure God would have been open to listening to another plan, especially if it meant He didn't have to send His Son to die on a cross. The truth is there is not, and never will be, a better or more designed plan. If there could have been a better plan, there would have been. God did everything and gave everything to make a way back to Him for you and me. There will be no excuses when that day comes if you have not accepted the path He made; only remorse will remain.

Did God do this to His Son without permission? Jesus said this before the crucifixion:

> And he went a little farther, and fell on his face, and prayed, saying, O my Father, if it be possible, let this **cup pass** from me: nevertheless not as I will, but as thou wilt.
>
> Matthew 26:39

Jesus surrendered to his Father's plan, and because of this and this alone, God said our path to Him is made whole! The real question is, Are you on that path? God did this for everyone's life, whether he or she wanted it or not. The question is, Will you take it?

Many of us want God to see the kind of person we are, to be fair, and to realize we are generally good, at least better than most people. Here is the problem with that logic: God has gone well beyond fairness and instead has paid your debt in full through His Son. He has seen your works, and while you may be better than some, you're not as good as others, and we all fall short of the glory of God.

Isaiah 64:6 (NASB) states:

> For all of us have become like one who is [Isaiah 6:5] unclean, and all our [Isaiah 46:12; 48:1] righteous deeds are like a **filthy** garment; and all of us [Psalm 90:5, 6; Isaiah 1:30] wither like a leaf, and our [Isaiah 50:1] iniquities, like the wind, take us away.

No one person has ever lived a life of righteousness and perfectness except Jesus, who never sinned in thought or action. He is the only worthy One. He is *the* One who lived the perfect life with no blemish, not just in action, but also in thought. Take the time to reflect on your life and acknowledge your thoughts every day. Are they clean, without blemish? And what are your thoughts made of? Many of us have grand thoughts of others, especially the ones we love. We think good and blessed things when the world is pleasing us, but when we are not pleased, what happens? When we are around rude or obnoxious people, where do our thoughts go? When we do this and we are in these situations, we all see what our hearts and minds are really made of. They are made of ourselves, and what makes us, in our own opinion, acceptable and good enough.

Jesus was the opposite. You see, He lived for others, suffered for all, and died to make the way not for Himself, but for everyone else.

So let's get back to the redemption of our parents' mistakes and our own, for that matter.

This is God's mathematical formula:

Greatest sacrifice (A father's son's life) + A perfect sacrifice (Jesus) without force = Forgiveness (righteousness and peace with God)

You see, God will know no sin. He knows what sin is, just as light knows what darkness is. Sin is the absence of God, just as darkness is the absence of light. Darkness has no measure or weight. Darkness is nothingness, just as sin is the absence of God. When Jesus was coming to the end of His life on the cross, He said, "My God, why hast thou forsaken me?" This is in **Matthew 27:46**: "And about the ninth hour Jesus cried with a loud voice, saying, Eli, Eli, lama sabachthani? That is to say, My God, my God, why hast thou **forsaken me?**"

Notice that before and after this, Jesus had always called God His Father, or Abba, but at this time, He was His God. He said this because Jesus had to take on all the sin and shame of the world, and for the first time, God was separated from His Son. God will not let sin be a part of Him, as there will be no sin in heaven.

Revelation 21:4 says:

> And God shall wipe away all tears from their eyes;
> and there shall be no more death, neither sorrow, nor
> crying, neither shall there be any more pain: for the
> former things are passed away.

Death, sorrow, pain . . . these are the things sin causes in every way. Jesus was able to take on this sin because He was part man, born of Mary, and all God in spirit. The sin attached to Jesus in the flesh, and what happened then? Just as God said, all sin leads to death, even His own Son's.

Romans 5:12 tells us, "Wherefore, as by one man **sin** entered into the world, and **death** by **sin**; and so **death** passed upon all men, for that all have **sin**ned."

Did Jesus die on the cross? Yes, he did—but oh, the spirit did not die. The spirit, as the light, did penetrate death and darkness, and Jesus rose from this fleshly death, as light always has overcome darkness. Jesus overcame death for us all, and there is no physical body to be found. We can read about this in **1 Corinthians 15:4**: "And that he was buried, and that he **rose** again the **third day** according to the scriptures . . . ."

Recently, a TV newsman said if they found the bones and body of Jesus, it would be okay, and that we (Christians) could still be Christians and continue our religion. What a sad statement that was.

I will only believe in all or nothing. My soul depends on His perfection, on the fact that **He did rise from the dead and overcome death, for if He didn't, nor will I.**

Read **Romans 8:2**: "For the law of the Spirit of life in Christ Jesus hath made me free from the law of **sin** and **death**."

This is the formula we follow as children of God. It is not a changeable formula or law; it is solid truth. It is everlasting, just as 1 + 1 will always equal 2. That is truth and a fact, and it will always be.

When you have surrendered your soul to the living God, you are attached to Jesus and are dead to this world. You may live in this world and still be breathing its air, but you are not of this world any longer, according to **2 Corinthians 5:17**, which states, "Therefore if any man be in Christ, he is a **new creature**: old things are passed away; behold, all things are become **new**."

You are not only dead to the world with Christ, as He died, but because of this, you also will rise, as Christ rose. You see, if you are subject to one thing in Christ, you are subject to all. God based this not on what we have or have not done in our lives, but on what Jesus did in His life for us. Jesus came for a purpose, and His purpose was fulfilled to the perfect letter of the law.

Matthew 5:17 tells us, "Think not that I am come to **destroy** the law, or the prophets: I am not come to **destroy**, but to fulfil."

Is it so hard to believe that our God made a way for us to reach Him again and has made this way from the very beginning, before the first man was ever made? God knew the choice Adam and Eve would make, and He has prepared the way for us all back to Him. **We do not live in a perfect world, but we do have the means to obtain a perfect world and a perfect peace.**

Why should we not honor Jesus' death for this? We honor death every day when we praise our soldiers for fighting for us and for our country. We honor heroes for rushing into a building and saving a child.

We celebrate the greatest sacrifice of all, which is life for life, yet when it comes to God, we ignore His greatest Sacrifice of all— His only, perfect Son, who died for you and me. And through that Sacrifice, He is still today rescuing the lost, the sick, the helpless, and whomever will ask and receive.

Matthew 11:28 says, "Come unto me, all ye that labour and are heavy laden, and I will give you rest."

So why am I being punished for mistakes my parents made? The same reason my kids will reap what I have sown for them in many ways. Why is there sickness in the world on the innocent for no apparent reason? It is because we brought sin among them in this world, and we continue to do so every day with the choices we make, just as Adam and Eve did.

Why doesn't God just fix it all now and make everything perfect? God said He will do this, and He will be here with us as He reigns.

Read **John 14:3**: "And if I go and **prepare** a **place** for you, I will come again, and receive you unto myself; that where I am, there ye may be also."

God says He wants none to perish, not one. I'm so glad He did not come back the day before I gave Him my heart! **It is the souls He waits on, yours and mine.** The suffering, the pain, the sickness, the disease—as bad as these are in this world, YOUR soul is the reason. It is precious to Him, and He is asking and waiting for it. He hates what we have done with this world, His creation, but your soul is worth the wait, the suffering, and the death. The innocent who die, the innocent who's lives seem to be the worst of the worst in our world, they willgo directly to heaven. The babies who starve will never starve again for eternity. The children who are abducted, molested, and murdered will go to a place so peaceful and perfect that they will not have lost out on anything, but will have gained everything. **You see, life is what is changeable. Life on this earth is where circumstances lead to decisions, good or bad. However, God is unchangeable, regardless of the circumstances around Him. That is what makes Him righteous and true. Why does He let it continue? He lets it continue for YOU.**

CHAPTER 3

<u>What Is Truth?</u>

───❦───

B efore we get too far, let's get to the real question at hand: What is truth? Is it real? Can we measure it? Is it the same for us all? Can we all be so different and still believe there is something out there that every single person on the face of this planet, in heaven and in hell, can say is the same? Can we be sure it is the same, no matter what circumstances or situation we may find ourselves in?

To begin, I will tell you my experience with truth. As I was growing up in Columbia, South Carolina, my grandmother took on the responsibility of raising my older brother and me. I can remember, even when I was only five, I always knew she loved me. In all my years, I have never doubted her love for me. It was strange at the time because while she always told me she loved me, it was the other things that made her love real to me—real and factual. It was making me breakfast before school. It was rubbing my feet and back at night. It was the way she was always there. Though she was not necessarily saying or doing anything, it was what she represented in my life. It was the sacrifice she made for all the things she deserved, but gave to my brother and me instead. At that time in my life, she was what *truth* was to me.

As I grew older, I started to realize, as we all do, the situation I was really in. I had no father around (he was living, but not near us). I also realized my mother was in the same town but not living with us. My mother loved my brother and me very much and was a part of our lives; however, it is not the same when you're not living with your natural parents. Many of my friends realized this as well—that life was not perfect, and you better adapt. So that is what I did. My grandmother worked every day while I was at home with my great-grandmother. I spent most days going to elementary school and a good Baptist church, just like many other kids (at least in my world), and at that time in my life, that is what I thought the truth was.

My point in talking about my childhood is twofold. I want to share with you what I thought truth was. I also want to publicly express my gratitude to my mother and grandmother for their sacrifices. Thank you for indulging me.

The definition of "truth" pertains to my past in that many people believe the truth is only as real as what you believe personally— what your situation is, where you reside, how you live, what your history was, and what your values are today. This is evident in the numerous "religions" and the many cultures that make up the earth. We are all different, and we all have different values. We all grow up differently, and *your* truth is not necessarily *mine*. The question is,

Is that a correct statement? **Is your truth different from mine?** If this is true, we must say that there is no real guideline and that truth is based on happenings. It would be impossible to say that there is a common truth for us all. This question also was found in Jesus' days on earth, and is still a question we ask today.

In the Bible, there is an example where Jesus was about to be crucified. Pilate, the Roman judge over that area, felt obligated to sentence Jesus to death because of the pressure the Jews were putting on him. If a revolt was to happen and word got back to Caesar that Pilate could not control his people or the Jews, then he surely would be relieved of his duty one way or another. Neither Pilate nor his wife wanted Jesus to die. They felt He had done nothing to deserve this, and they did not want to be the ones to make this decision.

Let's take a look at **John 18:33-38**:

[33]Then Pilate entered into the judgment hall again, and called Jesus, and said unto him, Art thou the King of the Jews? [34]Jesus answered him, Sayest thou this thing of thyself, or did others tell it thee of me? [35]Pilate answered, Am I a Jew? Thine own nation and the chief priests have delivered thee unto me: what hast thou done? [36]Jesus answered, My kingdom is not of this world: if my kingdom were of this world, then would my servants fight, that I should not be

delivered to the Jews: but now is my kingdom not from hence. [37]Pilate therefore said unto him, Art thou a king then? Jesus answered, Thou sayest that I am a king. To this end was I born, and for this cause came I into the world, that I should bear witness unto the truth. Every one that is of the truth heareth my voice. [38]Pilate saith unto him, What is truth? And when he had said this, he went out again unto the Jews, and saith unto them, I find in him no fault at all.

In this story, Jesus makes a bold statement to Pilate, saying He represents the truth, and then Pilate asks, "What is truth?" What Pilate was saying to Jesus is that truth is not defined to us all, but we each must find our own truth. Just as I stated before, what many of us believe today in our world is that there is no real truth. We tend to believe that truth is based on the environment, and the history of what we, as individuals, have been taught and what society has taught us to believe. What is factual and what is opinion is wherever we are living and how we are taught while growing up. Many people believe that one person's truth and what he or she believes to be right and wrong are not the same as what everyone else should believe to be right and wrong. Many people believe that because we live in different cultures, and we are raised differently, we have different morals, so no one way is correct.

The problem with this worldly assumption of truth that Pilate and many of us have is **Jesus IS claiming He represents the only truth.** Jesus is saying He represents what truth is for us all, and it is not where you live, whether you were abused as a child, whether you are handicapped, or whether you live in poverty or richness or sickness. Jesus says He is the truth, and He came not only to tell us this, but also He lived it out in His life. If what He says is right, then we, as a world, can look to one place for the answers to life. No matter where we live, how we were brought up, or what our present circumstances are, we can all come together in one accord and say that Jesus is the only Way, not just to heaven, but the Way we should believe and live on earth.

John 14:6 says, "Jesus saith unto him, I am the way, the truth, and the life: no man cometh unto the Father, but by me."

Truth statement: If Jesus is the truth, then anything that contradicts Him is false.

"Truth" defined would be something that is not false. Truth has no flaw; it is inherently perfection. Truth is not an opinion; if it could change in any way from one person to another, it would be false. If truth is everything it is supposed to be, it has to have a formula, or it can and will vary. And if it varies, it becomes an opinion, not a fact.

To go a step further, let's use a formula to prove this. Proven mathematics is one of the things in this world that are undisputable. When we have proved an accurate mathematical statement, we build upon it. We do not dispute it because when it has proved itself, there is nothing to dispute.

Around the globe, we don't question whether $1 + 1 = 2$. The answer to this equation will always equal 2, no matter what. As long as you do not change anything about the position of the numbers, it will remain constant.

It is the same with Jesus' claim to be the truth. It doesn't matter who you are or what you ever become, Jesus remains the truth, and He is constant. You may say it in many different languages, but it remains the same, no matter where you may be in the world. As $1+1 = 2$ and remains the same, no matter what happens around it, such it is with Jesus.

If there is a real truth, a guideline that is the same for us all, and it never changes from the emperor of China to the cannibal in the Amazon, we must all face with certainty the FIRST of many truths.

Truth statement: We either live in truth, or we live for ourselves. We are living for one of these, whether or not we accept it is the question..

As **Matthew 6:24** says, "No man can **serve two masters**: for either he will hate the one, and love the other; or else he will hold to the one, and despise the other. Ye cannot **serve** God and mammon."

If you can either say you're living for God, or decide you do not have a relationship with God, you are better off than someone who thinks there is a grey area and God will be fair.

Revelation 3:15-16 tells us:

I know thy works, that thou art neither **cold** nor **hot**:
I would thou wert **cold** or **hot**. So then because thou
art lukewarm, and neither **cold** nor **hot**, I will spue
thee out of my mouth.

We all evaluate our lives, though some do so more than others.
We all look at what our lives have been, what they are now, and
what we want them to become. When you evaluate your life, what is
it about? Did you have a great home growing up, or did you suffer
mental or physical abuse? Did you learn that life was about you and
what you did for yourself, or did you learn that life was about doing
for others? We were all made in God's image, but we are defined
and formed by our surroundings and our past in many ways. When
you take the time to evaluate what your life has been and what it is
about today, will you say it has been about yourself, or will you take
comfort in being saved?

Our parents, schools, and most of the entire world teach us from
birth to do what? They have taught us to be independent. They have
taught us how to live without having to depend on anyone, and to
rely on ourselves. Many of us find comfort in this because we have
talents that are better than others'. We end up serving ourselves
better than the rest, and we move ahead at a greater speed. Look at
the world we live in. If you are the best, you get the riches and the
fame, as well as the glory. If you look better than others, you get
more attention. We are a world of self. The contradiction and the

problem with this self-serving ideology is God teaches us to rely on Him, and not ourselves, in every way.

Luke 10:27 says, "And he answering said, Thou shalt love the Lord **thy** God with **all thy heart**, and with **all thy** soul, and with **all thy** strength, and with **all thy mind**; and **thy** neighbour as **thy**self."

You see, God teaches to rely on Him first, to love thy neighbor as thyself next, and then we come into the picture. This is the reason so many people will never come to Christ or accept His gift of salvation. We don't want this grace through His death, or we feel we don't need it, or, most of all, we would rather keep our own lives than give them away.

However, John 12:25 tells us, "He that loveth his **life** shall **lose** it; and he that hateth his **life** in this world shall **keep** it unto **life** eternal."

At this point, many people will say, "I am a good person, and I do good things for people," or, "I am not a bad human being; how could a perfect God allow me to spend eternity in hell?"

Let's begin with this: For whom did you do those good things? Why did you help your neighbor, give to that charity, or help the needy? It's true, many people do great and marvelous deeds in this world for others. I especially can look at the famous people who have so much to give. They give and help and take pride in knowing they have used their success to help others. This fits the profile of a Christian person. But you have to ask yourself, *For whom am I doing this?* If God is not your salvation, you are doing this for yourself and no other. You do these things to tell yourself or make yourself believe you are righteous and good. You are caring and compassionate; you are a friend to your neighbor. The truth says if God and salvation aren't the reason for these works, it all comes back to YOURSELF. You are serving yourself, and there is no reward in that.

Just read **Isaiah 64:6**: "But we are all as an unclean thing, and all our righteousness's are as filthy rags; and we all do fade as a leaf; and our iniquities, like the wind, have taken us away."

Until you surrender your life to the One who created you, you live for yourself and not the truth. No matter how great you are as a person, or what good deeds you do or have done, when you die, your good deeds die with you.

J.'s Story

Let me tell you of a friend I have. Let's call him J. He was brought up in a middle-class home with brothers and sisters as well as parents, who raised him to be not only a good person, but also a Christian. They always went to church and were very close as a family. J. did not make the same mistakes other kids did growing up. He did not want to try new things like drugs, alcohol, and so forth. J. knew the Bible very well, and he stuck by the rules and commandments, as he was taught to do. When J. was in his early twenties, he realized something that changed his life forever. He realized that even though he had acted like a good person and lived a relatively good life, he was a sinner and needed redemption. So J.

gave his heart to Christ, and now his actions are not the result of a life of teaching from his parents and church, but are out of love for the heavenly Father.

We can learn from J.'s testimony. He shows us that we may live our whole lives just going through the motions of a "good and faithful Christian" with no reward. The truth is, without accepting Jesus as our Lord and Savior, we are, in fact, just going through the motions. Those who have chosen not to accept Christ find it easier to continue to sin because they are only accountable to themselves. This is why so many good people will go to a devil's hell.

CHAPTER 4

God, Did You Do the Best You Could Do?

———∞∞∞———

Truth statement: God gave His all and earned His name as God; with Him it is all or nothing.

Luke 10:27 commands us to love God: "Thou shalt love the Lord **thy** God with **all thy** heart, and with **all thy** soul, and with **all thy strength**, and with **all thy** mind; and **thy** neighbour as **thy**self."

As I stated, if truth is perfection, without a flaw, then so must Jesus be. What does that mean to me? It means that Jesus (the Son), God (the Father), and the Holy Spirit (the Comforter), as well as the Holy Bible, are perfect in every way, without blemish, or it is all false and will collapse upon itself. This means the Bible (The Word of God) is all right or all wrong.

The key to this is that if you are God's child and have been saved, whether you are a prince of England or a dishwasher in New York, you are just as important to God as anyone else. God is looking at you through what I call Jesus goggles. **It also means that we**

41

all have to get to salvation through the same Person. We may not get there by the same circumstances, but we will through the same man. We are all on the same playing field now, all being judged the same by the same Judge. You see, Jesus' death on the cross not only accomplished salvation for us all, but also made it possible for God to judge us all based on the same measure.

[9]I am the door: by me if any man enter in, he shall be saved, and shall go in and out, and find pasture. [10]The thief cometh not, but for to steal, and to kill, and to destroy: I am come that they might have life, and that they might have it more abundantly. [11]I am the good shepherd: the good shepherd giveth his life for the sheep. [12]But he that is an hireling, and not the shepherd, whose own the sheep are not, seeth the wolf coming, and leaveth the sheep, and fleeth: and the wolf catcheth them, and scattereth the sheep. [13]The hireling fleeth, because he is an hireling, and careth not for the sheep. [14]I am the good shepherd, and know my sheep, and am known of mine. [15]As the Father knoweth me, even so know I the Father: and I lay down my life for the sheep.

John 10:9-15

So no matter what you're surroundings are or what your circumstances may be at this time, salvation is the same for us all, and this allows God to judge us all righteously, under the same conditions. No one can say to God, "You judged this person differently than you judged me."

Notice I have not brought up fairness. Fairness is the basis of how we like to be judged. We like people to be judged based on their efforts and what they have done, good or bad. We will look at a man who has stolen money. Some say he is a thief and deserves punishment; others will say he was experiencing hard times and stole the money for his children to eat, and he deserves help. You see, we decide what is right and wrong based on circumstances, not on the law itself. Our courts are loaded down with cases with very smart and articulate attorneys. They decide the law based on how they present, not the actual act that was committed. Many murderers are released today on technicalities in our flawed legal system because we have no real truth; we only have our opinions. When someone describes things in a way that distorts the truth, we make decisions based on ourselves and what we think is right or wrong.

Why doesn't God operate like this? Why does He not judge each person for his own works or non-works? Then the ones who make it, make it, and the ones who don't, just won't. If God did things like this (fairly, we would say), then I am better than my neighbor. The ideology that I am not a bad person would seem to help many of us justify ourselves with God. The problem with this is if God did do it this way, we will not all be judged the same way. Each person would not have the same opportunity as the other. Every one of us would have different circumstances in this life that would need to be taken into consideration.

You see, through the death of God's only Son, who lived the perfect life without sin, God made it so that one Man accomplished and overcame all mistakes man could not overcome, such as not obeying the law, acting on temptation, and experiencing death, to name a few.

Romans 5:12 and 15 tell us:

[12]Wherefore, as by one man sin entered into the world, and death by sin; and so death passed upon all men, for that all have sinned: [15]But not as the offence, so also is the free gift. For if through the offence of one many be dead, much more the grace of God, and the gift by grace, which is by one man, Jesus Christ, hath abounded unto many.

Now that God gave His Son for us, He has done more than show fairness in His judgment; He has done more than look at our circumstances. He has done more than make us earn salvation. God has made it so He can judge us all equally under one circumstance because if we have broken the law in one way, we have broken it in every way. **Romans 3:23 describes this:** "For **all** have sinned, and

come short of the glory of God."

Now, the Bible says we are all judged on the basis of either accepting or rejecting Jesus Christ's death for us. That is the truth that will be the same for us all. This will set you free of the idea of who is a better person. God will judge us all based on more than fairness, more than equality. He will judge us based on our choice to receive His Son as our pardon for sin. His judgment and His righteousness in judgment could never be overturned because He has gone above and beyond. We are all judged under the same measure: Either we accepted His Son's death for our sins, or we did not.

So if this is true, what does it mean to give my all and receive Christ? Does that mean He also will give me His all? A man could ask Jesus to prove to him He was God's Son, and he would believe. Jesus would say, "You believe, and I will show you." Many of you will say now that Christianity is a "mind over matter" issue. You may say because we have found something we can hold on to, this is what changes our lives and makes us better as Christians. For us, it was God who got us through, but for someone else, it could be their job or their spouse that helped them to get better. Basically, it is the idea that because that helped you, great, but don't tell me it's the same for us all.

The problem with the "mind over matter" issue is that, as we just read, all are under sin, and all have fallen short. Not one is good.

If this is true, then we all need something to overcome struggles in this life, including our upcoming death and such struggles as lying, making mistakes, hurting others, abusing drugs, overeating, drunkenness, or whatever other issues you may face. These are all just symptoms of a greater problem. We will all continue to struggle in this life, no matter how many self-help books we read. The struggle is far deeper than quitting a bad habit or becoming a better person. We all have issues we fight within this life, and no matter who you are, the final result of all of them is death, as Romans 6:23 says: "For the wages of **sin** is **death**; but the gift of God is eternal life through Jesus Christ our Lord."

Many of these sins are our own doing, but some are given to us from our parents. I mentioned my father was an alcoholic before he died. I never once made him drink, yet I had to deal with the shame of having a father who, though he was an awesome dad when he wasn't drunk, was the worst father ever when he was. These things may have come from our parents or brothers or someone else, but they still are our problems now. God says He has a place where none of that exists, and He has gone to prepare it!

The Bible tells us this in John 14:2: "In my Father's house are many **mansion**s: if it were not so, I would have told you. I go to prepare a place for you."

No self-help mind over matter can do that. The Bible says God has made us for His pleasure and for His glory, for His family. He is not talking about the years we spend on earth; He is talking about eternity in heaven with Him. A hundred years on this earth can't compare to eternity. Yet it gives us a chance to choose or not to choose

Christ. So how do I give Him my all? The Bible says when you give yourself to God through the death of His Son, and you accept His Son's death as your sacrifice, you have given your all. The thief on the cross is a perfect example of this. Read this Scripture passage:

[33]And when they were come to the place, which is called Calvary, there they crucified him, and the malefactors, one on the right hand, and the other on the left. [34]Then said Jesus, Father, forgive them; for they know not what they do. And they parted his raiment, and cast lots. [35]And the people stood beholding. And the rulers also with them derided him, saying, He saved others; let him save himself, if he be Christ, the chosen of God. [36]And the soldiers also mocked him, coming to him, and offering him vinegar, [37]and saying, If thou be the king of the Jews, save thyself. [38]And a superscription also was written over him in letters of Greek, and Latin, and Hebrew, THIS IS THE KING OF THE JEWS. [39]And one of the malefactors which were hanged railed on him, saying, If thou be Christ, save thyself and us. [40]But the other answering rebuked him, saying, Dost not thou fear God, seeing thou art in the same condemnation? [41]And we indeed justly; for we receive the due reward of our deeds: but this man hath done nothing

amiss. [42]And he said unto Jesus, Lord, remember me when thou comest into thy kingdom. [43]And Jesus said unto him, Verily I say unto thee, Today shalt thou be with me in paradise.

Luke 23:33-43

The one thief got saved, and one did not. Neither one did anything in their lives to deserve paradise, but one will see it. There are three reasons one will see paradise, and the other will not. First, one admitted he was at fault and that Jesus was not. Second, he believed that Jesus was dying for him, and third, he believed Jesus was the Son of God and that Jesus was going to God's kingdom. You see, salvation has nothing to do with your works and everything to do with what Jesus did.

Now that we have discerned what the truth says about what I must give, or in this case receive, to obtain salvation, we ask what God says He will give us if we do. Will He give us His all in return?

God says His all is to adopt you and make you a child in His family. You become His child, and He becomes your eternal Father; he becomes your Dad.

Galatians 3:26 says, "For ye are all the **children** of **God** by faith in Christ Jesus."

Truth statement: You are either God's child, or you are not.

A lot of kids live on the street where I live. My wife and I try to treat these kids with respect and try to show them we care for their well-being. Sometimes they eat with us, and sometimes they even go on trips with us, but they know, just as we know, they are not our children. Even though I care for them, it is not the same way I care for my own child. You see, I am bonded to my children because I am solely responsible for them, whereas I am not for the other kids. This same principle applies with God. By accepting His Son's sacrifice and asking to be a son or daughter of Christ, you join the family. You become not only a child of God's, but a joint heir to all God has given Jesus.

Romans 8:17 tells us, "And if **children**, then heirs; heirs of **God**, and joint-heirs with Christ; if so be that we suffer with him, that we may be also glorified together."

I am a joint heir!

Yes, God does love everyone, and yes, His love for us all is the same. He says He wishes no one would perish. The problem is that those who choose their own way in life and do not need salvation are not part of the family. They don't want to be part of the family. As much as God wants these children to come, they must choose to come, and that fulfills true love through free will. You see, Adam and Eve were placed in the garden and chose to disobey, but when Jesus returns, it will be for those who chose salvation. **God does not** want to force His children to love Him; He wants them to *choose* to love Him. At the end of it all, God will have His family, and His family will have Him, forever. This is His perfect plan, which will come to completion. I pray you choose wisely.

Jeff's Story: "A New Addition for the Family"

I had a friend named Jeff, who was in his late 30s. Jeff was a great guy with a loving family. He had been divorced once before, but that was in the distant past. He was finishing up his master's program in health care administration and had life in the palm of his hand. I had lunch with Jeff one day, and I was a close enough friend to bring up some personal things. I asked how his family was, and he began to tell me how much he loved his wife and his children. He continued to tell me how involved his wife and kids were in their church. He told me of messages his daughter would leave for him at night when he would come home late, and there would be a Scripture or a note telling how much she loved her dad and how much Jesus loves him. Then I asked Jeff if he went with them to church, and he said he did, but not all the time.

Then Jeff said something that God Himself would respect. He didn't tell me his opinions about God or what he thought about religion. Jeff looked at me and told me church was not his thing. He told me his passion was his job, his school, and his family. Jeff spoke the truth. He did not make excuses for himself. He knew what made him happy, and it was his career. By the way, he was an awesome administrator. The doctors respected him, his staff loved him, and higher administration wanted to see him excel as well. For those of you not in the health care business, these are the keys to success. It seemed Jeff had it all—a family, his career, and money. These are the ingredients for a successful life in this world. He was a well-loved person and did great works for his family and friends. So I guess the question is, How could God not allow a man with all this to be in heaven when his time on earth was up?

About two months after Jeff and I had lunch, I heard he had a problem one night while coming home with his wife and had to go to the emergency room. After several exams, Jeff was diagnosed with two brain tumors and three chest tumors. How could this happen? Why would God allow this to be? Was He punishing Jeff? Did Jeff do something wrong in his life to deserve this? I can only imagine what other things he thought of in this almost unbelievable time in his life. Jeff knew what this meant, and he realized very quickly that what he had worked so hard for in his life—his career—was coming to an end very abruptly. I went to see Jeff the day after he was admitted to the hospital. I went to present him with some books on God and cancer, and was hoping for something. I wasn't sure what; I was just hoping, but he was not in his room. The next day, I went again to visit, not sure what to expect. When I entered the room, I saw the most peculiar thing. I saw Jeff smiling, welcoming me into his room. I started to speak, but he interrupted me with the most delightful news. He said, "Before you say anything, I just want you to know that yesterday my wife, the pastor, and I went down to the chapel, and I gave my heart to Christ." Then he said, "I realize there is no significance to this to the world; I am faced with this terminal illness. But the great thing is I really did give my heart to Christ." Jeff did not just make a commitment because he was afraid of dying; he made a commitment because he needed the Lord! Jeff lived for almost six months from that day, and though they were faced with this albatross of death, he and his wife spoke of how Jeff's salvation brought them closer as a couple and a family. He said he was a better father and a better husband. But most importantly, he was a son of the living God! You see, when real salvation takes place, it will truly overcome the worst of the worst situations, especially death. **Your focus will not be on the things that life is taking away, but on what God has given you.**

The truth is that salvation is a real, true birth, and it is the same for us all. We may not have the same circumstances leading us to salvation, but the Person giving it to us as well as the Holy Spirit, which will live in us, are the same. They never change. No matter who you are or what your circumstances may be, they stay the same.

CHAPTER 5

If God Is Right, Must Everything Else Be Wrong?

―――∞∞∞―――

J esus states He is the Truth, and there is only one way to the Father and to heaven, and that is through Him. If that is true, we must say that either Christianity is false, or all other religions that reject that statement are false. They cannot both be true.

So many times, members of my family and many friends ask: "What makes your religion right? You believe you are right, but so do the Muslims, the non-converted Jews, the Hindus, and the Buddhists. How can you be so arrogant as to make a claim that you are right, but millions of others who were brought up in their religion are wrong? Why can't they all be right?" My friends and family members make a good point.

The problem with their logic on this is they believe there is no real truth, so all can be right in some way or another. Jesus said He is the Truth, the Way, and the Light, so if He is Truth, and as we said, the Bible teaches that it is the Holy truth without blemish, then either the Bible is truth and everything that contradicts the Bible is false, or the others are all wrong in some way. Because Jesus claims He is the only Way, any other way is false.

Mathematically, if I say that $2 + 2 = 4$, you could add that $3 + 1 = 4$ as well. So there are other ways to 4. But the point is not whether there are other ways to get to 4; it is about Jesus' saying He is the only Way, and to disagree with this would be to say that $2 + 2$ does not $= 4$. Someone is either right or wrong.

Truth statement: The road to salvation is narrow, but broad are the other paths, which lead to destruction.

Matthew 7:13 says, "Enter ye in at the strait gate: for wide is the gate, and **broad is** the **way**, that leadeth to destruction, and many there be which go in thereat."

My goal is not to bash other religions; it is to find which religion is the truth. For example, if I were in the woods, there would be several paths I could take, but only one that would lead me out of the woods; all the others would lead me to destruction. It would be foolish to judge each path based on how pleasant it would be to go down because the end result would be destruction. The paths may seem to have very nice views, and they may seem to be pleasant to walk down, but I would need the path that would lead me out of the woods and home. Religions may have great qualities, but it is not the qualities we need; it is the truth. The religion without a flaw is what we must have. That is the path we take. Many people do not like the path of Jesus because it requires things like forgiveness, truth about yourself, and acceptance of what you are. In addition, this path will change you. It also requires doing things that contradict our flesh, such as being kind to someone who doesn't deserve it. Part of the problem is the leaders and teachers of the church have failed us in many ways with their rule-based religions, and the effect of their erroneous opinions on how to live a godly life. The ceremonies many follow were never brought by Jesus or God, but by man.

Don't judge God and Jesus completely by the acts of Their so-called followers, but judge God and Jesus on what They are and what They stand for. For example, I would not say football is a bad sport because some players cheat and use steroids. Nor can you say Jesus is not truth because a priest molests a child. The only truth comes from the Word of God, and that is the Bible. If the Bible is wrong or false in any way, then its claim of truth is false, which makes it all false. To make this clearer, let's talk about the major religions to see if they contradict one another in any way. I will describe them briefly, as all I have to show is one contradiction to show that either they are all wrong, or one is right, but because they contradict one another, they can't all be right.

1) **Scientology.** Scientologists say their religion is the study of the truth. I am not sure they understand what truth is because even on their website, they say, "In Scientology no one is asked to accept anything as belief or on faith. That which is true for you is what you have observed to be true."

Now, this contradicts the Bible in many ways, but what I find most interesting is they are trying to define "truth" by saying it doesn't exist. **Their argument of no real truth is based on the study of a word they do not believe exists.**

Their fundamentals may be good, they may do good things and represent good causes, but they contradict the Bible, so either one is true, and one is false, or they are both false. Jesus said He is the truth, and you must accept Him to obtain the salvation He has for each of us.

2) Islam. This is such a large religion and goes back to Abraham, who Muslims believe, as do Christians, was the father of Isaac and Ishmael. Muslims believe Muhammad, not Jesus, is the savior, which is where the contradiction is.

My point in this is to show that both religions contradict one another, so again, either they are both wrong, or one is right, and one is wrong. But they cannot both be correct. The Bible says the truth is Jesus is the One who lived a perfect life, thus being able to die for our sins. Muhammad could not do this because he needed a savior for his own sins he had committed in his life. Jesus was born of God in the flesh by Mary, He knew no sin, and He died as a pure Sacrifice. Muhammad was born of a sinful man and a sinful woman.

In **2 Corinthians 5:21**, we read, "For he hath made him to be **sin** for us, who **knew no sin**; that we might be made the righteousness of God in him."

3) Hinduism. Hinduism is a religion that originated in the Indian subcontinent. Hinduism often is referred to as **Sanātana Dharma** by its practitioners, a Sanskrit phrase meaning "the eternal law." Hindu beliefs vary widely, with concepts of god and/or gods ranging from pantheism to monotheism to polytheism, with Vishnu and Shiva being the most popular deities. Other notable characteristics include a belief in reincarnation and karma, as well as personal duty, or dharma.

This religion contradicts the Bible on many different levels, but the one that is the most significant is based on the fact that this religion has nothing to do with Jesus, and all things are accomplished through us. They do believe in a god or many gods as well as reincarnation, but do not dignify Jesus as the path to freedom. As I stated before, the religion may help people become peaceful as well as bring good qualities, but if at the end it is not true, what good is it?

4) Buddhism. Buddhism is a family of beliefs and practices considered by many to be a religion. Buddhism is based on the teachings attributed to Siddhartha Gautama, commonly known as "The Buddha" (the Awakened One), who lived in the northeastern region of the Indian subcontinent and likely died around 400 BCE. Buddhists recognize him as an awakened teacher who shared his insights to help sentient beings end their suffering by understanding the true nature of phenomena, thereby escaping the cycle of suffering and rebirth (saṃsāra). Among the methods various schools of Buddhism apply toward this goal: ethical conduct and altruistic behavior, devotional practices, ceremonies, and the invocation of Bodhisattvas that help them achieve Nirvana, renunciation of worldly matters, meditation, physical exercises, study, and the cultivation of wisdom.

This is a religion and a way of life. But it contradicts the Bible in many ways as well in how to obtain peace and eternal security. It contradicts the Bible in that it has nothing to do with Jesus. It has many good qualities, but partial truth is a whole lie.

5) Judaism. Judaism (j̅o̅o̅dəĭz'əm, j̅o̅o̅dē–) is the religious beliefs and practices and the way of life of the <u>Jews</u> **Jews** [from Judah], traditionally, descendants of Judah, the fourth son of Jacob, whose tribe, with that of his half brother Benjamin, made up the kingdom of Judah; historically, members of the worldwide community of adherents to Judaism .

This is the religion of the Jews, who believe the Messiah has not yet come. They believe in the Old Testament, but refuse to accept Jesus Christ was the Messiah. This is a huge contradiction to the Bible. Many Jewish people even believe Jesus was a lunatic.

I would like to take a moment here and acknowledge the fact that three religions—Islam, Judaism, and Christianity—make up most of the religious people of the world, and they all believe God made the world, as the Bible states. Jesus says again, He is the only Way, so anything or anyone that says different is contradicting what

Jesus said the truth is. They can't all be right.

Lastly, even if all these ways of life and religions were added together, they still would not outnumber the largest religion of the world, and that is . . .

6) Self-religion. This is the oldest and largest religion ever known to mankind. This religion has some guidelines, but they change, depending on the person or people.

It can be based on some religions, but is usually founded in what the person has come up with in his or her own mind on how to live life, and what is right or wrong. It also can be based on many different religions combined. This religion feeds the person's senses and mind. It allows the person to have his or her own belief system, or no beliefs in God at all, like an atheist.

I have heard many people say they don't believe in God, and they don't have a religion, so let's look at the definition of "religion."

"Religion" is defined as the outward act or form by which men indicate their recognition of the existence of a god or of gods having power over their destiny, to whom obedience, service, and honor are due; the feeling or expression of human love, fear, or awe of some superhuman and overruling power, whether by profession of belief, by observance of rites and ceremonies, or by the conduct of life; a system of faith and worship; a manifestation of piety; as, ethical religions; monotheistic religions; natural religion; revealed religion; the religion of the Jews; the religion of idol worshipers.

This means we all believe in a religion, and the many people who claim no religion are actually their own gods, not far from what Satan chose.

Let's read Revelation 12:9:

And the great dragon was cast out, that old serpent, called the Devil, and Satan, which deceiveth the whole world: he was cast out into the earth, and his angels were cast out with him.

This religion helps people cope with life in their own way. This is the religion that many people fall under because they will not choose any one religion. They have their own ideas about what is right and wrong, and it could be made up of many different religions or maybe just what they believe personally. This is the religion for the ones who master the art of rationalizing, the ones who do not take the time to find out if any religion is true, so they decide for themselves the truth. This is the religion the antichrist will use to reach the world. The Bible says he will give a false peace to the nations. He will say it is okay to be whatever you want, as long as it makes you happy. **Have we not become a society of self-pleasure?** Has it not started already? The humanists are already putting billboards up that say "God probably doesn't exist, so go ahead and enjoy your life."

The Scripture says they, the unsaved, will believe a lie.

Second Thessalonians 2:9-12 states:

[9]Even him, whose coming is after the working of Satan with all power and signs and lying wonders, [10]and with all deceivableness of unrighteousness in them that perish; because they received not the love of the truth, that they might be saved. [11]And for this cause God shall send them strong delusion, that they should believe a lie: [12]That they all might be damned who believed not the truth, but had pleasure in unrighteousness.

Even at the end of the world, God will give to those who did not choose Him what they wish, which is themselves. Those who have chosen themselves and what they desire will be given over to this delusion, and damnation will follow.

You see, self-religion contradicts the Bible and Jesus in every way. The Bible and the life of Christ are about everyone else, whereas self-religion is about self. The sadness that self-religion brings is that all who worship themselves make themselves, and not God, righteous. They do for others only to say they are good. They give to others to say they are helpers. All that they do, as good as it may be, will only serve to justify themselves. Jesus came to say there is only one justified, and that is God.

CHAPTER 6

Salvation

———∞∞∞———

Truth statement: True salvation, once given, can never be taken back.

Ephesians 1:13 tells us:

> In whom ye also trusted, after that ye heard the word
> of truth, the gospel of your **salvation**: in whom also
> after that ye believed, ye were sealed with that holy
> Spirit of promise.

These are just a few of the questions we ask ourselves about salvation: What is true salvation? How do I get this salvation? What happens when I receive it? Can I lose it? Is it the same for everyone when he or she receives it?

"Salvation" means the state of being saved or preserved from harm, or the act of delivering from sin or saving from evil.

As we read before, Jesus said salvation can only happen through Him and His death, which He allowed to happen on the cross. If what He says is true, He will be the reason no harm or evil will come to you after your earthly death. He also will be the only reason you will be in heaven with Him, and that heaven is a place He has already prepared for you and all of His children.

Matthew 10:28 says, "Fear not them which kill the body, but are not able to kill the **soul**: but rather fear him which is able to destroy both **soul** and body in hell."

The truth says that God created you for His pleasure. Just as parents want to have a family, so does God want to share all He has with His family. He wants to give you His love, His friendship, and all that He created. He wants to share these wonderful things with us, His children.

The problem is just as Adam and Eve rebelled, we have all rebelled against God. He knew from the beginning the rebellion would take place, and a need for salvation then would have to take place if we were to ever be with Him again—that is, be with Him as part of His family, back to His original design, all of His children together with Him in a perfect place.

Before this could happen, though, He had to make a way, a way of escape from this sin and evil that had overcome the world and His children. This is the reason salvation became salvation, and the reason it must occur before we can ever be close to our Father again. True salvation is when you have surrendered (turned over or given up) your entire life and all you are, all you have, and all you will ever be to Him, your Creator, your God, your Father. You accept your sinfulness as well as the sacrifice Jesus made on the cross for your sins. Lastly, you will need to have faith that Jesus rose from that death, and because He did, there is hope and truth that says you will too. Know this, though: This faith and hope only comes after you have given Him your all. Only then will He put that faith and hope in you. The reason they come after is because He wants you to know these are things that come from Him, and not from yourself. He also does this to show you He is alive and well, and most of all, He loves you and will never, ever leave you.

So if I decide I want this salvation, how do I get it, and know it has really happened? A great example of true salvation is the story of the thieves on the cross. We can read about it in **Luke 23:39-43**:

> [39]And one of the malefactors which were hanged railed on him, saying, If thou be Christ, save thyself and us. [40]But the other answering rebuked him, saying, Dost not thou fear God, seeing thou art in the same condemnation? [41]And we indeed justly; for we receive the due reward of our deeds: but this man hath done nothing amiss. [42]And he said unto Jesus, Lord, remember me when thou comest into thy kingdom. [43]And Jesus said unto him, Verily I say unto thee, Today shalt thou be with me in paradise.

You see, both thieves prayed to God. One prayed to get him out of the mess he was in. First, He tried to cast doubt onto Jesus by saying, "If you are Christ . . .," and then he tempted Him by telling Him to use His power to free them. Isn't this the same prayer that so many of us pray when we get in a bad situation? We say, "Okay, God, if You're really there, help me." But that is not a prayer for salvation; that is a prayer of greed. That prayer is about not being accountable for what you have done, for your sins. The second thief is the one who had it right. He rebuked the first thief and acknowledged the TRUTH, which is that he was guilty, as we all are, and he realized that Christ was innocent. Then he did the only thing left to receive true salvation, and that was believe. He believed by asking God to remember him. He accepted himself as a sinner, and then he had the confidence that Jesus was who He said He was. What was the response from Jesus? "You will be with Me in paradise"!

That thief never lived a godly life, never gave money, and never made miens to people for his mistakes. Yet he obtained salvation, just as anyone else has or ever will. His prayer was riotous because he wasn't looking for a way out; he was accepting his sin, and his need for and belief in Christ. He said, "Remember me when you get to your kingdom." With these few simple words, this thief fulfilled the duties in obtaining salvation.

Today, many churches and people try to make it much more difficult for sinners to reach God. They teach us to be good, act right, and perform certain ceremonies. They have all kinds of ways of trying to make God happy with us. The problem is He is only happy with us when we have received His gift, His sacrifice through Jesus. The Holy Spirit then is living in us, salvation has occurred, and that salvation allows God to have joy in us. This was done through His works, not ours.

So what happens when you receive this salvation? The truth says that only when you have truly received God's grace and forgiveness for your sins, you become His child.

Galatians 4:6 says, "Because ye are **sons, God** hath sent forth the Spirit of his Son into your hearts, crying, Abba, Father."

And **Philippians 2:15** tells us, "That ye may be blameless and harmless, the sons of God, without rebuke, in the midst of a crooked and perverse nation, among whom ye shine as lights in the world."

If you want this salvation, you must know that God created you knowing you would need forgiveness for the sins in your life. All the thoughts and actions that you have committed in your life are against His Laws (The Ten Commandments), which are the natural laws of God.

When you are ready to look deep into your heart, and realize and admit you are a sinner, you make it possible for God to forgive you. Remember, just because you may not have been able to forgive yourself for the things you have thought and done, or forgive others for what they have done, does not mean God can't. You may not think it possible for God to forgive you, nor would you forgive yourself or anyone else for these deeds, but God says He can, and

He will. God says He will continue to forgive everyone who will receive it. God says He wrote the book on forgiveness.

God realizes, as we should all realize, you cannot truly forgive someone until you can find love in your heart for that person again.

Luke 23:34 says, "Then said Jesus, **Father, forgive them**; for they know not what they do. And they parted his raiment, and cast lots."

Many of us think, *How can He forgive those who have committed so many sins?*

First, let's realize this forgiveness was not without a cost. It was not without payment through His only begotten Son. Jesus prayed and gave us forgiveness before we ever even asked for it. He gave us forgiveness before we deserved it, even after putting Him on the cross to die.

Giving us forgiveness was not just for us; it is part of God's formula of perfection. Jesus would not go to the grave with unforgiveness in His heart. **Forgiving is how He overcame death and rose on the third day.**

Remember the reporter who said, "Even if Jesus was buried somewhere, and he didn't rise, we could still worship him"? Let's just say that reporter has no idea what His Resurrection means. If Jesus did not rise from the dead, nor will I.

There is no easy way to truth and perfection. Our sin, just as anyone's sin, has consequences. These sins must be dealt with if we are ever to be close to a perfect God.

As **John 3:16** says, "For God so loved the world, that he gave his only begotten Son, that whosoever believeth in him should not perish, but have everlasting life."

When I get this salvation, could I ever lose it? The truth says it is not yours to lose. Jesus is the One who lived the sin-free life, not us. Jesus is the reason we will be in heaven one day, through His sacrifice on the cross, not ours. He is the reason salvation can take place, and just as you had nothing to do with earning your salvation, there is nothing you can do to lose it. Salvation is not yours to lose; this is why our sins are forgiven as far as the east is from the west.

Read what the Bible says in **Psalm 103:12**: "As far as the east is from the west, so far hath he removed our transgressions from us."

So if we are saved, and our salvation can't be taken away, **why not live in sin and the flesh, knowing we will still go to heaven?** This is a great question and was answered by Paul in the New Testament.

Romans 6:1-2 says, "[1]What shall we say then? Shall we continue in sin, that grace may abound? [2]God forbid. How shall we, that are dead to sin, live any longer therein?"

This means if you are truly saved, while sinful things may tempt you, and you may even fall back into these things, you will not love sin as you did before. The Bible says when you are saved, you are changed, you are dead to your former life, and a new life has risen in you. This means you will hate the things you once loved and love the things you once hated. The flesh will always want to sin, but your new nature, the Holy Spirit, will convict you of it, and your love for it will be gone.

Lastly, if salvation is real, and we can't lose it, is it the same for us all, or is it different? The truth says that no matter who you are, what color you are, what family you are part of, or where you came from, salvation is the same.

Let's read Ephesians 4:1-7:

Unity in the Body of Christ

[1]I therefore, the prisoner of the Lord, beseech you that ye walk worthy of the vocation wherewith ye are called, [2]With all lowliness and meekness, with long-suffering, forbearing one another in love; [3]endeavouring to keep the unity of the Spirit in the bond of peace. [4]There is one body, and one Spirit, even as ye are called in one hope of your calling; [5]one Lord, one faith, one baptism, [6]one God and Father of all, who is above all, and through all, and in you all. [7]But unto every one of us is given grace according to the measure of the gift of Christ.

The circumstances that got you to salvation could be very different, but we all must go through the same One, Jesus Christ, to get to this salvation. The actual salvation is the same, just as the Holy Spirit is the same. It will live in you as it lives in me. What will vary after salvation has taken place are the gifts and talents. God made you like no other, and what you can do for Him is just as special. This is God's desire, that you not only come to Him willingly, but you surrender your life to Him wholly. This is salvation, and it is yours to have. The question is, Do you realize you even need it?

CHAPTER 7

The Father, the Son, and the Holy Spirit: Where Am I?

―――∞∞∞―――

While growing up, living with my grandmother, in many ways, I always felt she was my everyday mom. I also had another mom, the one who gave birth to me. She also helped raise me and loved me very much, but I did not live with her every day. My dad was around very little. I did have a stepdad, who treated me as if I were his son, but that did not make him my biological father.

This is not what happens when you are truly saved by the grace of Jesus Christ and He becomes your Father. You become HIS child, never to depart, never to be given away or separated by any circumstances. He becomes your Father in every sense of the word, physically and spiritually. You may have an earthly father, but God becomes your earthly and eternal Father. He not only gives you a new birth, but he also raises you and is accountable for you throughout this earthly life and the eternal life to come. His Word says He is the perfect Father in every way, and you're His child in every way. **Second Corinthians 6:18** says, "And will be a Father unto you, and ye shall be my sons and daughters, saith the Lord Almighty."

A story that helps describe this new birth and adoption comes from Jesus, who was speaking to a religious man named Nicodemus.

[1]There was a man of the Pharisees, named Nicodemus, a ruler of the Jews: [2]The same came to Jesus by night, and said unto him, Rabbi, we know that thou art a teacher come from God: for no man can do these miracles that thou doest, except God be with him. [3]Jesus answered and said unto him, Verily, verily, I say unto thee, Except a man be born again, he cannot see the kingdom of God. [4]Nicodemus saith unto him, How can a man be born when he is old? Can he enter the second time into his mother's womb, and be born? [5]Jesus answered, Verily, verily, I say unto thee, Except a man be born of water and of the Spirit, he cannot enter into the kingdom of God. [6]That which is born of the flesh is flesh; and that which is born of the Spirit is spirit. [7]Marvel not that I said unto thee, Ye must be born again. [8]The wind bloweth where it listeth, and thou hearest the sound thereof, but canst not tell whence it cometh, and whither it goeth: so is every one that is born of the Spirit. [9]Nicodemus answered and said unto him, How can these things be? [10]Jesus answered and said unto him, Art thou a master of Israel, and knowest not these things? [11]Verily, verily, I say unto thee, We

speak that we do know, and testify that we have seen; and ye receive not our witness. [12]If I have told you earthly things, and ye believe not, how shall ye believe, if I tell you of heavenly things? [13]And no man hath ascended up to heaven, but he that came down from heaven, even the Son of man which is in heaven. [14]And as Moses lifted up the serpent in the wilderness, even so must the Son of man be lifted up: [15]That whosoever believeth in him should not perish, but have eternal life. [16]For God so loved the world, that he gave his only begotten Son, that whosoever believeth in him should not perish, but have everlasting life. [17]For God sent not his Son into the world to condemn the world; but that the world through him might be saved. [18]He that believeth on him is not condemned: but he that believeth not is condemned already, because he hath not believed in the name of the only begotten Son of God. [19]And this is the condemnation, that light is come into the world, and men loved darkness rather than light, because their deeds were evil. [20]For every one that doeth evil hateth the light, neither cometh to the light, lest his deeds should be reproved. [21]But he that doeth truth cometh to the light, that his deeds may be made manifest, that they are wrought in God.

John 3:1-21

Nicodemus was an educated man as well as a religious leader. He came to Jesus this night presumably so that no one would see him. Notice that Jesus seems to always help those who **come to Him, who need Him**. Jesus did not go to Nicodemus; Nicodemus came to Him. Jesus says He stands at your door and knocks, and when you come to Him, when you search for His ways, you open that door.

Mark 2:17 says, "When Jesus heard it, he saith unto them, They that are whole have no **need** of the **physician**, but they that are sick: I came not to call the righteous, but sinners to repentance."

Jesus gave salvation to those who needed and wanted it. Through His life on earth, He always helped those who wanted and needed help. He did not spend His time helping or teaching the prideful souls that assumed they already knew everything about God, salvation, and life.

Today, many people say Christians are ignoring scientific evidence that speaks of evolution. Those same people are the ones who ignored God's truth through His Son, Jesus, and will continue to ignore Him until they see Him face to face.

As **Romans 14:11** says, "For it is written, As I live, saith the Lord, every knee shall bow to me, and every tongue shall confess to God."

So when Nicodemus came to Him and realized that the things Jesus had been doing were of God, he was looking for answers. Did Jesus answer? Yes, He did. Nicodemus may not have gotten the answers he wanted, just as God does not always give us the answers we want. He did, however, walk away with one thing for sure, the true answer from the One who claimed to be Truth. Notice also how Nicodemus asked his questions. He asked questions in an argumentative way, as did most of the Pharisees to Jesus. He asked in such a way as if to say, "How is this possible?" He asked not for assurance, but he asked in doubt. He asked not out of help or a need, but out of disbelief because he thought he already had the answers.

For example, if I tell my son how x-rays are taken, that the picture on an x-ray film comes from a ray called x, and the rest, from light, while he cannot see these substances, I can show him the end result, which is a photograph of anatomy. You see, I am the x-ray tech. I am the one educated in this science. My son may know what a picture is, but he has no idea how it got there. When Jesus told Nicodemus the solution and the properties of salvation, Nicodemus did not want to hear and accept truth; he wanted to cast doubt and disbelief. When people asked Jesus things out of acceptance and not doubt, notice that He gives them simple, truthful answers. Nicodemus did not get such a simple answer because he didn't really want an answer as much as he wanted to cast doubt. He did not come out to seek the truth by Jesus because he was not willing to accept anything other than what he had been taught. He did not come out of a need for a Savior as much as he came to find fault. However, he found none because there is no fault with Jesus, for He was perfect in every way, as God is. The good news is Jesus must have made a change, at least in thought, with Nicodemus. Nicodemus was one of the ones who helped with the burial of Christ, and in some way, I believe the truth must have sunk in.

You see, the truth says we are all born as children of God, even though we are born into sin. We are God's children, and a child who dies will go to heaven because he or she has never reached the age of accountability. I will touch on this age of accountability, and when it begins, shortly.

Even though we are God's children from birth, and He knows everything about us, we are born into sin, and we must not only choose Christ for our salvation, but also accept His gift of grace and accept the sacrifice His Son made on the cross for us all.

Romans 5:12 says, "Wherefore, as by one man sin entered into the world, and death by sin; and so death passed upon **all** men, for that **all** have **sinned**."

Furthermore, **Romans 3:22-31** says:

[22]Even the righteousness of God which is by faith of Jesus Christ unto all and upon all them that believe: for there is no difference: [23]For all have sinned, and come short of the glory of God; [24]being justified freely by his grace through the redemption that is in Christ Jesus: [25]Whom God hath set forth to be a propitiation through faith in his blood, to declare his righteousness for the remission of sins that are past,

through the forbearance of God; ^{26}to declare, I say, at this time his righteousness: that he might be just, and the justifier of him which believeth in Jesus. ^{27}Where is boasting then? It is excluded. By what law? Of works? Nay: but by the law of faith. ^{28}Therefore we conclude that a man is justified by faith without the deeds of the law. ^{29}Is he the God of the Jews only? Is he not also of the Gentiles? Yes, of the Gentiles also: ^{30}Seeing it is one God, which shall justify the circumcision by faith, and uncircumcision through faith. ^{31}Do we then make void the law through faith? God forbid: yea, we establish the law.

Without this passage of spiritual birth, the truth says you will never be at peace and live with God. When this (salvation) birth takes place, you will call heaven your home, and God will be your Father. He will give you peace, and He will send the Holy Spirit to live in you through all the days of this life. The Holy Spirit also will be a witness to you on the Day of Judgment.

That is what **Hebrews 10:15-19** tells us:

^{15}Whereof the Holy Ghost also is a witness to us: for after that he had said before, ^{16}This is the covenant that I will make with them after those days, saith the Lord, I will put my laws into their hearts, and in their minds will I write them; [17]and their sins and iniquities will I remember no more. [18]Now where remission of these is, there is no more offering for sin. [19]Having therefore, brethren, boldness to enter into the holiest by the blood of Jesus . . . .

<u>Truth statement:</u> Salvation and the Holy Spirit are the same in each of us, and the Father loves all of His children the same.

These Scriptures tell of our Comforter, who abides with us:

And I will pray the Father, and he shall give you another **Comforter**, that he may abide with you for ever.

John 14:16

But the **Comforter**, which is the Holy Ghost, whom the Father will send in my name, he shall teach you all things, and bring all things to your remembrance, whatsoever I have said unto you.

<u>John 14:26</u>

But when the **Comforter** is come, whom I will send unto you from the Father, even the Spirit of truth, which proceedeth from the Father, he shall testify of me.

<u>John 15:26</u>

Nevertheless I tell you the truth; It is expedient for you that I go away: for if I go not away, the **Comforter** will not come unto you; but if I depart, I will send him unto you.

John 16:7

Truth statement: **God never abandoned us; we are the ones who left Him.**

The Bible says we serve one God, one Trinity, consisting of God the Father, the Son, and the Holy Ghost. These three components operate the same way in me as they do in you. The Holy Spirit that abides in me is the same Spirit that will or does abide in you. The formula continues like this: God created us, Jesus sacrificed Himself for us, and God says, "I will leave you with the Holy Spirit until I come again." God says, "I will never leave you nor forsake you."

This world and the people in it will always let you down, sooner or later. But the trinity will not, for it will never leave. So, moving forward, if **a) God created the world, b) the Son gave His life to save the world, and c) the Holy Spirit is said to be left to comfort us as we go through this world,** we can see that all three parts of the Trinity fulfill the provision from God to His children.

First **Corinthians 8:6** tells us, "But to us there is but one God, the Father, of whom are all things, and we in him; and one Lord Jesus Christ, by whom are all things, and we by him."

This world is all we know now, but this is not the world God made in the beginning, nor is it the one He has planned for us for eternity.

God did create a perfect world in the beginning, and Adam and Eve, and we, have turned it into what it is today. This world for the saved has now become a means to a perfect world. This means to a perfect world is for those who are saved and called His children. We will live there because we chose to receive Christ and to obey the Father at least for salvation purposes alone. This is unlike Adam and Eve, who were placed in the garden and chose to sin and die. Instead, we chose to give our lives up to the acceptance of Christ, so that we may live forever. More importantly, we will be with our Father forever.

Read what John 12:25 says: "He that loveth his life shall lose it; and he that hateth his life in this world shall keep it unto life eternal."

So when are you accountable? Is there an age that is the same for everyone? Are there people who will never be accountable?

So when are you accountable? The truth says you are accountable when you have heard the Word and message of Christ, and reject it, knowing you should have accepted it. You do not become accountable at a certain age, but when you have obtained an understanding of what you have heard. It works both ways. You hear the Word, see your sin, repent, and believe. The other option: You hear the Word, deny it, and rationalize in disbelief.

Ephesians 1:13 says, "In whom ye also trusted, after that ye **heard** the **word** of truth, the gospel of your salvation: in whom also after that ye believed, ye were sealed with that holy Spirit of promise."

Furthermore, the Bible, in Luke 8:4-17, says:

[4]And when much people were gathered together, and were come to him out of every city, he spake by a parable: [5]A sower went out to sow his seed: and as he sowed, some fell by the way side; and it was trodden down, and the fowls of the air devoured it. [6]And some fell upon a rock; and as soon as it was sprung up, it withered away, because it lacked moisture. [7]And some fell among thorns; and the thorns sprang up with it, and choked it. [8]And other fell on good ground, and sprang up, and bare fruit an hundredfold. And when he had said these things, he cried, He that hath ears to hear, let him hear. [9]And his disciples asked him, saying, What might this parable be? [10]And he said, Unto you it is given to know the mysteries of the kingdom of God: but to others in parables; that seeing they might not see, and hearing they might not understand. [11]Now the parable is this: The seed is the word of God. [12]Those by the way side are they that hear; then cometh the devil, and taketh away the word out of their hearts, lest they should believe and be saved. [13]They on the rock are they,

which, when they hear, receive the word with joy; and these have no root, which for a while believe, and in time of temptation fall away. [14]And that which fell among thorns are they, which, when they have heard, go forth, and are choked with cares and riches and pleasures of this life, and bring no fruit to perfection. [15]But that on the good ground are they, which in an honest and good heart, having heard the word, keep it, and bring forth fruit with patience. [16]No man, when he hath lighted a candle, covereth it with a vessel, or putteth it under a bed; but setteth it on a candlestick, that they which enter in may see the light. [17]For nothing is secret, that shall not be made manifest; neither any thing hid, that shall not be known and come abroad.

Have you heard the Word and received it on good ground, or have you heard the Word and denied it, thinking more of men's ways than God's?

Are some never accountable, have some never heard the Word of God, or are some mentally unable to choose? Yes, many people we see today have no way of understanding God and what He has done for them. There are psychotics and the insane. There are the mentally handicapped, who go through this earth as the least, but many of whom will be the first in heaven.

A time will come when Jesus returns and will abide with us on this earth for a thousand-year reign. At this time, anyone who has never heard the Word before will hear it and actually be with it. For the people with mental disorders who will have passed away, and the people who have never heard of Christ or God's Word, this could be a time God has made when they will be able to choose as well. And when Christ is here with us, there will be no sickness or death or mental disorders of any sort.

Revelation 20:1-15 tells of Jesus' return:

[1]And I saw an angel come down from heaven, having the key of the bottomless pit and a great chain in his hand. [2]And he laid hold on the dragon, that old serpent, which is the Devil, and Satan, and bound him a thousand years, [3]and cast him into the bottomless pit, and shut him up, and set a seal upon him, that he should deceive the nations no more, till the thousand years should be fulfilled: and after that he must be loosed a little season. [4]And I saw thrones, and they sat upon them, and judgment was given unto them: and I saw the souls of them that were beheaded for the witness of Jesus, and for the word of God, and which had not worshipped the beast, neither his image, neither had received his mark upon their foreheads, or in their hands; and they lived and reigned with Christ

a thousand years. ⁵But the rest of the dead lived not again until the thousand years were finished. This is the first resurrection. ⁶Blessed and holy is he that hath part in the first resurrection: on such the second death hath no power, but they shall be priests of God and of Christ, and shall reign with him a thousand years. ⁷And when the thousand years are expired, Satan shall be loosed out of his prison, ⁸and shall go out to deceive the nations which are in the four quarters of the earth, Gog, and Magog, to gather them together to battle: the number of whom is as the sand of the sea. ⁹And they went up on the breadth of the earth, and compassed the camp of the saints about, and the beloved city: and fire came down from God out of heaven, and devoured them. ¹⁰And the devil that deceived them was cast into the lake of fire and brimstone, where the beast and the false prophet are, and shall be tormented day and night for ever and ever. ¹¹And I saw a great white throne, and him that sat on it, from whose face the earth and the heaven fled away; and there was found no place for them. ¹²And I saw the dead, small and great, stand before God; and the books were opened: and another book was opened, which is the book of life: and the dead were judged out of those things which were written in the books, according to their works. [13]And the sea gave up the dead which were in it; and death and hell delivered up the dead which were in them: and they were judged every man according to their works. [14]And death and hell were cast into the lake of fire. This is the second death. [15]And whosoever was not found written in the book of life was cast into the lake of fire.

During this time, Satan will be chained up, but after the thousand years, he will be loosed for a season and will cause yet another revolt. However, this time he will be cast into the lake of fire, along with death itself, not to rule, but to suffer. You see, God says He will judge us all based on the same playing field, whether or not you accepted Christ. Will you be part of this roll call?

Jason's Story

Jason was born a typical child, with all the characteristics of a normal life before him. As a baby, when Jason was dropped by his mother, he fell to the ground and suffered a blow to his head. He was rushed to the hospital, and his life was changed forever. Jason almost lost his life, but instead, he survived and lives today. Growing up, Jason did not grow to understand as others did, yet he physically grew normally. Jason was like the other children in that he could listen and understand what was being asked of him, and could do these things up to a certain level. His thinking skills when it comes to problem-solving and educational studies are those of someone younger than he, at age twenty-seven. He can do physical activities, such as running, playing sports, and working, but not at normal levels. When Jason was growing up as a child, he had seizures as well as outrage acts. He was mean to other children at times, and was very self-involved. One day Jason realized he was a sinner, and he asked God to forgive him. Just as God promised to us all, Jason received the Holy Spirit. I did not know him before his salvation, but those who did said Jason was in many ways a problem child.

After his salvation, in the time I have spent with Jason over the years, I find it hard to believe he was the way they say he was. The Jason I have known for many years is a young Christian man who is compassionate about his God. He loves people and his family very much, and reflects the Christian qualities more than most Christians I know. You see, the Holy Spirit is the same in Jason as it is in me. It knows no limits, physically or mentally. Jason cannot tell you answers to math or science problems, or give you directions to a destination, but he can out-answer many Christian friends I know on Scripture and the things of God. He prays more than most people and loves the things of the Lord. Jason was accountable because he knew right from wrong, and he heard the Word and believed and accepted it. The Holy Spirit that lives in him today has just as much power as anyone else because it is the same Spirit, and it knows no bounds.

CHAPTER 8

Salvation Received—What Next?

———∽∾∞∾∽———

When I was about eleven years old, I snuck into my great-grandmother's room, knowing where she kept her pocketbook. I opened it up and saw ten dollars. I went to take it, but realized it was way too much money, and she would notice if it were missing. I put it back, and as I was getting up, I turned around and saw, much to my surprise, she was standing there at the doorway. She had been watching me the whole time. She didn't spank me or cuss at me; she didn't even put me on restriction. She just said one simple truth, and that has stayed with me since. She looked at me at that moment, and with sadness in her eyes, she said, "I never would have thought you would do that to me," and then she walked away. I ran out of the house that morning and spent the most miserable day wondering how I was going to make it up to her. I was hoping she would forgive me, and I was trying to think of what to say to her. Most of all, I knew I got caught, and she probably lost some love for me. When I got home, with tears in my eyes, I told her I was so sorry, and I would never do that again. She hugged me, kissed me, and said okay. She never brought it up again, and she never loved me less than she had before. That day I learned not only what it means to get true forgiveness, but also how it feels when you have really repented and received forgiveness. Have you ever felt like that toward God for your sins? Have you come to Him with fear and trembling, wanting His forgiveness for your sins? If not, then you have no salvation or forgiveness, just the sin.

Second Corinthians 7:15 says, "His inward affection is more abundant toward you, whilst he remembereth the obedience of you all, how with **fear** and **trembling** ye received him."

You may wonder, *Now that I have been saved and forgiven, with a true love for God/Christ/the Holy Spirit in my life, what happens?*

What can we expect from this Trinity, and will it be consistent?

Am I supposed to live a certain way now, and what do I have to give up or change about myself and/or my life?

What happens when I mess up? Does He punish me?

Does God promise that if I do well, He will protect me from all harm?

First things first: What can we expect from God, Jesus, and the Holy Spirit, and will it be consistent? The Trinity is one made up of three, so I will refer to all three as God, knowing they all must be perfect, or none are. God tells us many things about what you can expect from Him when you are saved and counted as His child. As your Father, as a Friend, and as your Judge, He is accountable.

As a Father, God says He knows how to give you good

gifts, not just in heaven, but now, here on earth. We read this in **Matthew 7:11**: "If ye then, being evil, know how to **give good gifts** unto your children, how much more shall your Father which is in heaven **give good** things to them that ask him?"

In addition, He tells you what you mean to Him and what He has done for you.

¹There is therefore now no condemnation to them which are in Christ Jesus, who walk not after the flesh, but after the Spirit. ²For the law of the Spirit of life in Christ Jesus hath made me free from the law of sin and death. ³For what the law could not do, in that it was weak through the flesh, God sending his own Son in the likeness of sinful flesh, and for sin, condemned sin in the flesh: ⁴That the righteousness of the law might be fulfilled in us, who walk not after the flesh, but after the Spirit. ⁵For they that are after the flesh do mind the things of the flesh; but they that are after the Spirit the things of the Spirit. ⁶For to be carnally minded is death; but to be spiritually minded is life and peace. ⁷Because the carnal mind is enmity against God: for it is not subject to the law of God, neither indeed can be. ⁸So then they that are in the flesh cannot please God. ⁹But ye are not in the flesh, but in the Spirit, if so be that the Spirit of God dwell

in you. Now if any man have not the Spirit of Christ, he is none of his. [10]And if Christ be in you, the body is dead because of sin; but the Spirit is life because of righteousness. [11]But if the Spirit of him that raised up Jesus from the dead dwell in you, he that raised up Christ from the dead shall also quicken your mortal bodies by his Spirit that dwelleth in you. [12]Therefore, brethren, we are debtors, not to the flesh, to live after the flesh. [13]For if ye live after the flesh, ye shall die: but if ye through the Spirit do mortify the deeds of the body, ye shall live. [14]For as many as are led by the Spirit of God, they are the sons of God. [15]For ye have not received the spirit of bondage again to fear; but ye have received the Spirit of adoption, whereby we cry, Abba, Father. [16]The Spirit itself beareth witness with our spirit, that we are the children of God: [17]And if children, then heirs; heirs of God, and joint-heirs with Christ; if so be that we suffer with him, that we may be also glorified together.

Romans 8:1-17

Furthermore, He tells you how important you are to Him and how well He knows you. Read what **Luke 12:5-7** has to say about this:

[5]But I will forewarn you whom ye shall fear: Fear him, which after he hath killed hath power to cast into hell; yea, I say unto you, Fear him. [6]Are not five sparrows sold for two farthings, and not one of them is forgotten before God? [7]But even the very hairs of your head are all numbered. Fear not therefore: ye are of more value than many sparrows.

Lastly, He says He will show you His love always and will never leave you. Hebrews 13:5-8 states:

[5]Let your conversation be without covetousness; and be content with such things as ye have: for he hath said, I will never leave thee, nor forsake thee. [6]So that we may boldly say, The Lord is my helper, and I will not fear what man shall do unto me. [7]Remember them which have the rule over you, who have spoken unto you the word of God: whose faith follow, considering the end of their conversation. [8]**Jesus Christ the same yesterday, and to day, and for ever.**

God will never leave you, and that is a constant. Jesus said, "I must go so that I can send the Comforter." You see, Jesus knew even before His death that through His death not only would He give the gift of salvation to the world, but he also would make it possible for the Holy Spirit to dwell in all those who have become His children by receiving this salvation. You see, the Holy Spirit is what makes the difference in a person—not himself or herself, not his or her works, but the works of the Spirit. The truth says that the Spirit will be a witness to you at the judgment that is to come.

As **Romans 8:16** says, "The Spirit itself beareth **witness** with our spirit, that we are the children of God."

Back to the question: Is God constant in all things to me? He says He will always be a constant, loving father, He will always be there for you, and He will never leave you. God works in many ways we cannot see, but the reliability and accountability never change for His children. You may separate yourself from Him, but He will not leave you, for you are His child, and His Word is always constant. Never changing, it is always carrying the power for our changing lives.

Just read **John 15:7**: "If ye abide in me, and my **word**s abide in you, ye shall ask what ye will, and it shall be done unto you."

It seems in society that only the most trustworthy of our friends and family members are constantly dependable, and even then they fail us. Isn't dependability all the time what we want in God? The problem is we are putting God on *our* playing field and *our* world. We need to realize we are all actually on His playing field, all of existence, including the world, universe, galaxy, and beyond.

God is the One who says He made the universe, but we expect Him to follow our rules, in our world, based on how we treat imperfect people. However, God plays by His rules (truth and only truth). He is never flawed and never wrong; that is what makes Him perfect. God is constant in what He does and what He is, but He can do things in many different ways without losing His perfection. The reason God can do this is because He reacts with the same thing every time, no matter what He is reacting to: truth. God is not held by time, as we are. You may cry out to God and say: "Where are You? I need this, and I need that. Why did You do this? Why did You do that?" God will show you all these things, as He says He will do, but it is based on two principal conditions.

First, are you one of His children? If you are not one of His children, know that the accountability to be the Father He is to the saved is not the same when it comes to the unsaved. I love the children I work with, and I try to spend time with them as well as the other kids in my neighborhood, but at the end of the day, I am not responsible for them. It is their parents who are accountable. Their fathers and mothers are the ones who will make sure the children are safe, fed, and put to bed. God is willing to take you in and make you His child. He wants that accountability, but it is up to you whether you will choose Him. If you don't, that is your wish, not His.

The second condition is, are you the problem? Is it you who have separated yourself from God? You see, we want to blame God for not acting as we think He should. We want Him to do all things on our timeline, yet that is not a promise He has ever made. We need to realize He does things on His timeline, not ours. He is the

All-knowing, not us. He is the One who makes promises that can never be broken, but they will be by the rules of truth, and they will happen when He decides they are right. The problem we have is we don't see the big picture, and God does. While many times, we can look back and see what He has done in our lives and how it worked out, we can't see what's ahead.

For example, I may want to take the short route to my destination. But God sends me a different way, and I decide I don't like that way. I know that my way is the quickest and the easiest to get to my destination, but God is telling me to go a different route. I can argue and complain and refuse to understand why. I can even disobey and suffer the consequences, but what I never saw was the one thousand-car pileup He led me away from, the wreck I might have been part of, the wreck that would have taken my children, my life, and my job away. Because God is all-knowing, He sees ahead and prepares the way for His children, either to continue here on earth, or to enjoy a life everlasting with Him.

What does God promise us? God promises these things:

1. To make you His child if you accept Christ as your Savior.

2. To be the perfect Father always and every time. Remember, a perfect father's job is to help the child grow, to be an example to the child, and to love the child. God promises these things, and He has never failed, nor will He ever fail in giving these things to His children. The child many times does not understand why the father has done, or allowed, one thing or another, nor does the child agree

with what the father has done at particular times, but just because the child does not understand does not take away from the perfection of the father.

A story in the Bible describes these things.

> [1]And Saul, yet breathing out threatenings and slaughter against the disciples of the Lord, went unto the high priest, [2]and desired of him letters to Damascus to the synagogues, that if he found any of this way, whether they were men or women, he might bring them bound unto Jerusalem. [3]And as he journeyed, he came near Damascus: and suddenly there shined round about him a light from heaven: [4]And he fell to the earth, and heard a voice saying unto him, Saul, Saul, why persecutest thou me? [5]And he said, Who art thou, Lord? And the Lord said, I am Jesus whom thou persecutest: it is hard for thee to kick against the pricks. [6]And he trembling and astonished said, Lord, what wilt thou have me to do? And the Lord said unto him, Arise, and go into the city, and it shall be told thee what thou must do. [7]And the men which journeyed with him stood speechless, hearing a voice, but seeing no man. [8]And Saul arose from the earth; and when his eyes were opened, he saw no man: but they led him by the hand, and brought

him into Damascus. [9]And he was three days without sight, and neither did eat nor drink. [10]And there was a certain disciple at Damascus, named Ananias; and to him said the Lord in a vision, Ananias. And he said, Behold, I am here, Lord. [11]And the Lord said unto him, Arise, and go into the street which is called Straight, and enquire in the house of Judas for one called Saul, of Tarsus: for, behold, he prayeth, [12]And hath seen in a vision a man named Ananias coming in, and putting his hand on him, that he might receive his sight. [13]Then Ananias answered, Lord, I have heard by many of this man, how much evil he hath done to thy saints at Jerusalem: [14]And here he hath authority from the chief priests to bind all that call on thy name. [15]But the Lord said unto him, Go thy way: for he is a chosen vessel unto me, to bear my name before the Gentiles, and kings, and the children of Israel: [16]For I will shew him how great things he must suffer for my name's sake. [17]And Ananias went his way, and entered into the house; and putting his hands on him said, Brother Saul, the Lord, even Jesus, that appeared unto thee in the way as thou camest, hath sent me, that thou mightest receive thy sight, and be filled with the Holy Ghost. [18]And immediately there fell from his eyes as it had been scales: and he received sight forthwith, and arose, and was baptized. [19]And when he had received meat, he was strengthened. Then was Saul certain days with the disciples which were at Damascus. [20]And straightway he preached Christ in the synagogues, that he is the Son of God. [21]But all that heard him were amazed, and said; Is not this he that destroyed them which called on this name in Jerusalem, and came hither for that intent, that he might bring them bound unto the chief priests? [22]But Saul increased the more in strength, and confounded the Jews which dwelt at Damascus, proving that this is very Christ. [23]And after that many days were fulfilled, the Jews took counsel to kill him: [24]But their laying await was known of Saul. And they watched the gates day and night to kill him. [25]Then the disciples took him by night, and let him down by the wall in a basket. [26]And when Saul was come to Jerusalem, he assayed to join himself to the disciples: but they were all afraid of him, and believed not that he was a disciple. [27]But Barnabas took him, and brought him to the apostles, and declared unto them how he had seen the Lord in the way, and that he had spoken to him, and how he had preached boldly at Damascus in the name of Jesus. [28]And he was with them coming in and going out at Jerusalem. ²⁹And he spake boldly in the name of the Lord Jesus, and disputed against the Grecians: but they went about to slay him. ³⁰Which when the brethren knew, they brought him down to Caesarea, and sent him forth to Tarsus. ³¹Then had the churches rest throughout all Judaea and Galilee and Samaria, and were edified; and walking in the fear of the Lord, and in the comfort of the Holy Ghost, were multiplied.

Acts 9:1-31

Paul believed he was the worst sinner, and he later even called himself the chief of sinners. I am sure he felt he did that which was the worst you could do: kill Christians for being Christians. At this time, when he was named Saul, he hated Christians and spoke viciously of them. He made it a point to persecute them, as he did not have Christ in his life, nor did he care to until the day Christ came to him. Then, at that moment, Saul realized he had met his God. When we meet God, we will all bow before Him and His deity.

Jesus asked Paul one thing, and that was, "Why do you persecute me?" Jesus showed Saul his sin, and that is what led him to become a child of God's. Notice what happened next: God caused Saul to become blind for three days. Was that the right thing for a Father to do to his son? Not only was it right, but it was necessary. Saul had to realize his weakness as a human before his Maker.

Also in the story, we have a child of God's named Ananias, and he does not like what God has asked him to do. He does not agree with God, and doesn't understand why He has mercy on a person who has done so much to hurt the cause of Christ. The Lord tells him to do what He says, and, of course, it all works out to God's glory in the end. In the ending of this story, you can see that only after Saul had been given the Holy Spirit and was baptized did he have a love for Christ and a zeal to preach His word. The change that will occur in your life after your salvation also will be from the Holy Spirit. As a side note, remember, God changed Saul's name to Paul, and Paul ended up writing two-thirds of the New Testament, as well as leading the work of Christ to the gentiles. God sees the big picture.

After you accept Christ, you may wonder, *So, now am I supposed to act a certain way? Do I have to give up anything?*

The good news about this answer is that when you are saved, the truth says you gain everything and lose nothing.

Romans 8:5 tells is, "For they that are after the flesh do mind the **things** of the flesh; but they that are after the Spirit the **things** of the Spirit."

This doesn't mean you will not be tempted and don't still have a fleshly desire for sin. What it does mean is you will no longer love the sin as you did before you were saved. Salvation has changed your nature from the inside out. God made you specifically for His pleasure, and no one else in the world is like you, so why would you think He would want you to be or act like anyone else? God also tells us the proper attitude we should have as His child toward Him and our neighbor. He says we should love Him with all our hearts and love our neighbors as ourselves. If you can do those two things, the rest follows suit. If you love your parents, you will try and please them. If you love your spouse, you will want to do the things that make your spouse happy. This is because you get joy from loved ones' joy. If you think that by following a bunch of rules and ceremonies, in some way you will please God, you are sadly mistaken. Read the following Bible story.

Matthew 19:16-22 says:

[16]And, behold, one came and said unto him, Good Master, what good thing shall I do, that I may have eternal life? [17]And he said unto him, Why callest thou me good? There is none good but one, that is, God: but if thou wilt enter into life, keep the commandments. [18]He saith unto him, Which? Jesus said, Thou shalt do no murder, Thou shalt not commit adultery, Thou shalt not steal, Thou shalt not bear false witness, [19]Honour thy father and thy mother: and, Thou shalt love thy neighbour as thyself. [20]The young man saith unto him, All these things have I kept from my youth up: what lack I yet? [21]Jesus said unto him, If thou wilt be perfect, go and sell that thou hast, and give to the poor, and thou shalt have treasure in heaven:

and come and follow me. [22]But when the young man heard that saying, he went away sorrowful: for he had great possessions.

The rich man thought he had it all together, didn't he? He believed if he followed enough rules and did all the things God says to do, he was good enough in God's eyes and would go to heaven. The problem is if he did do all those things, he would have been accepted as riotous, but he didn't, and he did have sin in his life. The problem lies in the fact that he had hidden his sin of money before Christ, as many of us do today. He put his love of money ahead of his love for God. He went away sorrowful because he had great possessions, and that was the God of his heart; that is what he served.

You may ask, "What happens when I mess up? Will He punish me, or will He protect me from all harm, no matter what? Does He only protect me when I am doing well?"

These are great questions because in many cases, it seems that bad things happen to good people. Christians die and get hurt every day. When you become a Christian, God does not promise that you will live a life without trials and tribulation. He does not say that you will not get hurt or suffer for serving Him. In fact, He says to be prepared for this. Remember, He may allow pain and suffering, but He says He will love you and help you, as His child. God promises us eternal life with Him, so if He allows one of His children to die, he or she is with Him forever. Is that supposed to be a bad thing?

When God allows this to happen, in many cases, we see it as a bad thing, when in reality it is the greatest thing that can happen to a child of God. Returning to the Father is greatest of rewards; you get to go home.

You may ask, "If I do good or bad, will He do more or less?"

This is where we get back into the formula God has in effect. Mathematically, if you follow the rules of truth, not that you will be perfect and not make mistakes, but if you love the Lord and follow after Him, He says He will give you joy and peace, even in the hardest times.

This does not mean hard times won't come. In fact, through the hard times, God will make you stronger and more receptive to the blessings He has for you. God says He will be a loving Father, and a truly loving father will chastise his children when they do wrong. He also will reward them for doing right.

Hebrews 12:6-14 tells us:

> 6For whom the Lord loveth he chasteneth, and scour-geth every son whom he receiveth. 7If ye endure chas-tening, God dealeth with you as with sons; for what son is he whom the father chasteneth not? 8But if ye be without chastisement, whereof all are partakers, then are ye bastards, and not sons. 9Furthermore we have had fathers of our flesh which corrected us, and we gave them reverence: shall we not much rather be

in subjection unto the Father of spirits, and live? [10]For they verily for a few days chastened us after their own pleasure; but he for our profit, that we might be partakers of his holiness. [11]Now no chastening for the present seemeth to be joyous, but grievous: nevertheless afterward it yieldeth the peaceable fruit of righteousness unto them which are exercised thereby. [12]Wherefore lift up the hands which hang down, and the feeble knees; [13]and make straight paths for your feet, lest that which is lame be turned out of the way; but let it rather be healed. [14]Follow peace with all men, and holiness, without which no man shall see the Lord.

Remember, chastisement comes from a parent because of our actions and is not without cause. When you are His child, He is accountable for you, and He takes His parental responsibility seriously. Part of God's formula of living in this world and receiving blessings and chastisement is based on our actions. He wants you to do well as His child, and He will bless you for good and chastise you for bad. The question is, *How do I get myself to a point of doing more good as a son or daughter, and not make so many mistakes?*

The best example I can give related to this is something I went through while jogging.

THE DOG

I was running into my neighborhood one early winter morning after finishing a long run. As I entered into the neighborhood, I had my headset on with music playing in my ears, and my hood was over my head to keep the heat in. When I looked up in front of me, I saw a petite woman holding a very large dog, a mastiff, I believe. The woman was not strong enough to keep the dog from running toward me, but she was strong enough to hold it back so I could run far around them both. After I passed them and was far enough away to realize how close I had come to a not-so-great ending to my run, the Holy Spirit spoke to me. It said to me: "That is what I should be like in you. I should be a great force to be reckoned with when Satan and the demons come to tempt." The truth says Satan goes to and fro on the earth, looking for whom he can devour. The Spirit showed me if you spend your life walking with Christ and feeding the spirit with His Word and your prayer, when temptation comes, you will be a mastiff, not a Chihuahua, with a lot of mouth but no bite. We are all tempted and tested, and we all fail, but when the Spirit is strong, your walk will be more determined, and the failures will be less.

So why do the innocent die without cause? Why do the good die young? Because the righteous are not of this world. Our kingdom has not yet come. We live in a wicked world with a wicked prince. God has allowed us to stay in this world not to hurt us, but to love us. I hope you can see the beauty in the prayer Jesus made for us before

He was crucified. Jesus never had a prayer that His Father denied. Have peace; this prayer was for you.

1These words spake Jesus, and lifted up his eyes to heaven, and said, Father, the hour is come; glorify thy Son, that thy Son also may glorify thee: 2As thou hast given him power over all flesh, that he should give eternal life to as many as thou hast given him. 3And this is life eternal, that they might know thee the only true God, and Jesus Christ, whom thou hast sent. 4I have glorified thee on the earth: I have finished the work which thou gavest me to do. 5And now, O Father, glorify thou me with thine own self with the glory which I had with thee before the world was. 6I have manifested thy name unto the men which thou gavest me out of the world: thine they were, and thou gavest them me; and they have kept thy word. 7Now they have known that all things whatsoever thou hast given me are of thee. 8For I have given unto them the words which thou gavest me; and they have received them, and have known surely that I came out from thee, and they have believed that thou didst send me. 9I pray for them: I pray not for the world, but for them which thou hast given me; for they are thine. 10And all mine are thine, and thine are mine; and I am glorified in them. [11]And now I am no more in the world, but these are in the world, and I come to thee. Holy Father, keep through thine own name those whom thou hast given me, that they may be one, as we are. [12]While I was with them in the world, I kept them in thy name: those that thou gavest me I have kept, and none of them is lost, but the son of perdition; that the scripture might be fulfilled. [13]And now come I to thee; and these things I speak in the world, that they might have my joy fulfilled in themselves. [14]I have given them thy word; and the world hath hated them, because they are not of the world, even as I am not of the world. [15]I pray not that thou shouldest take them out of the world, but that thou shouldest keep them from the evil. [16]They are not of the world, even as I am not of the world. [17]Sanctify them through thy truth: thy word is truth. [18]As thou hast sent me into the world, even so have I also sent them into the world. [19]And for their sakes I sanctify myself, that they also might be sanctified through the truth. [20]Neither pray I for these alone, but for them also which shall believe on me through their word; [21]that they all may be one; as thou, Father, art in me, and I in thee, that they also may be one in us: that the world may believe that thou hast sent me. [22]And the glory which thou gavest me

I have given them; that they may be one, even as we are one: **[23]I in them, and thou in me, that they may be made perfect in one; and that the world may know that thou hast sent me, and hast loved them, as thou hast loved me.**

John 17:1-23

CHAPTER 9

Our Wicked and Wonderful World

Love not the world, neither the **things** that are in the world. If any man **love** the world, the **love** of the Father is not in him.

1 John 2:15

Let us be perfectly clear on this subject concerning the world. The truth says God made this world and gave it to man to be over. God provided for man, but man ruled the land.

Read the following Scriptures:

And out of the ground the LORD God formed every beast of the field, and every fowl of the air; and brought them unto **Adam** to see what he would call them: and whatsoever **Adam** called every living creature, that was the name thereof.

Genesis 2:19

And unto **Adam** he said, Because thou hast hearkened unto the voice of thy wife, and hast eaten of the tree, of which I commanded thee, saying, Thou shalt not eat of it: cursed is the ground for thy sake; in sorrow shalt thou eat of it all the days of thy life.

Genesis 3:17

In the beginning, all was created perfectly, with no sin, no shame, no sickness, and no death. Adam and Eve both walked in an intimate and close relationship with God every day. Neither animals, nor people killed one another, and peace reigned and would have for eternity. This was the world God initiated and created. We also know the end of this perfect world occurred when Satan tempted Eve. She was tempted because she wanted to be as God is, knowing both good and evil. What Satan did was cast doubt, doubt that what God had said would really happen. She gave in to this doubt, as did Adam. The Scripture says as soon as they ate the fruit, they realized they were naked. At that very moment, shame and sin entered the world. The death God said would come if they disobeyed began that very moment. Spiritually, they died immediately; their intimacy with God was no more. Physically, their bodies would now know pain, and eventually would die, as ours do today. God said, "You will surely die if you eat of it." What else happened? They were sent from the garden into a world that Satan could go to and from, looking for whom he can devour. Satan had won this battle, but God has declared He will have the overall victory.

Genesis 3:14-15 says:

[14]And the LORD God said unto the serpent, Because thou hast done this, thou art cursed above all cattle, and above every beast of the field; upon thy belly shalt thou go, and dust shalt thou eat all the days of thy life: [15]And I will put enmity between thee and the woman, and between thy seed and her seed; it shall bruise thy head, and thou shalt bruise his heel.

Life was no longer perfect, as it was before, as God had created it. Life became a world full of sin, shame, death, and war—all because they chose to disobey and believe a lie over God's truth. The fact that they doubted God would kill them, for this did not change God, just as the doubts and unbelief of many in this world will not change who He is. Because millions of people decide not to follow the truth does not mean God isn't true; it just means you would rather have it your way than His.

Notice I did not say Adam and Eve disobeyed the Father, even though they did. I said they chose the wrong way to go in their lives. They chose *their* way instead of God's way. I tend to have compassion on Adam and Eve because they chose something they knew nothing about. On the other hand, we know what sin is, and we choose it every day. What is even worse is as a society, we are now saying that a sin is not a sin; we are replacing truth with lies and passing these lies down to our children. Every generation moving forward is making up their own truth. More and more, we change the natural truth to our own.

Just read these two Scriptures:

Woe unto them that **call** evil good, and good evil; that put **darkness** for **light**, and **light** for **darkness**; that put bitter for sweet, and sweet for bitter!

Isaiah 5:20

If we say that we have fellowship with him, and walk in **darkness**, we lie, and do not the truth.

1 John 1:6

All this being said, does this take away from God's perfection and omnipotence, knowing He has control over everything, yet allowing the world to get into the shape it is in?

It seems we have decided as a society and as a religion that because God says He is omnipotent, or all-powerful, as well as all-knowing, He is the Controller of this world.

In many cases, this is why people refuse to believe God is perfect or that He even exists, because we judge Him based on the things of this world. War, famine, the innocent dying every day, the unfairness in our society, as well as the haves and have-nots. It actually seems that the world is running either on its own or by someone who does not care. To say the least, it seems to be run by a God who shows us that the strongest and most talented get ahead and the weak and the unfortunate are left behind.

In contrast to this, the world itself, if you took all the people out of it and judged it solely based on its scenery, would be a wonderfully beautiful place. The world offers us so much beauty, even through the years of death and war and killings. So the question remains: Which is it, wicked or wonderful?

This world and universe we live in are both defiantly wicked and definitely wonderful. It is wonderful in so many ways, specifically in ways that man has not defiled yet. The creation of the universe, the stars, the sun, and the moon are majestic, to say the least. The beauty of animal life is portrayed on television as well as in our own back yards. The natural birth of animals, with the interaction of all the species, all coincide with our lives every day. The beauty in the creation is endless, and artists will never run out of paintings and music to portray the beauty that surrounds us. There are times in our lives, although brief, it seems, when we are content with what we have. For example, it is wonderful to laugh until you cry, or to enjoy a holiday with your family when no one is sick or hurt or mad. Watching the birth of your child and looking into your new baby's eyes for the first time bring a lot of joy as well. Other things that could be counted as wonderful include dreaming of things to come or escaping this world through movies and books. Some moments everything seems wonderful . . . and then what happens? In every case with everyone, the wicked comes in, and the peace seems to part. Have you ever noticed that no matter who you are or where you live, peace seems to come in spurts? Some have mastered the art of fighting these wicked things off, but the negativity and the evilness in this world are always waiting around the corner. Even the lives of the saved, who have eternal peace with God, seem to be anything but peaceful. Many people get a glimpse of something wonderful, and then the wicked seems to roll right in.

The wicked steals this beauty from us as the lion devours the elk or the wolf consumes the lamb. As men and women, we devour the earth every day with our sins. The truth says the sins of man have taken God's wonderfulness away and left us with this wickedness. The world has a destiny back to wonderfulness, but before the world reaches this destiny, the wicked will reign, and the destiny of the world's destruction will come first. I hear the world and the leaders in every aspect trying to pull us all together to make the world a better place. The problem with this idea is that if we all come together and the world becomes this euphoric happy place where we all can live in peace, then the Bible is wrong. The truth from God is no longer truth. That is because the truth says the world will not get better, will not heal. The Bible says the end will not be happy, but devastating.

Read what **1 Thessalonians 5:3** says: "For when they shall say, Peace and safety; then sudden **destruction** cometh upon them, as travail upon a woman with child; and they shall not escape."

God does not have a plan under which if everyone does well and works together, He will start us all with a clean slate and give us more time in this world. God's truth says that we are not of this world, and He has a new heaven and earth for us. God wants to walk with us and be at one with us. He has made all the arrangements for this to happen, and this happens only through His Son, Jesus Christ's sacrifice. Our focus should not be on seeing how perfect we can make this world. Instead, it should be on anticipating the perfection of an eternal world with our Father, who wants to be with us, as He was in the beginning.

Please in no way confuse what I am saying about the earth in which we live now. We *should* work together; we *should* love one another and try to do the best we can to beautify our lives as well as the lives of our neighbors, from right next door to all around the world. The reason you're doing this is not because you expect the world to change its ways, but because Christ is in you. Because of that, you are bringing something perfect into an imperfect world. If you profess to be a Christian, the fruit of Christ you produce will be enough to make this world a better place in which to live until the last days to come.

Before we move on, let's pretend for a moment. Let's just say, as a world, we did it; we all pulled together and made it perfect. We had no war, no famine, no crime, and no rudeness. We all worked together. Thus, we didn't even need courts. You see, the problem with trying to make this happen is unless you take sin and our wickedness out of the world, none of this can take place. We are born with a rebellious nature, and we are taught to do good. We know how to rebel all by ourselves; our nature is to have things our way. So in this perfect world, while we are all working together without God, who will be in charge? Will there never be the poor and the rich, or the hungry? This world that so many people are trying to get to with their own actions is impossible to obtain. It has no answers to these questions; we have been trying to have this world without God for so long already. It comes down to the fact that we want to have our sin and our joy all at the same time. We want this world to be about self, our lives, and then others.

So let's see what the truth has to say about the contradiction of what Christ is versus the world in which we live today.

But I say unto you, That ye resist not evil: but whosoever shall smite thee on thy right **cheek, turn** to him the other also.

Matthew 5:39

The world says: Fight back, make them respect you, show you have pride, and forgive only if they deserve it and have asked for it abundantly.

And he answering said, Thou shalt **love** the **Lord** thy God **with all** thy heart, and **with all** thy soul, and **with all** thy strength, and **with all** thy mind; and thy neighbour as thyself.

Luke 10:27

The world says: Love yourself, or no one else will. Care for those who care for you. Put your family first, and the rest comes next.

¹Then was Jesus led up of the Spirit into the wilderness to be tempted of the devil. ²And when he had fasted forty days and forty nights, he was afterward an hungred. ³And when the tempter came to him, he said, If thou be the Son of God, command that these stones be made bread. ⁴But he answered and said, It is written, Man shall not live by bread alone, but by every word that proceedeth out of the mouth of God. ⁵Then the devil taketh him up into the holy city, and setteth him on a pinnacle of the temple, ⁶and saith unto him, If thou be the Son of God, cast thyself down: for it is written, He shall give his angels charge concerning thee: and in their hands they shall bear thee up, lest at any time thou dash thy foot against a stone. ⁷Jesus said unto him, It is written again, Thou shalt not tempt the Lord thy God. ⁸Again, the devil taketh him up into an exceeding high mountain, and sheweth him all the kingdoms of the world, and the glory of them; ⁹and saith unto him, All these things will I give thee, if thou wilt fall down and worship me. ¹⁰Then saith Jesus unto him, Get thee hence,

Satan: for it is written, Thou shalt worship the Lord thy God, and him only shalt thou serve.

Matthew 4:1-10

The world says: If you're hungry, eat. If you want to rebel, rebel. If you want power and fame and riches, bow down to the world, and maybe you'll get it.

Wherein in time past ye walked according to the course of this **world**, according to the **prince** of the power of the air, the spirit that now worketh in the children of disobedience.

Ephesians 2:2

In whom the god of this **world** hath blinded the minds of them which believe **not**, lest the light of the glorious gospel of Christ, who is the image of God, should shine unto them.

2 Corinthians 4:4

[1]These words spake Jesus, and lifted up his eyes to heaven, and said, Father, the hour is come; glorify thy Son, that thy Son also may glorify thee: [2]As thou hast given him power over all flesh, that he should give eternal life to as many as thou hast given him. [3]And this is life eternal, that they might know thee the only true God, and Jesus Christ, whom thou hast sent.

[4]I have glorified thee on the earth: I have finished the work which thou gavest me to do. [5]And now, O Father, glorify thou me with thine own self with the glory which I had with thee before the world was. [6]I have manifested thy name unto the men which thou gavest me out of the world: thine they were, and thou gavest them me; and they have kept thy word. [7]Now they have known that all things whatsoever thou hast given me are of thee. [8]For I have given unto them the words which thou gavest me; and they have received them, and have known surely that I came out from thee, and they have believed that thou didst send me. [9]I pray for them: I pray not for the world, but for them which thou hast given me; for they are thine. [10]And all mine are thine, and thine are mine; and I am glorified in them. [11]And now I am no more in the world, but these are in the world, and I come to thee. Holy Father, keep through thine own name those whom thou hast given me, that they may be one, as we are. [12]While I was with them in the world, I kept them in thy name: those that thou gavest me I have kept, and none of them is lost, but the son of perdition; that the scripture might be fulfilled. [13]And now come I to thee; and these things I speak in the world, that they might have my joy fulfilled in themselves. [14]I

have given them thy word; and the world hath hated them, because they are not of the world, even as I am not of the world. [15]I pray not that thou shouldest take them out of the world, but that thou shouldest keep them from the evil. [16]They are not of the world, even as I am not of the world. [17]Sanctify them through thy truth: thy word is truth. [18]As thou hast sent me into the world, even so have I also sent them into the world. [19]And for their sakes I sanctify myself, that they also might be sanctified through the truth. [20]Neither pray I for these alone, but for them also which shall believe on me through their word; [21]That they all may be one; as thou, Father, art in me, and I in thee, that they also may be one in us: that the world may believe that thou hast sent me. [22]And the glory which thou gavest me I have given them; that they may be one, even as we are one: [23]I in them, and thou in me, that they may be made perfect in one; and that the world may know that thou hast sent me, and hast loved them, as thou hast loved me. [24]Father, I will that they also, whom thou hast given me, be with me where I am; that they may behold my glory, which thou hast given me: for thou lovedst me before the foundation of the world. [25]O righteous Father, the world hath not known thee: but I have known thee, and these have known that thou hast sent me. [26]And I have declared unto them thy name, and will declare it: that the love wherewith thou hast loved me may be in them, and I in them.

John 17:1-26

Now, I think we can see by the Scripture verses whose world we live in. God allows these things to happen, and there is no escaping that, but in God's formula, He can use the wickedness we bring to the world and make goodness from it. Notice I did not say He caused the bad things to occur, but because He is perfect, He can bring goodness from these evil, wicked things. Jesus left us with this prayer and the Father's love to see us through this world, not to keep us in it. We are destined for the new kingdom, the kingdom of Christ!

Romans 8:28 says, "And we know that all **things** work together for good to them that **love** God, to them who are the called according to his purpose."

I get so tired of people saying God did this to punish these people. The truth is in many ways, God gave this world to mankind. We are the ones who chose the wickedness; He did not. We are the ones who defile the world He gave to us, not only for ourselves, but for our children. Though we are a generation of destruction and chaos, we are asking God to make this place (our world) perfect. As a whole, we want to continue to live the way we live. We are eating horrible things, doing horrible things to our bodies, and not working out but expecting some magic pill to help us lose weight and become healthy. Doing this is a contradiction. We do these things in our lives, so why do we expect God, the Definer of truth, to help us lie to ourselves and bless our sins?

In our world, we have so many different cultures and ways of life. If we are all allowed to live our own way based on our own beliefs, there could never be any truth. We are a society that is the result of what we decide is best, whether it is about sexual preferences or the laws we enact. We have taken the truth away from these decisions and made them based on preferences for the most powerful. We want to live our lives in sin, yet we expect God to bless that with truth. This is like telling a mathematician that you want to come up with the number 2, but you are using the formula 1 - 1.

So how can God's goodness come from wicked things?

This also pertains to the formula of God and truth. Truth is not changed because someone lied and changed it. The truth still exists; someone just made up a lie and took that as the truth, when, in fact, it is not the truth. An example would be how the Pharisees took Jesus and all He said, which was true, and tried to make it into a lie.

Read the following story.

[9]And when he was departed thence, he went into their synagogue: [10]And, behold, there was a man which had his hand withered. And they asked him, saying, Is it lawful to heal on the sabbath days? that they might

accuse him. [11]And he said unto them, What man shall there be among you, that shall have one sheep, and if it fall into a pit on the sabbath day, will he not lay hold on it, and lift it out? [12]How much then is a man better than a sheep? Wherefore it is lawful to do well on the sabbath days. [13]Then saith he to the man, Stretch forth thine hand. And he stretched it forth; and it was restored whole, like as the other. [14]Then the Pharisees went out, and held a council against him, how they might destroy him. [15]But when Jesus knew it, he withdrew himself from thence: and great multitudes followed him, and he healed them all.

Matthew 12:9-15

The truth was this man needed help, and Christ didn't care what day it was, or whether it was the Sabbath. They didn't want to believe it because it interfered with their way of thinking, so they decided they would kill him, and eventually they did. So how did God and the truth get goodness out of the death of Christ? I believe you know that after three days, Christ rose from the dead, showed Himself to many, overcame death, and sent the Holy Spirit to dwell in His children. God allowed the death of His only Son, but He also made a great goodness from our wicked act, not His. *We* are the ones who murder and rape—not God and not Christ, but us. We are the ones who lie and steal—not God and not Christ. Because we sin, it doesn't make God or Christ or the truth any less perfect. In His perfection, God can bring goodness from the atrocities we cause, so that we can see His perfection in our inadequacies. This goodness He shows us through the wickedness of the world is to give us a chance to reach out to Him for salvation. When you acknowledge your sins and your bad decisions, God can make you into a vessel for Him. When you give Him your life, He will make you a new creature.

According to **2 Corinthians 5:17**, "Therefore if any man be in Christ, he is a **new creature**: old things are passed away; behold, all things are become **new**."

We need to realize the problem is we go to the evil. We don't turn away from it; we don't receive Christ and His gift. We still want to hold God accountable for our actions and our parents' actions. If you use the promises of God, then the formula will work every time, no matter what the circumstances.

If you tell the devil to flee, he will flee, but you can't tell him to flee if you're welcoming him in with your actions. That's because it's not what you say as much as what you do.

As far as being judged, God says the people who have turned from Him and not received salvation will be judged for their sins.

To me, it seems funny that we, as a society, accept our judges and laws to protect us from criminals, but we don't think God should judge us for our actions. We believe if a man rapes a woman, he should be punished and taken away from society, but God should

123

not judge us for our wrongdoings. But then who will judge the ones who never got caught, the ones society lets go?

The real problem is we don't accept that God is our Judge, but we have decided to be His judge instead.

The story below is about our judgment that has been tainted as a society. We need a righteous judge who already knows the truth before it has ever even been spoken.

The Story of M. and When the Guilty Are Let Go

M. was a fifteen-year-old girl who used to go to our church. She asked Christ into her heart a couple of years prior to this, and things seemed to be coming around for her. She was going through the rebellious stages in her life, and she did not have the perfect family, but her family loved her very much. As she was in ROTC class one day, her instructor told all the other students to leave for training, and M. was to stay back to clean a closet that stored the equipment. Then the leader took this opportunity to take her into that room and fondle and kiss her. He kept going in and out of the room to see if anyone was coming, and the last time he touched her private area, she was so scared she told him she was menstruating so he would stop. Then, he finally left the room. That evening at church, she came to me as well as her mother in tears and let us know what had happened. An arrest was made, and the trial started. They had a statement from the man, in which he admitted he had touched her breast, but said she prompted him. This was never allowed in the courtroom because he chose the right not to speak, pleading the Fifth Amendment. At the end of the trial, he was found not guilty and set free. A day later, a woman called the courthouse and said she had just heard about the trial and wanted to say he had raped her when she was in school, but she did not have the courage to speak out.

You see, society failed us in this case. There was a truth—that this teacher admitted to doing wrong—but because we have decided what truth should be allowed and not be allowed, we have come up with our own truth instead of the actual truth. We need to let real truth speak for itself, but because we won't, we all pay the price. Laws without the truth will hold no justice, only compromise and litigation. I know God will never give up on her, but it is not His fault this happened. The only good news in this event is if M. allows, God can and will bring goodness from this terrible occurrence.

CHAPTER 10

Tradition Vs. Truth: Tradition Is Winning . . . for Now

A s we all move forward in our lives, we seem to take what our ancestors have given us, add to or take away from that value, and pass it down to the next generation as truth. What if what we are passing down is tradition, and we are calling it truth from God when it's not? I will attempt to remove myself as much as possible from this chapter due to my opinion's getting in the way, but I will say that tradition in many ways has single-handedly tried to ruin the gospel as well as Christian testimonies and the church itself. Man's traditions have been replacing God's truth, and they continue to do so to this very day.

So let's decide if traditions and truth go hand in hand, or hand in foot. As you will see, Jesus had a lot to say regarding traditions, especially from the religious. To say the least, unless the tradition is from the truth, which is Christ and His Word, then the tradition is only as good as where it came from and who it is going to.

Let's look at the following traditions, and see if they're from man or God.

Tradition of slavery. Slavery has been used as part of our history and society as far back as history goes in many ways. It has spread all across the land, in every continent, and has impacted uncountable lives. So is it a truth from God, or a tradition man started? Is there a place for this, or should there have ever been a place for this in our history? The Bible talks in detail about what a servant is, should be, and should not be, but a servant is not a slave by God's truth.

Psalm 113:1 says, "Praise ye the LORD. Praise, O ye **servant**s of the LORD, praise the name of the LORD."

As we look at the Scripture, we see that many of the greatest men in the Bible had servants and were servants. The one most common factor they all shared is they were all servants to God, not slaves. They were set free from God, not imprisoned.

In discussing a servant and a slave, I will not go into detail as to one race over the next when it comes to slavery. So many races, from the Israelites to African-Americans, have been held captive in slavery over the years. However, certain races have received much more punishment and have gone through extraordinarily worse circumstances than other races. The truth is slavery is from man; it is our tradition, not God's. Men have been killing one another and trying to be over and outdo one another from the beginning, starting with Cain and Abel, the sons of Adam and Eve.

So in short, the tradition of slavery is an abomination to any society, whereas the truth of being a servant is from God to all societies. God has never wanted His children to be enslaved. On many occasions, He has allowed slavery to take place and even initiated the onset of it, but His will is not enslavement; it is freedom. He wants us to be free and to show that He allowed His Son to die for all of us so we could obtain that freedom. He does not differentiate — the white, the black, the brown, and the yellow are all being saved by the red blood of the Son of God.

This is the essence of God, giving not only to us, but also to the angels themselves, free will to serve Him or, by default, serve ourselves and Satan.

Read **Psalm 19:28-32**:

28My soul melteth for heaviness: strengthen thou me according unto thy word. 29Remove from me the way of lying: and grant me thy law graciously. 30I have chosen the way of truth: thy judgments have I laid before me. 31I have stuck unto thy testimonies: O LORD, put me not to shame. 32I will run the way of thy commandments, when thou shalt enlarge my heart.

King David, who wrote this, was chosen by God, just as Israel as a nation was chosen by God.

Second Thessalonians 2:13 says:

But we are bound to give thanks alway to God for you, brethren beloved of the Lord, because God hath from the beginning **chose**n you to salvation through sanctification of the Spirit and belief of the truth.

While God is the One who chooses you, you choose whether to follow. God chose Satan to be an angel, but Satan rebelled. God chose Adam and Eve, but they rebelled. God gives all men the opportunity, but the man or the woman must be willing to accept. God knows who will choose and who won't, but regardless of the choices we make, God does not change; we do. God is not dependent on me to fulfill His will. God needs only to depend on His might, His strength, as He is the Fulfiller of His own will. When I do fulfill His will, it is only because He gave me the strength to do so.

[1]I am the true vine, and my Father is the husbandman. [2]Every branch in me that beareth not fruit he taketh away: and every branch that beareth fruit, he purgeth it, that it may bring forth more fruit. [3]Now ye are clean through the word which I have spoken unto you. [4]Abide in me, and I in you. As the branch cannot bear fruit of itself, except it abide in the vine; no more can ye, except ye abide in me. [5]I am the vine, ye are the branches: He that abideth in me, and I in him, the same bringeth forth much fruit: for without me ye can

do nothing. ⁶If a man abide not in me, he is cast forth as a branch, and is withered; and men gather them, and cast them into the fire, and they are burned. ⁷If ye abide in me, and my words abide in you, ye shall ask what ye will, and it shall be done unto you. ⁸Herein is my Father glorified, that ye bear much fruit; so shall ye be my disciples. ⁹As the Father hath loved me, so have I loved you: continue ye in my love. ¹⁰If ye keep my commandments, ye shall abide in my love; even as I have kept my Father's commandments, and abide in his love. ¹¹These things have I spoken unto you, that my joy might remain in you, and that your joy might be full. ¹²This is my commandment, That ye love one another, as I have loved you. ¹³Greater love hath no man than this, that a man lay down his life for his friends. ¹⁴Ye are my friends, if ye do whatsoever I command you. ¹⁵Henceforth I call you not servants; for the servant knoweth not what his lord doeth: but I have called you friends; for all things that I have heard of my Father I have made known unto you. ¹⁶Ye have not chosen me, but I have chosen you, and ordained you, that ye should go and bring forth fruit, and that your fruit should remain: that whatsoever ye shall ask of the Father in my name, he may give it you. ¹⁷These things I command you, that ye love one another. [18]If the world hate you, ye know that it hated me before it hated you. [19]If ye were of the world, the world would love his own: but because ye are not of the world, but I have chosen you out of the world, therefore the world hateth you. [20]Remember the word that I said unto you, The servant is not greater than his lord. If they have persecuted me, they will also persecute you; if they have kept my saying, they will keep yours also. [21]But all these things will they do unto you for my name's sake, because they know not him that sent me. [22]If I had not come and spoken unto them, they had not had sin: but now they have no cloak for their sin. [23]He that hateth me hateth my Father also. [24]If I had not done among them the works which none other man did, they had not had sin: but now have they both seen and hated both me and my Father. [25]But this cometh to pass, that the word might be fulfilled that is written in their law, They hated me without a cause. [26]But when the Comforter is come, whom I will send unto you from the Father, even the Spirit of truth, which proceedeth from the Father, he shall testify of me: [27]And ye also shall bear witness, because ye have been with me from the beginning.

<u>John 15:1-27</u>

You may not think of yourself as a slave to anyone. However, when we reflect on our lives, we all do seem to be slaves to something. Whether it's drugs or alcohol, lust, food, our jobs, our spouses, our children, ourselves, our false gods, or the one true God. It seems no matter how good we have it or how smart we are or how beautiful we may be, we are slaves. Whatever it is that we hold on to in life that makes us feel alive and meaningful, valuable, we are slaves to. Slavery is as common today as it ever has been, and just as rewarding if enslaved by righteous things of God, and just as debilitating if enslaved by anything other than God and Christ Himself.

So what are you enslaved by at this very moment? Is it your thoughts of lust or greed? Maybe your wife or husband is all that consumes your mind. Could it be your children? Have you not realized that no matter what it is, you can never get enough of it, and it does not give you the complete and long-lasting peace you had hoped it would? If it does bring you peace, does it bring anyone else around you peace? The truth says to be a servant is an honorable thing, and as we all know, the truth will set you free.

Isaiah 58:6 says, "Is not this the fast that I have **chose**n? to loose the bands of wickedness, to undo the heavy burdens, and to let the oppressed go free, and that ye break every yoke?"

Colossians 3:23-24 tells us: "[23]And whatsoever ye do, do it heartily, as to the Lord, and not unto men; [24]knowing that of the Lord ye shall receive the reward of the inheritance: for ye serve the Lord Christ."

And **Mark 12:30** says, "And thou shalt **love** the **Lord** thy God **with all** thy heart, and **with all** thy soul, and **with all** thy mind, and **with all** thy strength: this is the first commandment."

When you are able to do these things, the foundation has been laid for all else to come. Godly wisdom, peace, power, and freedom all begin with this commandment.

Many people feel this is impossible to do, and for them, it is and always will be. The reason it is impossible is their love is for others or for themselves; it has been displaced to people or things that do not have the power of God.

God and Jesus showed us that serving God first and your neighbor second is where the reward and freedom for ourselves come from. Real fulfillment comes from seeing someone else happy due to something you may have done or been a part of. As a parent, that fulfillment is seeing our child have joy because of a birthday or a gift, even just a day that has given them happiness. The parent could have had a hundred birthdays for himself or herself, but never received the joy he or she received from the child's birthday. That is how God looks at us; He wants to give us these things. His joy comes from seeing His children satisfied and joyful in Him. The happiness we get from serving others is where we will obtain true peace. As the truth says, to be a real leader, you must first be the lowliest of servants, and then the leadership is earned and not given. That is the reason Jesus washed the feet of the disciples. Jesus came to serve as a Savior and, in return, will reign as a King.

Traditions in Our Church and the Religions Under the Crucifixion

Over the years as a Christian, this has been a real battle for me, trying to see what is truly from God in our churches and what has been brought by man. I have personally experienced many traditional rules and ceremonial practices that are the exact opposite of what God intended church or His Word to be. Racism, bigotry, condemnation, and rule-based religion, spoken and unspoken, are significant issues in our churches today. These things have led to why our churches have failed us over their history. The failure of unity has divided Christians from the beginning, from the crucifixion to the rising of our Savior, Jesus Christ, and continues to this very day.

_____**Matthew 12:22-30** states:

[22]Then was brought unto him one possessed with a devil, blind, and dumb: and he healed him, insomuch that the blind and dumb both spake and saw.

[23]And all the people were amazed, and said, Is not this the son of David?

[24]But when the Pharisees heard it, they said, This fellow doth not cast out devils, but by Beelzebub the prince of the devils.

[25]And Jesus knew their thoughts, and said unto them, Every kingdom divided against itself is brought to desolation; and every city or house divided against itself shall not stand:

[26]And if Satan cast out Satan, he is divided against himself; how shall then his kingdom stand?

[27]And if I by Beelzebub cast out devils, by whom do your children cast them out? therefore they shall be your judges.

[28]But if I cast out devils by the Spirit of God, then the kingdom of God is come unto you.

[29]Or else how can one enter into a strong man's house, and spoil his goods, except he first bind the strong man? and then he will spoil his house.

[30]He that is not with me is against me; and he that gathereth not with me scattereth abroad.

Satan knows that he has been defeated, but that will not stop him from trying to overcome man and lead as many souls as he possibly can to hell. Satan also knows the easiest way to take away from the truth is to cause confusion. How do you cause confusion? First, one does this by questioning the truth and not accepting it for what it is: fact.

Matthew 4:1-11 tells us:

[1]Then was Jesus led up of the Spirit into the wilderness to be tempted of the devil.

[2]And when he had fasted forty days and forty nights, he was afterward an hungred.

[3]And when the tempter came to him, he said, If thou be the Son of

God, command that these stones be made bread.

[4]But he answered and said, It is written, Man shall not live by bread alone, but by every word that proceedeth out of the mouth of God.

[5]Then the devil taketh him up into the holy city, and setteth him on a pinnacle of the temple,

[6]And saith unto him, If thou be the Son of God, cast thyself down: for it is written, He shall give his angels charge concerning thee: and in their hands they shall bear thee up, lest at any time thou dash thy foot against a stone.

[7]Jesus said unto him, It is written again, Thou shalt not tempt the Lord thy God.

[8]Again, the devil taketh him up into an exceeding high mountain, and sheweth him all the kingdoms of the world, and the glory of them;

[9]And saith unto him, All these things will I give thee, if thou wilt fall down and worship me.

[10]Then saith Jesus unto him, Get thee hence, Satan: for it is written, Thou shalt worship the Lord thy God, and him only shalt thou serve.

[11]Then the devil leaveth him, and, behold, angels came and ministered unto him.

As you can see, in the first two cases, Satan first tempts Christ with doubt: "If you're truly the Son of God, then . . . ." Notice what Satan did to Eve in the garden:

¹Now the serpent was more subtil than any beast of the field which the LORD God had made. And he said unto the woman, Yea, hath God said, Ye shall not eat of every tree of the garden? ²And the woman said unto the serpent, We may eat of the fruit of the trees of the garden: ³But of the fruit of the tree which is in the midst of the garden, God hath said, Ye shall not eat of it, neither shall ye touch it, lest ye die. ⁴And the serpent said unto the woman, Ye shall not surely die: ⁵For God doth know that in the day ye eat thereof, then your eyes shall be opened, and ye shall be as gods, knowing good and evil. ⁶And when the woman saw that the tree was good for food, and that it was pleasant to the eyes, and a tree to be desired to make one wise, she took of the fruit thereof, and did eat, and gave also unto her husband with her; and he did eat. ⁷And the eyes of them both were opened, and they knew that they were naked; and they sewed fig leaves together, and made themselves aprons.

Genesis 3:1-7

Eve was first given doubt that what God said was really true. If they ate of that fruit, they would die. And every day, Satan does this to us. He makes us wonder, *Does God exist? Does He care for me? Is He here with me now?* Satan's answers to these questions are no, no, and no. However, God's answers are yes, yes, and yes! Which one we believe is evident in our attitude and testimony every time we act or speak.

When there is doubt, faith is vanished. God says that unless you come to Him as a little child, you shall not enter into heaven. What He is saying here is that a child has unwavering faith. When a parent tells a child something, he or she believes it. Good examples are the Easter bunny and Santa Clause—children believe and never question them until when? They question when the truth comes back void because there is no truth in either instance. With Christ, the truth never stops or wavers, so the initial faith is always sustained, at least from Christ's end.

The second way we get confused is by bringing in man's glory and opinions, man's preference on how that truth should be handled. Catholics, Baptists, those at the Church of God, Methodists, Presbyterians, independents, Anglo-Saxons, Pentecostals all stem from the same truth—which is a creating God, a crucified Jesus and a risen Savior, who overcame death. When you then add in our opinions and traditional ceremonies, we tend to change these solid truths as we go. See the Scripture passage below, telling of when Jesus confronted religious leaders about their traditions.

[1]Then came to Jesus scribes and Pharisees, which were of Jerusalem, saying,

[2]Why do thy disciples transgress the tradition of the elders? for they

wash not their hands when they eat bread.

³But he answered and said unto them, Why do ye also transgress the commandment of God by your tradition?

⁴For God commanded, saying, Honour thy father and mother: and, He that curseth father or mother, let him die the death.

⁵But ye say, Whosoever shall say to his father or his mother, It is a gift, by whatsoever thou mightest be profited by me;

⁶And honour not his father or his mother, he shall be free. Thus have ye made the commandment of God of none effect by your tradition.

⁷Ye hypocrites, well did Esaias prophesy of you, saying,

⁸This people draweth nigh unto me with their mouth, and honoureth me with their lips; but their heart is far from me.

⁹But in vain they do worship me, teaching for doctrines the commandments of men.

¹⁰And he called the multitude, and said unto them, Hear, and understand:

¹¹Not that which goeth into the mouth defileth a man; but that which cometh out of the mouth, this defileth a man.

¹²Then came his disciples, and said unto him, Knowest thou that the Pharisees were offended, after they heard this saying?

¹³But he answered and said, Every plant, which my heavenly Father hath not planted, shall be rooted up.

¹⁴Let them alone: they be blind leaders of the blind. And if the blind lead the blind, both shall fall into the ditch.

¹⁵Then answered Peter and said unto him, Declare unto us this

parable.

¹⁶And Jesus said, Are ye also yet without understanding?

¹⁷Do not ye yet understand, that whatsoever entereth in at the mouth goeth into the belly, and is cast out into the draught?

¹⁸But those things which proceed out of the mouth come forth from the heart; and they defile the man.

¹⁹For out of the heart proceed evil thoughts, murders, adulteries, fornications, thefts, false witness, blasphemies:

²⁰These are the things which defile a man: but to eat with unwashen hands defileth not a man.

Matthew 15:1-20

What Satan did was take the religious ones, the ones that were looked upon as the model children of God, and make them into vessels of power, not from God, but from themselves. Satan let them keep their religious ceremonies, and he took away their heart for God and left them with only the shell of religion. When people were trying to please God through following the law instead of drawing man toward God, it drove man away. Similarly, today, many people don't go to church because they don't feel worthy or welcomed enough to enter the doors. We have made our churches into halls of prestigiousness and accomplishments, halls of doing right and following the law, halls sinners can only look up at and feel worse about themselves, not better. The other halls we have made—halls of wealth and good times, where people can come, and if they do this or that, life will bring them roses—are a matter of mind over matter, not the mind of God.

Mark 2:17 tells us, "When Jesus heard it, he saith unto them, They that are whole have no need of the **physician**, but they that are sick: I came not to call the righteous, but sinners to repentance."

As this verse points out, Christ's hall and sanctuary are made for the sinner, not the righteous. They are made not for the strong, but for the weak; not for the one who could accomplish the most, but for the one who could serve the most. Christ's hall is decorated in a humbling, pure birth, with only the basics for life. A stained cleansing blood covers the wall to show that this house was made for the filthy to become clean. Finally, the house is glorified and covered in victory from a risen living Savior, who overcame death in this world for Himself and for all those willing to receive Him.

Note that these changes we add to the truth have consequences. I know a man whose wife got diagnosed with cancer in her thirties. As she was in her last stages, she called a priest, as she was Catholic, and asked him to help her. His response was, "There is nothing I can do." He said due to his rules and regulations, he could not help her because as a Catholic, you have to go through certain things to become ready for salvation. However, if he had followed the truth, he could have led her to Christ in that very moment . . . but he stopped listening to the truth and was focused on tradition. I am glad the truth says, "If you call on Me, I will come," not, "If you do a bunch of stuff first, call on Me then."

Revelation 3:20 says, "Behold, I stand at the **door**, and knock: if any man hear my voice, and open the **door**, I will come in to him, and will sup with him, and he with me."

Our churches need to stop adding things to our truth, a truth that needs no additions. If our churches hope to ever accomplish unity among ourselves, we will have to put away the traditional things and come with only the truth, a truth in our crucified and risen Savior, Jesus Christ. **Make no mistake when thinking of heaven as one unified body of Christ, serving one unified Holy Trinity. We will serve as one unit without division.**

Let's discuss just a few of the traditions that have split many a church.

Tradition of Music

The world of music and sound is endless, it seems, with new styles of music coming out each year. We have all seen music change over the years, not to mention the changes from the history of the world. Music seems to be broken down not only by continents and nations, but also by differences in northern and southern states. The instruments used for this music vary, and there are a multitude of sounds, fashions, and sizes.

The question is, What defines music as being good or bad? I will speak specifically in regards to the traditional logic of music in our churches and religions, but this really covers all music. We have all heard the hymns that continue over the years; there are so many wonderful songs that praise the Lord. Many leaders in our churches today say that the only music they deem acceptable is this style of godly music. So the question is, What is godly music, and what is not? For example, I have heard that Christian rock 'n' roll is not godly. *Why is that?* I ask myself. *Is it the instruments? Maybe it's the lyrics. Is it how the music is played?* I will address these questions, but at the end of the day, it always seems to come full circle back to preference. My fellow Christians always say, "God is separate from the world, so why are we bringing the worldly music into a godly environment? Why bring rock 'n' roll, which is assumed to be ungodly and worldly, and try to make it godly? Regarding this, or any other, type of music, let's see what the truth has to say.

It came even to pass, as the trumpeters and singers were as one, to make one sound to be heard in praising and thanking the LORD; and when they lifted up their voice with the trumpets and cymbals and instruments of **music**k, and praised the LORD, saying, For he is good; for his mercy endureth for ever: that then the house was filled with a cloud, even the house of the LORD.

2 Chronicles 5:13

Now his elder son was in the field: and as he came and drew nigh to the house, he heard **music**k and dancing.

Luke 15:25

143

So can Christian rock 'n' roll music be acceptable to God? The Bible says it can. If the words are clear, and it praises God in a truthful way, then it is a joyful noise to God, whom it is written for anyway. Any song, no matter what instruments are used or whose voice is heard, is acceptable if it is used to praise God and Jesus Christ. You may not like the instruments or the voice, and you may not understand where the person is coming from, but you get to choose whether or not to listen to it. The problem is when we start deciding what is acceptable, and what is not, to God based on our standards and not His, we are pushing judgment on others regarding what we feel is acceptable. God sees the heart; He looks to see the origin of the song, the lyrics, and the meaning behind the song.

First Chronicles 28:9 says:

And thou, Solomon my son, know thou the God of thy father, and serve him with a perfect **heart** and with a willing mind: for the LORD searcheth all **heart**s, and understandeth all the imaginations of the thoughts: if thou seek him, he will be found of thee; but if thou forsake him, he will cast thee off for ever.

Music was created from God, and just like the other gifts God has given to us, we get to choose to use it to glorify Him or to glorify ourselves. A personal example is I love to listen to Fleetwood Mac, especially the music with Stevie Nicks. The good thing about this music is that it is beautiful in so many ways to me and many others who enjoy the group's style. The lyrics are encrypted many ways to symbolize the most basic things about life and love and whatever else. The voices used to sing these songs are original and like no others. Growing up with this music meant a lot to me, and when I was sad or depressed, it made me feel better. When I was happy, it made me even happier. Looking at this music from this standpoint, what could be wrong with it? The Beatles, AC/DC, and The Rolling Stones were all masters of their musical industries, so what is wrong with this music?

The problem with this music, and any other music like it, whether it is rock, country, or jazz, is what is at the heart of what they are writing. Where is it from, and what does it encourage us to do? Does it consist of ungodly things from men and women at a time in their lives when they were writing songs that were from their ungodly lives? As a society, we've opened our eyes and ears to artists who have very ungodly characteristics, and we have allowed their very ungodly lives to enter into our lives.

For many of us, music seems to serve a purpose. In some ways, music is a way of relaxing and getting away from the stresses of this world. In other ways, it is a way of expressing ourselves and speaking about what we feel with lyrics and notes. Just like everything else God made, music was to be enjoyed by men and women. And just like with everything else, some people have chosen to use it to glorify God, and some have used it to glorify themselves. Don't blame the instruments or the sound; blame the singer, the orchestrator, the definer of the song. So before judging someone for his or her musical preference, find out if he or she celebrates God and godly things, or just himself or herself and the things of this world.

The Tradition of Women

What a beautiful topic to discuss concerning the most beautiful thing God ever created (that is my opinion, of course). Women were made specifically for a reason, and that was to be with and to complete a man. The woman is the second piece of the union that made two separate people feel as if they were one together. God could have just used dust to make Eve, as He had done to make Adam, but He didn't. He made her from one of Adam's ribs so they would be of one body, joined for life. We know women's roles have changed from the beginning of the garden all the way to this very day, and they will continue to change in the future, no doubt. What I will focus on is what God says about women, and what have we, as men and women, made the women into.

Genesis 3:20 says, "And **Adam** called his wife's name **Eve**; because she was the mother of all living."

Furthermore, we read in **Genesis 2:18-25**:

[18]And the LORD God said, It is not good that the man should be alone; I will make him an help meet for him.

[19]And out of the ground the LORD God formed every beast of the

field, and every fowl of the air; and brought them unto Adam to see what he would call them: and whatsoever Adam called every living creature, that was the name thereof.

20And Adam gave names to all cattle, and to the fowl of the air, and to every beast of the field; but for Adam there was not found an help meet for him.

21And the LORD God caused a deep sleep to fall upon Adam, and he slept: and he took one of his ribs, and closed up the flesh instead thereof;

22and the rib, which the LORD God had taken from man, made he a woman, and brought her unto the man.

23And Adam said, This is now bone of my bones, and flesh of my flesh: she shall be called Woman, because she was taken out of Man.

24Therefore shall a man leave his father and his mother, and shall cleave unto his wife: and they shall be one flesh.

25And they were both naked, the man and his wife, and were not ashamed.

Notice when I said God made Eve second, I did not say He did so to serve Adam; He did so to complete Adam, just as Adam completed Eve. Man's traditions over the years have seemed to place women under men, second to them, and to serve them. Is this true, and is it from God? How about women working or being submissive to their husbands in every way?

We all realize women have a role to play in society, just as men do. Before the Fall of man and woman, neither knew of shame or nakedness; they walked with God in the dew of the morning. In fact, they were at peace with one another, and the union they enjoyed was prepared and graced by God every day. The woman's role was equal to Adam's in every way. One was not preferred more than the other, and God designed the two to be very different from each other, but still in perfect harmony together.

From the beginning, man and woman were made to be together for joy and peace. It was one more wonderful design God put into motion when He created a perfect world for us to live in.

After the Fall of man and woman, the roles changed drastically.

Read **Genesis 3:6-24**:

[6]And when the woman saw that the tree was good for food, and that it was pleasant to the eyes, and a tree to be desired to make one wise, she took of the fruit thereof, and did eat, and gave also unto her husband with her; and he did eat.

[7]And the eyes of them both were opened, and they knew that they were naked; and they sewed fig leaves together, and made themselves aprons.

[8]And they heard the voice of the LORD God walking in the garden in the cool of the day: and Adam and his wife hid themselves from the presence of the LORD God amongst the trees of the garden.

[9]And the LORD God called unto Adam, and said unto him, Where art thou?

[10]And he said, I heard thy voice in the garden, and I was afraid, because I was naked; and I hid myself.

[11]And he said, Who told thee that thou wast naked? Hast thou eaten of the tree, whereof I commanded thee that thou shouldest not eat?

[12]And the man said, The woman whom thou gavest to be with me, she gave me of the tree, and I did eat.

[13]And the LORD God said unto the woman, What is this that thou hast done? And the woman said, The serpent beguiled me, and I did eat.

[14]And the LORD God said unto the serpent, Because thou hast done this, thou art cursed above all cattle, and above every beast of the field; upon thy belly shalt thou go, and dust shalt thou eat all the days of thy life:

[15]And I will put enmity between thee and the woman, and between thy seed and her seed; it shall bruise thy head, and thou shalt bruise his heel.

[16]Unto the woman he said, I will greatly multiply thy sorrow and thy conception; in sorrow thou shalt bring forth children; and thy desire shall be to thy husband, and he shall rule over thee.

[17]And unto Adam he said, Because thou hast hearkened unto the voice of thy wife, and hast eaten of the tree, of which I commanded thee, saying, Thou shalt not eat of it: cursed is the ground for thy sake; in sorrow shalt thou eat of it all the days of thy life;

[18]Thorns also and thistles shall it bring forth to thee; and thou shalt eat the herb of the field;

[19]In the sweat of thy face shalt thou eat bread, till thou return unto the ground; for out of it wast thou taken: for dust thou art, and unto dust shalt thou return.

[20]And Adam called his wife's name Eve; because she was the mother of all living.

[21]Unto Adam also and to his wife did the LORD God make coats of skins, and clothed them.

[22]And the LORD God said, Behold, the man is become as one of us, to know good and evil: and now, lest he put forth his hand, and take also of the tree of life, and eat, and live for ever:

[23]Therefore the LORD God sent him forth from the garden of Eden, to till the ground from whence he was taken.

[24]So he drove out the man; and he placed at the east of the garden of Eden Cherubims, and a flaming sword which turned every way, to keep the way of the tree of life.

God gave each party of the rebellion a just punishment and gave them the role they would play throughout their earthly lives. Man has taken hold of this, and as a worldly tradition, we have decided to treat women as inferior to men. The Word of God says the man was to become over the woman, not treat her as inferior to him, not make her a slave to him, not make her a weak vessel. God gave the charge of the one flesh that they still were to the man. He gave the authority of the couple to the man; he was to be the leader, not the master.

Speaking traditionally, first in our history, the woman was to obey the man and give him rule over her life as well as the family. She was to be submissive in every way and was to be guided by her father and then turned over to her husband when married.

As we all have seen, man has abused that authority that was given him, and instead of leading the wife and family in a spiritual way, the man in many cases has decided to abuse the wife and the family. Man has used the leadership God gave him to meet his own desires. Many traditional men take this Scripture and decide that the woman must give him all sexual gratification whenever he likes, and that the children and wife must honor him as the leader, even if he is not much of one. Man has taken the leadership but left the working role that comes along with it—the honoring God, and leading the family in prayer and things of God—and the man wonders why he gets no respect in his own house.

Read **Ephesians chapter 5** and **Colossians chapter 3**; a few of the key verses follow.

For the **husband** is the head of the wife, even as Christ is the head of the church: and he is the saviour of the body.

Ephesians 5:23

Therefore as the church is subject unto Christ, so let the wives be to their own **husband**s in every thing.

Ephesians 5:24

Husbands, love your wives, even as Christ also loved the church, and gave himself for it.

Ephesians 5:25

Nevertheless let every one of you in particular so love his wife even as himself; and the wife see that she reverence her **husband**.

Ephesians 5:33

Wives, submit yourselves unto your own **husband**s, as it is fit in the Lord.

Colossians 3:18

Husbands, love your wives, and be not bitter against them.

Colossians 3:19

Furthermore, **1 Peter 3:7** tells us:

Likewise, ye **husband**s, dwell with them according to knowledge, giving honour unto the wife, as unto the weaker vessel, and as being heirs together of the grace of life; that your prayers be not hindered.

The role of the woman is still to complement the man, as he should complement her. The woman is to be respected and honored. When that is done, the woman will want to follow the man and be submissive to his leadership. If these Scriptures were taken with the correct understanding, the woman's role is respectful and rewarding for all. However, once man put his two cents in and used it to his advantage, the woman became weak and enslaved.

Of course, due to this, women revolted and changed their role in spite of men, as any person does when enslaved long enough. Remember, it does not take every man to make something bad happen. One man can commit an act, and many could suffer. This has led to the following tradition, which is sweeping through our societies all over the world.

Today, a second tradition related to women that has taken its hold on America, and the world, is that they can be more powerful than men, and they don't even need men. Man has become a bumbling fool who knows nothing much, just a glorified caveman. The woman is being taught that she can become the man of the house, of the church, and of the office. With this new tradition that women have come up with, due mostly to men's failure to do their job, the man is now expendable. Women have decided they will do things their own way. To accomplish this, they use their beauty and their bodies; others use their intellect and wisdom. Essentially, women have taken the gifts God gave them to please men and used them for their own greed. Look at our society; turn on your television, and you'll notice advertisers are using **sex to sell**. Women found out a long time ago that men could be persuaded by affecting their sex drive and their wallets. Women now use their bodies and beauty to gain power, money, and fame, and they use their minds to try and become the leaders. I see these young beautiful girls becoming stars, either through their singing talents or their acting abilities. First they get on shows on such networks as The Disney Channel and come into our lives in a clean way, but as soon as they get older, they allow it to happen. Someone persuades them, or they decide for themselves, to use their bodies and beauty to obtain their goals in life: more money, more power, and more fans. Our society tells them the less they wear, the more seductive they can be, and the more we will like them. Society tells them that if they stay clean, their career will be over. This is true, by the way. Men will tend to like them more, but not for their talents or their inner beauty; men will like them only for their bodies.

The reason this tradition will not bring women true joy is because a woman's true accomplishment, just as a man's, will only be fulfilled when a person loves the beauty on the inside, not just on the outside, when a woman can be successful without giving up her morals. Many women want to be respected for their minds and talent, but the majority are using their bodies to get ahead. If women are tired of being looked at as sexual entities and want to be respected for their inner beauty, they must change the younger generation of girls. Stop presenting yourselves to society as women who believe that if you've got it, you should use it, and use it as long as you can to get what you can.

Tradition of What to Wear

I went to a church once where the women all wore skirts because jeans were considered inappropriate. The problem is the skirts were all tight and were more revealing than the jeans. You see, what we wear is a reflection of who we are or who we want to be. The clothes are a covering for our bodies because of the sin and shame of nakedness in public that dates all the way back to Adam and Eve.

Read **Genesis chapters 2 and 3**, some verses of which are included here:

And they were both **naked**, the man and his wife, and were not ashamed.

Genesis 2:25

And the eyes of them both were opened, and they knew that they were **naked**; and they sewed fig leaves together, and made themselves aprons.

Genesis 3:7

And he said, I heard thy voice in the garden, and I was afraid, because I was **naked**; and I hid myself.

Genesis 3:10

Many men's traditions regarding clothes, especially for their little girls, dictate that you should not wear anything revealing that would entice someone else in a sexual way, especially in church. The problem with this is that men and women want to look good. No matter how many layers we put on, we want people to acknowledge us as being beautiful. We all want to be beautiful in one way or another. **We all want to be loved.**

Beyond man's traditions, God's truth about clothes is that you should dress modestly. Notice I did not say ugly or boring, but *modestly*. The truth says that the outside of the vessel is not as important as the inside. When you are happy with God on the inside, your desire to please everyone else on the outside to make yourself feel good won't be as much of a priority. Your dependability on your looks will not own you, but instead, you will own it. So the question is, What should you wear? Wear what you want, knowing that you don't just represent yourself, but you represent what your Father in heaven has done for you. What you wear speaks about who you are, how you feel, and how you want others to perceive you. The answer to *What should I wear?* is there every time you put on your clothes; you just have to ask yourself, *Why am I wearing this?*

Tradition of Marriage

As we all know, marriage has been a part of society forever. The combining of a couple to be together forever is a sacred principle from God, and He tells us clearly what it should be and when it should end. From God's perspective, He made man and woman to be together forever, with no earthly end, as we can see with the first husband and wife, Adam and Eve.

Genesis chapter 2 describes this.

And the LORD God caused a deep sleep to fall upon Adam, and he slept: and he took one of his ribs, and closed up the **flesh** instead thereof.

Genesis 2:21

And Adam said, This is now bone of my bones, and **flesh** of my **flesh**: she shall be called Woman, because she was taken out of Man.

Genesis 2:23

Through the years, society has made its own marriage traditions and defined what marriage is supposed to be. All around the world, marriages vary differently, and I will not go into too much detail, as everyone has a reason for doing what he or she does. I will say that whether it is a marriage that has been set up before the couple is two years old, or the marriage is between the same sexes, the tradition of marriage from God has been changed by man. Just as everything else people come in contact with, we seem to have changed it up from its original intentions. This change is almost always to meet our needs. God never intended for perverted marriages or divorce to happen, but because of our flaws and irresponsible decisions, He allowed these things to be.

Matthew 19:3-9 states:

³The Pharisees also came unto him, tempting him, and saying unto him, Is it lawful for a man to put away his wife for every cause? ⁴And he answered and said unto them, Have ye not read, that he which made them at the beginning made them male and female, ⁵and said, For this cause shall a man leave father and mother, and shall cleave to his wife: and they twain shall be one flesh? ⁶Wherefore they are no more twain, but one flesh. What therefore God hath joined together, let not man put asunder. ⁷They say unto him, Why did Moses then command to give a writing of divorcement, and to put her away? ⁸He saith unto them, Moses because of the hardness of your hearts suffered you to put away your wives: but from the beginning it was not so. ⁹And I say unto you, Whosoever shall put away his wife, except it be for fornication, and shall marry another, committeth adultery: and whoso marrieth her which is put away doth commit adultery.

In regards to divorce, infidelity was the only way it was approved to become separated.

The truth says that when you are married, both became one, and there is no separation. What have we turned marriage into? It has become legal contracts and "stay with me until better," and not "for better or worse."

The truth says marriage is not between a man and a man, or a woman and a woman, but a man and a wife. It's not between a man and a woman in a relationship with another man and another woman, consentingly or not. This is not my truth, but the truth from a loving God, who created each one of us in His own image.

Rule-based Religion

Lastly, let's answer the questions "Why did all these foundational righteous things of God become traditional things of men? Why did women and men turn to these perversions of the truth?"

One major reason is the above title: "rule-based religion."

The problem we have in many churches, especially the more traditional ones, is that every person is not able to express himself or herself and his or her style, the way God made the person, whether it is with music or dress. We like to model the perfect Christians and make them our poster children for what we think a good Christian is supposed to be. "Don't drink, but you can smoke"; "Don't do drugs, but let's all go get fat from eating Sunday dinner."

There is a right way to live your life, and that is to walk with God in freedom, not imprisonment. God says, "If you love Me, you will follow My commandments."

This is stated in the following verses.

Jesus answered and said unto him, If a man **love me**, he will keep my words: and my Father will **love** him, and we will come unto him, and make our abode with him.

John 14:23

If ye **love me**, keep my commandments.

John 14:15

Our God knew that for us to really follow His law and live His way, it would have to be done out of a love for Him and not because we are told to do so. He knew that if I would ever love my enemy, it would be because I had a love for Him and knew that He loved me when I was His enemy.

He knew that if He told me to give up everything I owned and follow Him, I would do it because my love for Him is all that I own. God shows us the two greatest commandments are these:

[36]Master, which is the great commandment in the law?

[37]Jesus said unto him, Thou shalt love the Lord thy God with all thy heart, and with all thy soul, and with all thy mind.

[38]This is the first and great commandment.

[39]And the second is like unto it, Thou shalt love thy neighbour as thyself.

[40]On these two commandments hang all the law and the prophets.

Matthew 22:36-40

The reason it all hinges on these two things is because without doing them both with a true love in your heart, there is no value in either. This is the start of the formula, and without the start, the next step can never be reached.

So what God and the truth say I can do, tradition in many ways says I can't. Tradition says I am to go along with what has always been done. However, **God says, "If you follow Me, I will put the truth in your heart and mind, and no man will be able to take it away." God set you free to worship and love Him because you are different from anyone who ever was or ever will be. You are His child and like no other.**

Rod's Story

Many years ago, I made a friend; we will call him Rod. At first we said the normal hellos and moved on, as most neighbors do. I saw him running one day and because I had just started running myself, I asked if he wanted to run together sometime. We started to meet once a week, usually on Sunday mornings, and we would run a mile or two. He would listen to me talk about the Bible, and I would listen to him speak about the things going on in his life. He was going through a lot at that time, and it was a good opportunity for me to share what had made a change in my life.

After about two years of running together and getting to know each other, I, of course, knew he didn't attend a church regularly, so I invited him to mine. We had talked about his going to church, but for some reason, he had never made a commitment to one. He agreed to come to the church that Sunday after his run, and I was pretty excited for him, hoping what Christ had done for me He would also do for Rod. When we arrived that morning, we both walked into the church together. As I was going to the pulpit, Rod was following me in. As we came in, an older man who sat in the front pew scowled at my friend. The older man had always seemed to be unpleasant, but this was something different; there was hatred in his eyes, hatred projected toward someone whom he had never met before. I guess I need to mention that my friend Rod is black, and the church he came to, the one I invited him to with such high hopes, was a church where all members who attended were white. The church had never had a black member, nor had a black man ever been baptized at this church. To say the least, I was totally shocked at this older man's actions, but I thought maybe I was the only one who noticed.

Isn't it amazing how quickly Satan and the demons come after someone looking for peace in Christ? They waste no time trying to make a mockery of Christ and His church, of what Christ really stood for. Anyway, after the morning announcements, we retreated to Sunday school, and as we were walking back, Rod said jokingly, "I don't think your buddy liked me too much." Then, trying to downplay it, I said, "What are you talking about?" Rod looked at me and said, "Come on, you saw how he looked at me." And because I knew he was right and as embarrassed as I was for our church and members, I told Rod two things you should never do when it comes to a church.

First, don't ever judge Jesus and/or God based on people and their actions or ways. As followers of Christ, we should be examples of Christ, and as Christians, we should act in a loving way to everyone. The Lord knows we all mess this up more times than we should, but the evidence of our walk should be apparent. Judge God for God's actions, not ours.

Second, don't judge a church based on one member. I told him our church had a lot of kind people in it as well and to give it a chance. For the next two to three months, Rod, who was going through a divorce at the time, came to our church and listened to the Word of God. Many times when he came, that same old man would look back at him with that same evil scowl on his face. Rod finally called me one night and asked if the preacher and I would meet him at the church. We did, and that night, Rod gave his heart to Christ, He was baptized not long afterward. He was the first black man to ever be baptized at that church, and that day is when we really became a church for the first time. A church is a place where everyone can come and find Christ and the peace He offers. That includes all colors and creeds, especially the sinners, and everyone else, all undeserving of what Christ did. I have another friend who is saved and goes to another church. He told me once that his church would allow a black person to attend, be saved, and be baptized, but would not let him be a member of the church. I tell you this because it is the truth: No church will ever be respectful to God unless it is open to all of His children at any time to be a part of a family that is greater than one race or one culture. When we are saved, we are all members—and all equal—in one family, and that is the family of Christ.

CHAPTER 11

Must I Be Perfect?

———∞∞∞———

When this book is published and sent out, the people who read it will probably want to know who wrote it. The reason is they will want to put a face and name to what they are reading. Many readers, I am sure, will differ in their opinions of the quality of this book, as well as of the person writing it. After reading this book, many will want to judge me and my life to see if I am holding up to what I believe in. This is what I want you to know: The only thing good in me is Christ, and this book is not about my opinions or what I believe; this book is based on the truth, which is no respecter of man or opinions. Truth is factual, and that which is truth will not change.

First Timothy 1:15 tells us, "This is a faithful saying, and worthy of all acceptation, that Christ Jesus came into the world to save sinners; of whom I am chief."

My mistakes and sins are not a reflection on who God is or what Jesus says. My actions are not deciding whether or not the Bible is accurate. Just as you would never judge a math problem based on the person trying to solve it, you should never judge Jesus based on people. The math problem is a factual statement, and just because I am the one trying to get the correct answer, and I get it wrong, does not make the math problem wrong. What it means is that I am solving the problem wrong. The error is attributed to me, not the mathematical formula. The answer to the question "Must I be perfect?" is there has only been One who's been perfect, and that was and still is Christ. Even Christ Himself said there is only One good, and that is God. Perfection is based on what is *inside* of you, not on what's on the outside. Perfection is not about someone's opinion; it is about God's character, and perfection can only be obtained after the formula is complete.

Read **John 17:1-26**:

[1]These words spake Jesus, and lifted up his eyes to heaven, and said, Father, the hour is come; glorify thy Son, that thy Son also may glorify thee:

[2]As thou hast given him power over all flesh, that he should give eternal life to as many as thou hast given him.

[3]And this is life eternal, that they might know thee the only true God, and Jesus Christ, whom thou hast sent.

[4]I have glorified thee on the earth: I have finished the work which thou gavest me to do.

[5]And now, O Father, glorify thou me with thine own self with the glory which I had with thee before the world was.

[6]I have manifested thy name unto the men which thou gavest me out of the world: thine they were, and thou gavest them me; and they have kept thy word.

[7]Now they have known that all things whatsoever thou hast given me are of thee.

[8]For I have given unto them the words which thou gavest me; and they have received them, and have known surely that I came out from thee, and they have believed that thou didst send me.

[9]I pray for them: I pray not for the world, but for them which thou hast given me; for they are thine.

[10]And all mine are thine, and thine are mine; and I am glorified in them.

[11]And now I am no more in the world, but these are in the world, and I come to thee. Holy Father, keep through thine own name those whom thou hast given me, that they may be one, as we are.

[12]While I was with them in the world, I kept them in thy name: those that thou gavest me I have kept, and none of them is lost, but the son of perdition; that the scripture might be fulfilled.

[13]And now come I to thee; and these things I speak in the world, that they might have my joy fulfilled in themselves.

[14]I have given them thy word; and the world hath hated them, because they are not of the world, even as I am not of the world.

[15]I pray not that thou shouldest take them out of the world, but that thou shouldest keep them from the evil.

[16]They are not of the world, even as I am not of the world.

¹⁷Sanctify them through thy truth: thy word is truth.

¹⁸As thou hast sent me into the world, even so have I also sent them into the world.

¹⁹And for their sakes I sanctify myself, that they also might be sanctified through the truth.

²⁰Neither pray I for these alone, but for them also which shall believe on me through their word;

²¹That they all may be one; as thou, Father, art in me, and I in thee, that they also may be one in us: that the world may believe that thou hast sent me.

²²And the glory which thou gavest me I have given them; that they may be one, even as we are one:

²³I in them, and thou in me, that they may be made perfect in one; and that the world may know that thou hast sent me, and hast loved them, as thou hast loved me.

²⁴Father, I will that they also, whom thou hast given me, be with me where I am; that they may behold my glory, which thou hast given me: for thou lovedst me before the foundation of the world.

²⁵O righteous Father, the world hath not known thee: but I have known thee, and these have known that thou hast sent me.

²⁶And I have declared unto them thy name, and will declare it: that the love wherewith thou hast loved me may be in them, and I in them.

This was the prayer Jesus made for us before He was crucified. He left us with this as a way of giving us what He had while He was on earth. Jesus had the Father in Him, and He is saying this to the children who have chosen Him. He is saying that because He lived the perfect life and would sacrifice His life for us, the formula would be complete. God could live in us, and that part of us, the Holy Spirit, is perfect and will live inside of us continuously for the rest of our lives. Jesus, the Holy Spirit, and God are together in me, and I am no longer His enemy, but His son.

Read these two Scriptures:

I am crucified with Christ: nevertheless I live; yet not I, but Christ liveth in me: and the life which I now live in the flesh I live by the faith of the Son of God, who loved me, and gave himself for me.

Galatians 2:20

And I said unto him, Sir, thou knowest. And he said to me, These are they which came out of great tribulation, and have washed their robes, and made them white in the blood of the Lamb.

Revelation 7:14

So perfection can only come from God. God is the only One who claims perfection. He never makes a mistake, and is all-knowing and all-loving. He has never sinned, and never will. God is truth because He is perfect, and He is perfect because He is truth.

Let's see what God thinks about perfection as a human, and then maybe we can see if perfection is possible with us. The truth says Jesus Christ was the only Human born who lived a perfect life. At many times, His life was like ours, filled with chaos, with no money and noplace to even lay his head. The difference is He had no sin in Him and made no mistakes when it came to making the right choices. He not only followed God's law (the Ten Commandments), but also was always completely in the Father's will for His life.

Let's see what the truth says about Him.

Jesus' Life = Never Sinned

But with the precious blood of Christ, as of a **lamb** without blemish and without spot . . . .

1 Peter 1:19

Birth = Put Himself to Serve Us and Was Born of a Virgin; Also, Below the Angels

Behold, a virgin shall be with child, and shall bring forth a son, and they shall call his name Emmanuel, which being interpreted is, God with us.

Matthew 1:23

But we see Jesus, who was made a little lower than the **angels** for the suffering of death, crowned with glory and honour; that he by the grace of God should taste death for every man.

Hebrews 2:9

³Jesus knowing that the Father had given all things into his hands, and that he was come from God, and went to God;

⁴He riseth from supper, and laid aside his garments; and took a towel, and girded himself.

⁵After that he poureth water into a bason, and began to wash the disciples' feet, and to wipe them with the towel wherewith he was girded.

⁶Then cometh he to Simon Peter: and Peter saith unto him, Lord, dost thou wash my feet?

⁷Jesus answered and said unto him, What I do thou knowest not now; but thou shalt know hereafter.

⁸Peter saith unto him, Thou shalt never wash my feet. Jesus answered him, If I wash thee not, thou hast no part with me.

⁹Simon Peter saith unto him, Lord, not my feet only, but also my hands and my head.

¹⁰Jesus saith to him, He that is washed needeth not save to wash his feet, but is clean every whit: and ye are clean, but not all.

¹¹For he knew who should betray him; therefore said he, Ye are not all clean.

¹²So after he had washed their feet, and had taken his garments, and was set down again, he said unto them, Know ye what I have done

to you?

[13]Ye call me Master and Lord: and ye say well; for so I am.

[14]If I then, your Lord and Master, have washed your feet; ye also ought to wash one another's feet.

[15]For I have given you an example, that ye should do as I have done to you.

[16]Verily, verily, I say unto you, The servant is not greater than his lord; neither he that is sent greater than he that sent him.

John 13:3-16

Food = His Food Was the Word of God

And Jesus answered him, saying, It is written, That man shall not live by **bread alone**, but by every word of God.

Luke 4:4

Work = Carpenter

Is not this the **carpenter**'s son? Is not his mother called Mary? and his brethren, James, and Joses, and Simon, and Judas?

Matthew 13:55

Death in the Garden Following the Will of God

[36]Then cometh Jesus with them unto a place called Gethsemane, and saith unto the disciples, Sit ye here, while I go and pray yonder.

³⁷And he took with him Peter and the two sons of Zebedee, and began to be sorrowful and very heavy.

³⁸Then saith he unto them, My soul is exceeding sorrowful, even unto death: tarry ye here, and watch with me.

³⁹And he went a little farther, and fell on his face, and prayed, saying, O my Father, if it be possible, let this cup pass from me: nevertheless not as I will, but as thou wilt.

⁴⁰And he cometh unto the disciples, and findeth them asleep, and saith unto Peter, What, could ye not watch with me one hour?

⁴¹Watch and pray, that ye enter not into temptation: the spirit indeed is willing, but the flesh is weak.

⁴²He went away again the second time, and prayed, saying, O my Father, if this cup may not pass away from me, except I drink it, thy will be done.

Matthew 26:36-42

The Return of Christ = He Will Return for His Children, and He Will Never Leave Us Alone

¹Let not your heart be troubled: ye believe in God, believe also in me.

²In my Father's house are many mansions: if it were not so, I would have told you. I go to prepare a place for you.

³And if I go and prepare a place for you, I will come again, and receive you unto myself; that where I am, there ye may be also.

⁴And whither I go ye know, and the way ye know.

⁵Thomas saith unto him, Lord, we know not whither thou goest; and how can we know the way?

⁶Jesus saith unto him, I am the way, the truth, and the life: no man cometh unto the Father, but by me.

⁷If ye had known me, ye should have known my Father also: and from henceforth ye know him, and have seen him.

⁸Philip saith unto him, Lord, show us the Father, and it sufficeth us.

⁹Jesus saith unto him, Have I been so long time with you, and yet hast thou not known me, Philip? He that hath seen me hath seen the Father; and how sayest thou then, Show us the Father?

¹⁰Believest thou not that I am in the Father, and the Father in me? The words that I speak unto you I speak not of myself: but the Father that dwelleth in me, he doeth the works.

¹¹Believe me that I am in the Father, and the Father in me: or else believe me for the very works' sake.

¹²Verily, verily, I say unto you, He that believeth on me, the works that I do shall he do also; and greater works than these shall he do; because I go unto my Father.

¹³And whatsoever ye shall ask in my name, that will I do, that the Father may be glorified in the Son.

¹⁴If ye shall ask any thing in my name, I will do it.

¹⁵If ye love me, keep my commandments.

¹⁶And I will pray the Father, and he shall give you another Comforter, that he may abide with you for ever;

¹⁷Even the Spirit of truth; whom the world cannot receive, because

it seeth him not, neither knoweth him: but ye know him; for he dwelleth with you, and shall be in you.

[18]I will not leave you comfortless: I will come to you.

[19]Yet a little while, and the world seeth me no more; but ye see me: because I live, ye shall live also.

[20]At that day ye shall know that I am in my Father, and ye in me, and I in you.

[21]He that hath my commandments, and keepeth them, he it is that loveth me: and he that loveth me shall be loved of my Father, and I will love him, and will manifest myself to him.

John 14:1-21

The Final Battle of Christ

These shall make war with the **Lamb**, and the **Lamb** shall overcome them: for he is Lord of lords, and King of kings: and they that are with him are called, and chosen, and faithful.

Revelation 17:14

The Scripture shows God is perfect, His Son is perfect, and so His Word must also be perfect. Because of this perfection in each, we are able to use the Word of God to bring power into our own lives. That Word we use and the perfection will become noticeable in us. The final key to this perfection is that faith—belief that the truth is the truth, Jesus is Jesus, and God is God—is required. When you believe and act on this belief with faith and assurance, this leads not only to salvation, but also to all the other miracles both in the Bible and in our lives today.

Let's take a second to see how Jesus used faith as part of this perfection formula. Let's see how the Word of God was a power source for His life, and in turn can be for us.

[6]And it came to pass also on another sabbath, that he entered into the synagogue and taught: and there was a man whose right hand was withered.

[7]And the scribes and Pharisees watched him, whether he would heal on the sabbath day; that they might find an accusation against him.

[8]But he knew their thoughts, and said to the man which had the withered hand, Rise up, and stand forth in the midst. And he arose and stood forth.

[9]Then said Jesus unto them, I will ask you one thing; Is it lawful on the sabbath days to do good, or to do evil? To save life, or to destroy it?

[10]And looking round about upon them all, he said unto the man, Stretch forth thy hand. And he did so: and his hand was restored whole as the other.

[11]And they were filled with madness; and communed one with another what they might do to Jesus.

Luke 6:6-11

As it was then, it is now. We want truth and miracles too, but we only want them as long as it fits into our ideal. The Pharisees proclaimed to follow God, and they did, as long as God obeyed their laws and not His own true Laws.

[54]And when he was come into his own country, he taught them in their synagogue, insomuch that they were astonished, and said, Whence hath this man this wisdom, and these mighty works?

[55]Is not this the carpenter's son? Is not his mother called Mary? And his brethren, James, and Joses, and Simon, and Judas?

[56]And his sisters, are they not all with us? Whence then hath this man all these things?

[57]And they were offended in him. But Jesus said unto them, A prophet is not without honour, save in his own country, and in his own house.

[58]And he did not many mighty works there because of their unbelief.

Matthew 13:54-58

God and Jesus, as well as others, have performed many, many miracles that are stated in the Bible. So does that mean God's miracles are based on our actions? Yes, it does. In many ways, that is exactly right. When Israel rebelled and worshiped other idols and put the true God away, He caused things to happen in this world to convict them of their errors. Understand that I am not just talking about natural plagues; I am talking about God's allowing His people to fall to their enemies without protection because of their ways and choices. God has always protected the riotous, and He has always rewarded the good—maybe not with the reward we think is right, such as money and wealth, although He has done that as well. A greater reward is given, a reward of peace and good fortune, one of true joy. Today, when we see all types of disasters in this world, such as hurricanes, oil spills, volcanoes, and earthquakes, many people believe they are God's punishing us. However, the truth says Jesus Christ took the wrath of God for us.

Read these Scriptures:

The next day John seeth Jesus coming unto him, and saith, Behold the Lamb of God, which taketh away the **sin** of the **world**.

John 1:29

And he is the propitiation for our **sin**s: and not for ours only, but also for the **sin**s of the whole **world**.

1 John 2:2

This was the punishment we, not Jesus, deserved—the wrath was poured out on Christ. This is the difference between the old way God handled people, before Jesus died on the cross, and how He does now. The wrath has been dealt with already, and our punishment and debt have been paid. The final wrath comes in the end, when Christ judges us based on one truth: whether or not we received Jesus as Savior.

The Bible says:

For then must he often have **suffered** since the foundation of the world: but now once in the end of the world hath he appeared to put away sin by the sacrifice of himself.

Hebrews 9:26

For Christ also hath once **suffered** for sins, the just for the unjust, that he might bring us to God, being put to death in the flesh, but quickened by the Spirit.

1 Peter 3:18

So now we see the effects of our sin on the earth, the power it wields. We call out to God and say, "Why?" Or we cry and blame Him. We should be blaming ourselves, what we have done to the world to make this happen, what we have done to ourselves and our planet. Let's make no mistake, though the Bible also foretells the final wrath of God, and it is much worse than earthquakes and a few tornadoes.

[7]For nation shall rise against nation, and kingdom against kingdom: and there shall be famines, and pestilences, and earthquakes, in divers places.

[8]All these are the beginning of sorrows.

[9]Then shall they deliver you up to be afflicted, and shall kill you: and ye shall be hated of all nations for my name's sake.

[10]And then shall many be offended, and shall betray one another, and shall hate one another.

[11]And many false prophets shall rise, and shall deceive many.

[12]And because iniquity shall abound, the love of many shall wax cold.

[13]But he that shall endure unto the end, the same shall be saved.

[14]And this gospel of the kingdom shall be preached in all the world for a witness unto all nations; and then shall the end come.

[15]When ye therefore shall see the abomination of desolation, spoken of by Daniel the prophet, stand in the holy place, (whoso readeth, let him understand:)

[16]Then let them which be in Judaea flee into the mountains:

[17]Let him which is on the housetop not come down to take any thing out of his house:

[18]Neither let him which is in the field return back to take his clothes.

[19]And woe unto them that are with child, and to them that give suck in those days!

[20]But pray ye that your flight be not in the winter, neither on the sabbath day:

[21]For then shall be great tribulation, such as was not since the beginning of the world to this time, no, nor ever shall be.

Matthew 24:7-21

Let's circle back now to when a person was healed in the Bible. In most cases, Jesus said, "Your faith has made you whole." Though God can do anything He likes, especially when it comes to miracles, He allows us to be a part of this formula. In the Scripture passage earlier in this chapter, where Jesus was not honored in His own town, these people looked at Jesus as a person, not as the Son of God. They looked at Him as incapable because they saw Him as the boy who had lived as a neighbor. They did not see His sinless actions and His wisdom beyond those of an ordinary man. Their unbelief is what stopped miracles from happening, just as today our unbelief is what stops them from happening for us. When I got saved and the Word of God set me free, I received the Holy Spirit, and I was a changed person from the inside out. I was still tempted as before, but it was only from the flesh. The desire and the love for the life I lived before were not there anymore. Christ had taken my love for sin and changed it into a love for Him. He changed it to be a love for the riotous things of life. My point is that the people who knew me most didn't believe, they didn't want to believe, I had changed. They called it a phase at first, and they asked me all kinds of questions, not to be curious, but to be defiant. After all the smoke had cleared and time moved on, as it does, I had moved on to a different lifestyle, and many of them continued to live in theirs.

Second **Corinthians 5:17** says, "Therefore if any man be in Christ, he is a new creature: old things are passed away; behold, all things are become new."

I thank God every day that He had grace on me, that He didn't give up on me when He should have. I tried everything there was before giving my life over to Him. When it was all said and done, all that I had left to give Him was my leftovers, and He took them. Amen. He took them! I thank Him for giving me the people in my life who prayed for my soul to be saved. When I surrendered my life and believed in the truth, I saw the miracles begin to happen. I began to feel bad for others, the ones like the Pharisees, who will not hear and obey. They will not see miracles, only despair and regret. They won't believe because no matter how miserable their lives may be, they would rather keep them than give them up.

How does God give you the kind of miracle that is so important for your life and eternity? God puts the Holy Spirit in you, and that is what changes you into a newborn child of God. That part of you is perfect, and your actions cannot change that after it has been given. Your perfection is complete now, and when you die from this world, you will open your eyes in your Father's house, a house He made for you to live with you. You were made perfect by your salvation and the sacrifice Jesus made. Now you can live with a perfect God because you have been purified and have become perfected yourself.

Read what the following Scriptures say about this.

And Jesus, when he was baptized, went up straightway out of the water: and, lo, the heavens were opened unto him, and he saw the Spirit of God descending **like** a **dove**, and lighting upon him.

Matthew 3:16

And one of the elders answered, saying unto me, What are these which are arrayed in **white robes**? And whence came they?

Revelation 7:13

And I said unto him, Sir, thou knowest. And he said to me, These are they which came out of great tribulation, and have washed their **robes**, and made them **white** in the blood of the Lamb.

Revelation 7:14

For the **grace** of God that bringeth salvation hath appeared to all men.

Titus 2:11

That being justified by his **grace**, we should be made heirs according to the hope of eternal life.

Titus 3:7

So what the truth tells us is that perfection was and is achieved only by One, and that is God. Through God and the Word, Jesus lived a perfect, sinless life full of sacrifice. So now that we have God and His perfection in us and are made perfect, the real question is, Can we live this life perfectly? Is it possible to see perfection in us on this earth?

Let's take a look at the truth, and see what it says.

Truth statement: It is not about being perfect; it is about desiring the perfection in Him.

Therefore leaving the principles of the doctrine of Christ, let us go on unto **perfection**; not laying again the foundation of repentance from dead works, and of faith toward God.

Hebrews 6:1

And said, Verily I say unto you, Except ye be converted, and **become** as **little child**ren, ye shall not enter into the kingdom of heaven.

Matthew 18:3

The children are the ones with the secret to perfection. The closet thing to perfection we will ever find in this life is in a child. This is yet more proof of the contradiction between heaven and this world. Though children are around us every day, many of us just discount it. A child, born in the flesh, as we all are, does not need to be taught to do wrong. We spend our time in this world trying to teach children to do right. You can see perfection in a young child even before the child learns to say his or her first words, especially when it comes to faith. Children have complete faith and trust in their parents and will keep that faith and trust until the parents show them they can't be trusted. This may happen at an early age or later in life, but the parents always fail in one way or another, just as the child fails in one way or another. An example is my eighteen-month-old son. I can put him on a bed, and he will jump into my arms. If I let him hit the floor one time, he will probably not trust me to do the same the next time.

While children may have a sinful nature from birth, they also have the main ingredients God requires in perfection. They have undoubting faith with no unbelief, and they back that up with an innocence and action. When we can do this same thing with God, He will always respond, not because we deserve a response, but because we showed real faith.

Matthew 19:14 says, "But Jesus said, Suffer little **children**, and forbid them not, to come unto me: for of such is the kingdom of **heaven**."

Unless you become as that little child, believing with all your heart and trusting that God exists, that He had a Son who gave His life for your sins and has risen from death, you will never be free. You have no hope, no faith, no chance of salvation or a truly abundant life. Do you feel His call? Will you receive it? The perfection we question is attainable when you are saved and the Lord lives in you. That perfection is seen when you follow His guidance and obey Him. Then, He begins to mold you into a perfect vessel to be as He is. Can you live a perfect life? No, and that is because we sin every day. The important thing to remember is you can strive to live that life, and when you fail, try again. As you succeed and humble yourself, He will make you more beautiful every day. You will see as you grow, the only good in you will be from Him, and at least that part of you will always be perfect.

As time marches on, our bodies grow old, and the beauty fades . . . but the vessel inside shines brighter each day.

The Lives of F. and E.

Though not their close friend, I have known these two people in my life. While they did not know each other, in many ways, they lived identical lives. Both were good people, with many loving characteristics. If you were to measure them among others, they would be on the higher end of the spectrum. Both were hard workers and all-around nice guys. Both had families that loved them and people around them who cared for them greatly. *So what's the problem?* you ask.

The problem is neither one ever really received true salvation. Neither one confessed a love for Christ and said he received salvation. Both have since passed away. During their lives, both of them heard the Word of God and could have given their hearts to Christ. I pray they both did before they passed, but this was not part of their walk before this time. Again, these two individuals were both loving parents and people. Many people may see their death, whenever it occurs, as an atrocity that God would send them to hell despite their goodness here on this earth. But what they forget is God sees the heart. If we were to take either of these people and displayed their thoughts on any given day, we could see what God sees. The wickedness and sinfulness man carries with him is in all of us. These two both held onto their lives, their ways, their ideas on what death would bring. We can all agree none of us live a perfect life, as we all know we fall short. The difference between their lives and, say, the life of a murderer, who followed through with his sinful thoughts, who may be in prison, but who truly repented and received salvation, as the Bible says, is that man will be in heaven, and the other two will spend eternity in hell.

The confusion in this scenario is that we want to decide who deserves what based on *our* ideals, and not God's. We want to say this man should have peace because he has done enough good, or that man should go to hell because he was under the good-and-bad scale by one extra bad deed. We don't want to be judged by a holy God, and we don't want to give our lives over to Christ because to do this, we must follow their guidelines and not our own. We, as individuals, want to decide our own fairness. The problem is we, as individuals, are all different, and our ideas of fairness cannot be equal to all others' because of these differences. This is why God can allow a seemingly good person who lived a good life to go to hell. God has based salvation on receiving Christ, on giving up *your* life to Christ, who died for all of our sins. God's formula is simple in this way, as all will be judged equally based on the receiving of the sacrifice He and His Son made on the cross. Through this sacrifice, we are made perfect, and because Christ rose from the dead and overcame death, so will we. The formula holds true for all people, not based on how good we seem to be in this life, but on how great Christ was in His life. He is the One who has sacrificed for us so we could be perfected through Him.

CHAPTER 12

Free at Last, Free at Last.
Thank God, I Am Free at Last!

———∞∞∞———

Truth statement: I am FREE, not only saved from sin and death, but justified. Sin no longer rules my nature, even though it tries to rule my flesh.

John 8:32-36 says:

[32]And ye shall know the truth, and the truth shall make you free.

[33]They answered him, We be Abraham's seed, and were never in bondage to any man: how sayest thou, Ye shall be made free?

[34]Jesus answered them, Verily, verily, I say unto you, Whosoever committeth sin is the servant of sin.

[35]And the servant abideth not in the house for ever: but the Son abideth ever.

[36]If the Son therefore shall make you free, ye shall be free indeed.

The truth says that Jesus died on the cross not only for all the sin of the world, but also for all the shame of the world. He not only died for the murder, but also the son the murderer left behind. The shame this son, and his ancestry, will feel now will follow him all the days of his life. He not only died for the alcoholic, but also the daughter of the alcoholic, living with the shame that she never caused, yet is punished for every day. The sin was just one of the things for which Jesus died.

No wonder he sweat drops of blood before performing this act of sacrifice.

Luke 22:44 says, "And being in an agony he prayed more earnestly: and his sweat was as it were great **drops** of **blood** falling down to the ground."

Due to this act, I am no longer judged for my sins as it pertains to going to heaven. Now I am not only forgiven for my past sins, but also I am forgiven for my future sins. Can you see the formula of truth yet, the cleansing power of it? How could God get us back to the way it was in the beginning, before sin entered, and still allow us to have free will? The death of His Son accomplished all this, so we could one day live free of all sins, guilt, and shame. We are there because God chose us, and we accepted and received His gift. God calls all men, from before and in the future, to repentance, and all are given the choice to accept or reject this gift.

For I delivered unto you first of **all** that which I also received, how that **Christ died** for our sins according to the scriptures.

1 Corinthians 15:3

For the love of **Christ** constraineth us; because we thus judge, that if one **died** for **all**, then were **all** dead.

2 Corinthians 5:14

As far as the **east is from** the **west**, so far hath he removed our transgressions **from** us.

Psalm 103:12

[44]Let these sayings sink down into your ears: for the Son of man shall be delivered into the hands of men.

[45]But they understood not this saying, and it was hid from them, that they perceived it not: and they feared to ask him of that saying.

[46]Then there arose a reasoning among them, which of them should be greatest.

[47]And Jesus, perceiving the thought of their heart, took a child, and set him by him,

[48]and said unto them, Whosoever shall receive this child in my name receiveth me: and whosoever shall receive me receiveth him that sent me: for he that is least among you all, the same shall be great.

[49]And John answered and said, Master, we saw one casting out devils in thy name; and we forbad him, because he followeth not with us.

[50]And Jesus said unto him, Forbid him not: for he that is not against us is for us.

[51]And it came to pass, when the time was come that he should be received up, he stedfastly set his face to go to Jerusalem,

189

⁵²and sent messengers before his face: and they went, and entered into a village of the Samaritans, to make ready for him.

⁵³And they did not receive him, because his face was as though he would go to Jerusalem.

⁵⁴And when his disciples James and John saw this, they said, Lord, wilt thou that we command fire to come down from heaven, and consume them, even as Elias did?

⁵⁵But he turned, and rebuked them, and said, Ye know not what manner of spirit ye are of.

⁵⁶For the Son of man is not come to destroy men's lives, but to save them. And they went to another village.

Luke 9:44-56

So if all men are called, then it is your choice whether or not you will receive this call. God has shown Himself to this world in many ways. He has shown us through creation, prophecy, and fulfilled prophecy. He has sent messengers to tell us, warn us, and show us He is real. He sent His only Son to live with us, teach us, and pay for our sins with His own life. Even after that death, He overcame death itself, yet still gives us Himself in the Holy Spirit, to live in us every day.

We now know He is always with us, ready to show us His love and the work He has in store for us, His beloved children.

1 John 5

[1]Whosoever believeth that Jesus is the Christ is born of God: and every one that loveth him that begat loveth him also that is begotten of him.

[2]By this we know that we love the children of God, when we love God, and keep his commandments.

[3]For this is the love of God, that we keep his commandments: and his commandments are not grievous.

[4]For whatsoever is born of God overcometh the world: and this is the victory that overcometh the world, even our faith.

[5]Who is he that overcometh the world, but he that believeth that Jesus is the Son of God?

[6]This is he that came by water and blood, even Jesus Christ; not by water only, but by water and blood. And it is the Spirit that beareth witness, because the Spirit is truth.

[7]For there are three that bear record in heaven, the Father, the Word, and the Holy Ghost: and these three are one.

[8]And there are three that bear witness in earth, the Spirit, and the water, and the blood: and these three agree in one.

[9]If we receive the witness of men, the witness of God is greater: for this is the witness of God which he hath testified of his Son.

[10]He that believeth on the Son of God hath the witness in himself: he that believeth not God hath made him a liar; because he believeth not the record that God gave of his Son.

[11]And this is the record, that God hath given to us eternal life, and

this life is in his Son.

¹²He that hath the Son hath life; and he that hath not the Son of God hath not life.

¹³These things have I written unto you that believe on the name of the Son of God; that ye may know that ye have eternal life, and that ye may believe on the name of the Son of God.

¹⁴And this is the confidence that we have in him, that, if we ask any thing according to his will, he heareth us:

¹⁵And if we know that he hear us, whatsoever we ask, we know that we have the petitions that we desired of him.

This establishes the mathematical formula of truth. With these Scriptures, God gives His complete truth.

He created us, and we rebelled. We brought imperfection into a perfected place. When we don't believe, we call Him the liar.

Genesis 3:17 states:

And unto **Adam** he said, Because thou hast hearkened unto the voice of thy wife, and hast eaten of the tree, of which I commanded thee, saying, Thou shalt not eat of it: cursed is the ground for thy sake; in sorrow shalt thou eat of it all the days of thy life.

Then He clothed us in our shame. This is the time when sin for all mankind began, and it is still with us today.

Further, we read in **Genesis 3:21**, "Unto Adam also and to his wife did the LORD God make coats of skins, and clothed them."

The good news is instead of destroying us, He provided us with a way back to Him, back to the perfect and sinless place, as before. This came by a second choice—not a choice to rebel, but to concede, a choice to accept His love, not reject it as before.

Was this done without a price to be paid? Certainly not! The price for us would be great; the cost was one perfect life for many imperfect lives. Christ died for all, not for some.

We read in **1 Corinthians 15:22**, "For as in Adam all die, even so in Christ shall all be made alive."

So when Jesus Christ gave the ultimate sacrifice, this almost completed the formula. Christ had overcome the choice Adam and Eve had made, the choice that brought us into this mess. Christ's death enabled us to get back to the original perfection, and start a new relationship with the Father.

Genesis 3:15 says: "And I will put enmity between thee and the woman, and between thy seed and her seed; it shall bruise thy **head**, and thou shalt bruise his **heel**."

The last part of the formula still had to be completed. But then, after this completion, perfection, sinlessness, the eternal life with no death, pain, or suffering, and being with our Creator and Father would all be attainable. What would be this final piece, or ingredient, to the formula that would bring us to this true freedom—not freedom to rebel, but freedom to love and obey?

This ingredient would be needed to overcome death itself. Read these Scriptures to find out what it is:

Not to all the people, but unto witnesses chosen before God, even to us, who did eat and drink with him after he **rose from** the **dead.**

Acts 10:41

And I will pray the Father, and he shall give you another **Comforter,** that he may abide with you for ever.

John 14:16

But the **Comforter,** which is the Holy Ghost, whom the Father will send in my name, he shall teach you all things, and bring all things to your remembrance, whatsoever I have said unto you.

John 14:26

But when the **Comforter** is come, whom I will send unto you from the Father, even the Spirit of truth, which proceedeth from the Father, he shall testify of me.

John 15:26

Nevertheless I tell you the truth; It is expedient for you that I go away: for if I go not away, the **Comforter** will not come unto you; but if I depart, I will send him unto you.

John 16:7

The only way perfection through salvation can happen is if death is overcome by life. So now, not only are we able to overcome death, as Christ did, but also we are able to have Christ in us until the day He returns. Christ can live freely in you, without the fear of death, without shame or guilt, with only freedom from the burdens of this world.

The truth says:

For the **law** of the Spirit of life in Christ Jesus hath made me **free from** the **law** of sin and death.

Romans 8:2

When Jesus therefore had received the vinegar, he said, It **is finished**: and he bowed his head, and gave up the ghost.

John 19:30

When He said this, it meant the ingredients and actions to save us had been met. The only thing left now is for God to keep His end of the deal, the promise He had made to His perfect Son. Christ completed His job, and the reward for the completion was Jesus gets us, the true Christians of this world, the ones He said He will return to receive one day.

John 14:1-29 states:

¹Let not your heart be troubled: ye believe in God, believe also in me.

²In my Father's house are many mansions: if it were not so, I would have told you. I go to prepare a place for you.

³And if I go and prepare a place for you, I will come again, and receive you unto myself; that where I am, there ye may be also.

⁴And whither I go ye know, and the way ye know.

⁵Thomas saith unto him, Lord, we know not whither thou goest; and how can we know the way?

⁶Jesus saith unto him, I am the way, the truth, and the life: no man cometh unto the Father, but by me.

⁷If ye had known me, ye should have known my Father also: and from henceforth ye know him, and have seen him.

⁸Philip saith unto him, Lord, show us the Father, and it sufficeth us.

⁹Jesus saith unto him, Have I been so long time with you, and yet hast thou not known me, Philip? He that hath seen me hath seen the Father; and how sayest thou then, Show us the Father?

¹⁰Believest thou not that I am in the Father, and the Father in me? The words that I speak unto you I speak not of myself: but the Father that dwelleth in me, he doeth the works.

¹¹Believe me that I am in the Father, and the Father in me: or else believe me for the very works' sake.

¹²Verily, verily, I say unto you, He that believeth on me, the works

that I do shall he do also; and greater works than these shall he do; because I go unto my Father.

¹³And whatsoever ye shall ask in my name, that will I do, that the Father may be glorified in the Son.

¹⁴If ye shall ask any thing in my name, I will do it.

¹⁵If ye love me, keep my commandments.

¹⁶And I will pray the Father, and he shall give you another Comforter, that he may abide with you for ever;

¹⁷Even the Spirit of truth; whom the world cannot receive, because it seeth him not, neither knoweth him: but ye know him; for he dwelleth with you, and shall be in you.

¹⁸I will not leave you comfortless: I will come to you.

¹⁹Yet a little while, and the world seeth me no more; but ye see me: because I live, ye shall live also.

²⁰At that day ye shall know that I am in my Father, and ye in me, and I in you.

²¹He that hath my commandments, and keepeth them, he it is that loveth me: and he that loveth me shall be loved of my Father, and I will love him, and will manifest myself to him.

²²Judas saith unto him, not Iscariot, Lord, how is it that thou wilt manifest thyself unto us, and not unto the world?

²³Jesus answered and said unto him, If a man love me, he will keep my words: and my Father will love him, and we will come unto him, and make our abode with him.

²⁴He that loveth me not keepeth not my sayings: and the word which

ye hear is not mine, but the Father's which sent me.

[25]These things have I spoken unto you, being yet present with you.

[26]But the Comforter, which is the Holy Ghost, whom the Father will send in my name, he shall teach you all things, and bring all things to your remembrance, whatsoever I have said unto you.

[27]Peace I leave with you, my peace I give unto you: not as the world giveth, give I unto you. Let not your heart be troubled, neither let it be afraid.

[28]Ye have heard how I said unto you, I go away, and come again unto you. If ye loved me, ye would rejoice, because I said, I go unto the Father: for my Father is greater than I.

[29]And now I have told you before it come to pass, that, when it is come to pass, ye might believe.

We are now not only saved, but we are joint heirs to all Jesus has! We are free to live a life on this earth as well as for eternity. We know we have peace with our Creator, and His love is given to us every second of our lives. This love is forevermore, and when we have really received this love, we will, in turn, share His love for us with others.

Romans 8:17 tells us, "And if children, then **heirs**; **heirs** of God, and **joint-heirs** with Christ; if so be that we suffer with him, that we may be also glorified together."

God did not make us as joint heirs as some bonus to salvation. We are all unworthy of either. If Jesus would have died for our sins only, and we did not become joint heirs, salvation could not have taken place. But we are not judged by our sins any longer. Jesus Christ has become our Savior, and we are considered a part of Jesus. Not only do we receive heaven because of His sacrifice, but we also are heirs with Him to the Father's kingdom. If God is really going to allow us to come to heaven through Jesus, then He does it all the way or no way at all. I am now tied to Christ, just as a father is tied to his children genetically. And I cannot be separated!

_____Read what the truth <u>says:</u>

[31]What shall we then say to these things? If God be for us, who can be against us?

[32]He that spared not his own Son, but delivered him up for us all, how shall he not with him also freely give us all things?

[33]Who shall lay any thing to the charge of God's elect? It is God that justifieth.

[34]Who is he that condemneth? It is Christ that died, yea rather, that is risen again, who is even at the right hand of God, who also maketh intercession for us.

[35]Who shall separate us from the love of Christ? Shall tribulation, or distress, or persecution, or famine, or nakedness, or peril, or sword?

[36]As it is written, For thy sake we are killed all the day long; we are accounted as sheep for the slaughter.

[37]Nay, in all these things we are more than conquerors through him that loved us.

[38]For I am persuaded, that neither death, nor life, nor angels, nor principalities, nor powers, nor things present, nor things to come, [39]nor height, nor depth, nor any other creature, shall be able to separate us from the love of God, which is in Christ Jesus our Lord.

Romans 8:31-39

I hope you see the true freedom you have through this now—the freedom to live your life without the burdens or cares of this world owning you. Although you will still have these burdens, know you are free from them, and know they have become the Lord's burdens.

John 16:33 tells us, "These things I have spoken unto you, that in me ye might have peace. In the **world** ye shall have tribulation: but be of good cheer; I have **overcome** the **world**."

I understand it's just not that easy to live this way. In this world, we are surrounded by many things, and they consume our lives every day. Every morning, from the time we get up to the time we go to sleep, we are on a battlefield. It seems we are always struggling with ourselves or things we can't control. Read what God says about this world.

Love not the **world**, neither the things that are in the **world**. If any man love the **world**, the love of the Father is not in him.

1 John 2:15

In whom the god of this world hath blinded the minds of them which believe not, lest the light of the glorious gospel of Christ, who is the image of God, should shine unto them.

2 Corinthians 4:4

No doubt, this world has many beautiful things, and I believe most of us have had many happy moments. What we need to realize is there are two formulas working at the same time in this world—the formulas of evil and good—and they contradict each other.

The Formula of Evil

The "evil" formula on the outside looks great; it looks as if the ingredients that make up this formula are guaranteed success. Among them: money, lust, power, strength, looks, worldly wisdom, independence, and self-worship at its infinite point. The mightiest of these is the goal of happiness. The problem with this formula is that at first, it seems to be right. However, as you continue to use it, you'll find there is never enough. The happiness comes, but never lasts. Instead of the formula freeing you as it promised, it imprisons you slowly until you are completely concealed and chocking from it, until it has taken your last breath. The happiness it promised has faded to misery and, eventually, to death.

John 8:44 tells us:

Ye are of your father the devil, and the lusts of your father ye will do. He was a murderer from the beginning, and abode not in the truth, because there is no truth in him. When he speaketh a lie, he speaketh of his own: for he is a **liar**, and the father of it.

God's Formula

In contrast, God's formula is made of weakness in ourselves, but strength in Christ. It's made of riches in heaven, though not always on earth. It's made of love for others as ourselves.

On the surface, it looks like this formula won't work, but when applied, it actually frees us from the worldly prison. It lets us live freely with joy no matter the circumstances. **The reason it looks like it won't work is because we are using the correct formula in the wrong world.** The great thing about this is that the correct formula ends in truth, and the evil formula ends in a lie. Even though we live in a lying world, the truth overcomes the lie, and that is why we can live in a world that is opposite our new nature in Christ. While we will battle every day with these two formulas, at the end of it all, truth always overcomes the lie, just as God has already overcome Satan. God knows the truth because He is the truth.

Luke 15:7 says, "I say unto you, that likewise **joy** shall be in heaven over **one sinner** that repenteth, more than over ninety and nine just persons, which need no repentance."

The question is, How do you find the way to this formula? If this is the formula of freedom, how do you get it?

Every day, we all realize and see these two formulas working in our lives. Just look at the movies, which portray good versus bad, and pit heroes against villains. We know we want the right formula, the formula of truth, but we must apply the things against the world to obtain this formula.

Read what the truth says about repentance:

When Jesus heard it, he saith unto them, They that are whole have no need of the physician, but they that are sick: I came not to call the righteous, but sinners to **repent**ance.

Mark 2:17

And they went out, and preached that men should **repent**.

Mark 6:12

And he came into all the country about Jordan, preaching the baptism of **repent**ance for the remission of sins.

Luke 3:3

I came not to call the righteous, but sinners to **repent**ance.

Luke 5:32

Despite this, repenting is the hardest thing to do when you are unsaved. However, this is the most important ingredient in the formula, and without it nothing is completed. Salvation without repentance is like having open wounds, but calling yourself whole. These open, infected wounds in our lives are sins that eat at us like canker sours do the flesh. And if left untreated, these wounds of sin will lead to a total infection of the body and then death. The first thing you have to do before an open wound will heal is acknowledge there is a problem, and that problem needs a solution.

If you never acknowledge the wound exists, there is no help applied. Maybe you don't know where the wound is. Maybe you are not able to find its origin, and you only see the wound's symptoms. Well, just as we go through a battery of tests when we are ill to find the cause, so will God help you to find your source of illness. God goes to the root of the problem, the core of the issue. This could be a lost child or a parent who abused you. Maybe it's a spouse's cheating or not loving you. When God is the Physician, He always finds the issue, and He medicates it with Himself and the truth. No illness, not even death itself, can keep its sting when the one true God takes over.

This is the truth:

O **death**, where is thy **sting**? O grave, where is thy victory?

1 Corinthians 15:55

The Fletcher Story

Once I met a man named Fletcher, and we became friends. He was eighty-eight years old when he died, but for a few years, I was blessed to spend time with him. I would see him at church and visit him at his home. We worked on church projects together, and he was a pleasure to be around. We joked and laughed. He was a hard worker, and one thing was for sure: He loved Jesus. One night I took the kids from the church over to his house for a visit. At this time in Fletcher's life, he was just about to die. Coherent and in his right mind, he was sitting up in his favorite chair and was definitely happy to see us come visit. That night I asked him if he would give the kids some advice on how to live a good life. He looked at the kids and, with a soft voice, said, "I gave my heart to Christ eight years ago, and this has been the best eight years of my life." At that moment, the kids did not seem to see the volume of what he said, but I did, and it will forever be burned into my mind. For a man to say the last years of his life—the time of sickness and feebleness, the time of age and memory loss—have been the best years is a miracle in itself. When Fletcher got saved, God did not give him happiness; God gave Fletcher JOY and freedom. God gave him true joy and freedom, and these things cannot be contained or put away because of age or health. In other words, true joy and freedom can sing out in any circumstance in which this world may put you. Jesus said, "Fear not the world, for I have overcome the world."

CHAPTER 13

Suffering:
Where Is the Balance?

⟨∞⟩

At some point in our lives, suffering affects us all. However, as history shows us, some people will suffer much greater than others. Many will seem to never suffer, but this is only because their suffering is hidden from the world. To the individual, it is absolutely evident. For example, take someone born with a handicap that causes the person to have extreme pain. What about someone who is left on this earth who has lost his entire family in a car accident? The examples are endless, and they vary from the minute to the extreme, but the truth is, as long as we live in this world and as long as sin reigns, suffering will follow. The Bible tells us so.

And he began to teach them, that the Son of man must **suffer** many things, and be rejected of the elders, and of the chief priests, and scribes, and be killed, and after three days rise again.

Mark 8:31

And whether we be afflicted, it is for your consolation and salvation, which is effectual in the enduring of the same **suffering**s which we also suffer: or whether we be comforted, it is for your consolation and salvation.

2 Corinthians 1:6

So the question becomes, If we all will suffer, why does God allow a greater suffering for some than for others? Is there something we can do in our lives to make our suffering less, or even to help someone who is suffering more? We read that Jesus did suffer, but did He suffer for all or just some? Why does He not protect the innocent now, and why do they sometimes seem to suffer the most? Finally, is this God's plan? Did He plan all this suffering, and did it include all this awful stuff to get to the good?

Let's start with controlling suffering—can it be done?

At the time I was writing this book, I was reading about a famous young actress who was warned that if she did not follow a judge's rules, she would spend time in jail. Despite this, she decided not to follow them, and she was ordered to spend time in jail as a punishment for breaking the law. She was in control of her suffering in that instant. If she would have followed the judge's rules, she would not have suffered by receiving jail time. Suffering in many ways starts from *our* actions, not God's. We also will discuss when suffering was not brought on by our actions. At the end of the day, if we were to analyze all cases of suffering, much, if not most, of it is directly related to *our* poor choices, not God's ultimate plan.

Jude 1:7 states:

Even as Sodom and Gomorrha, and the cities about them in like manner, giving themselves over to fornication, and going after strange flesh, are set forth for an example, **suffering** the vengeance of eternal fire.

Sodom and Gomorrha caused their suffering by their actions, and the entire city paid for this lifestyle. So, yes, suffering can be controlled by an individual, whether or not by the person's actions. So if suffering is brought on by something out of our control, like a child's being born with a handicap or an accident that leaves someone in pain, it can be controlled, but how?

Suffering is a state of being that is synonymous with pain, anger, tears, despair, and loss. Suffering is comprised of emotions and circumstances in our lives that seem to control us, especially during the time of the suffering. Jesus suffered in this world, and He said we will suffer as well; that is, until His promised return. Read the following verse.

But rejoice, inasmuch as ye are partakers of Christ's **suffering**s; that, when his glory shall be revealed, ye may be glad also with exceeding joy.

1 Peter 4:13

Because suffering is inevitable in our lives, and is from our choices, our loved ones' choices, or maybe uncontrollable circumstances, how do we control suffering? You control suffering, which is directly related to sin, by one simple method, and that is through a shot of joy and peace. This should be injected into every area of suffering in your life. Where does this joy come from? It comes directly from the Holy Spirit, who is the Comforter Jesus sent to believers. This joy and peace I speak of cannot come from a human and last for any amount of time. This cure from suffering comes from God, Christ, and the Holy Spirit—and them alone. For those of you readers who were looking for a cure without Christ, good luck with that. Nobody's found one yet. So let's take a serious look at the truth and what it says.

But the **Comforter**, which is the Holy Ghost, whom the Father will **send** in my name, he shall teach you all things, and bring all things to your remembrance, whatsoever I have said unto you.

John 14:26

But when the **Comforter** is come, whom I will **send** unto you from the Father, even the Spirit of truth, which proceedeth from the Father, he shall testify of me.

John 15:26

Nevertheless, I tell you the truth; It is expedient for you that I go away: for if I go not away, the **Comforter** will not come unto you; but if I depart, I will **send** him unto you.

John 16:7

An example in the Bible shows us the type of joy and peace that is given when you have Christ and the Comforter with you.

[16]And it came to pass, as we went to prayer, a certain damsel possessed with a spirit of divination met us, which brought her masters much gain by soothsaying:

[17]The same followed Paul and us, and cried, saying, These men are the servants of the most high God, which shew unto us the way of salvation.

[18]And this did she many days. But Paul, being grieved, turned and said to the spirit, I command thee in the name of Jesus Christ to come out of her. And he came out the same hour.

[19]And when her masters saw that the hope of their gains was gone, they caught Paul and Silas, and drew them into the marketplace unto the rulers,

[20]and brought them to the magistrates, saying, These men, being Jews, do exceedingly trouble our city,

[21]and teach customs, which are not lawful for us to receive, neither to observe, being Romans.

[22]And the multitude rose up together against them: and the magistrates

rent off their clothes, and commanded to beat them.

[23]And when they had laid many stripes upon them, they cast them into prison, charging the jailor to keep them safely:

[24]Who, having received such a charge, thrust them into the inner prison, and made their feet fast in the stocks.

[25]And at midnight Paul and Silas prayed, and sang praises unto God: and the prisoners heard them.

[26]And suddenly there was a great earthquake, so that the foundations of the prison were shaken: and immediately all the doors were opened, and every one's bands were loosed.

[27]And the keeper of the prison awaking out of his sleep, and seeing the prison doors open, he drew out his sword, and would have killed himself, supposing that the prisoners had been fled.

[28]But Paul cried with a loud voice, saying, Do thyself no harm: for we are all here.

[29]Then he called for a light, and sprang in, and came trembling, and fell down before Paul and Silas,

[30]and brought them out, and said, Sirs, what must I do to be saved?

[31]And they said, Believe on the Lord Jesus Christ, and thou shalt be saved, and thy house.

[32]And they spake unto him the word of the Lord, and to all that were in his house.

[33]And he took them the same hour of the night, and washed their stripes; and was baptized, he and all his, straightway.

Acts 16:16-33

So after serving God, Paul seemed to get punished for doing so. At this moment, under these circumstances, he would have good reason to be angry with God. But instead of being bitter, Paul decided to inject joy into this bad situation, and what happened? The jail opened up. What is even more surprising is that given the opportunity to leave, he stayed and led a man and his entire family to the Lord. That is the joy and peace that suffering cannot contain.

Jesus has said that He will give you peace in these times of suffering if you call on Him. If He is your Savior, peace is guaranteed to come, one way or another. He does not say, "Maybe I will"; He says He will. Jesus offers us this refuge His way, a way of peace through the suffering, a way of comfort through the pain.

Matthew 11:28-30 states:

[28]Come unto me, all ye that labour and are heavy laden, and I will give you rest.
[29]Take my yoke upon you, and learn of me; for I am meek and lowly in heart: and ye shall find rest unto your souls.
[30]For my yoke is easy, and my burden is light.

This is not an easy task for solid Christians, not to mention people who don't know Christ at all. The formula of truth will not be changed because of our lack of faith or unbelief; it will just not work for us because of this lack. The simple truth is if we turn our sufferings, along with our lives, over to Christ, His formula begins to work. It will not only begin in the suffering, but also in every aspect of our lives, even the things we have not realized yet.

So why does God allow some to suffer more than others? Why does it seem the innocent suffer the most?

These are the questions from which many of us run. We say we don't know all things about God, and some things we will never understand. Wrong answer! First of all, we already have discussed that suffering is not something God wants us to endure, but He tells us we will. But He has made the ultimate sacrifice already to make sure we don't suffer in torment for eternity, which is His greatest concern. We also need to see God's Son, Jesus, who gave His life and suffered for us. He did this willingly and specifically for you.

The truth says:

For God sent **not** his Son into the **world** to **condemn** the **world**; but that the **world** through him might be saved.

John 3:17

[17]Therefore doth my Father love me, because I lay down my life, that I might take it again.
[18]No man taketh it from me, but I lay it down of myself. I have power to lay it down, and I have power to take it again. This commandment have I received of my Father.

John 10:17-18

¹The LORD is my shepherd; I shall not want.

²He maketh me to lie down in green pastures: he leadeth me beside the still waters.

³He restoreth my soul: he leadeth me in the paths of righteousness for his name's sake.

⁴Yea, though I walk through the valley of the shadow of death, I will fear no evil: for thou art with me; thy rod and thy staff they comfort me.

⁵Thou preparest a table before me in the presence of mine enemies: thou anointest my head with oil; my cup runneth over.

⁶Surely goodness and mercy shall follow me all the days of my life: and I will dwell in the house of the LORD for ever.

Psalm 23:1-6

So now that the suffering for eternity is taken care of, let's focus on the earthly time. God and Jesus tell us that suffering will be a part of this life, but they have sent the Comforter to help us. God does not want you to suffer, nor is it His will for you to suffer. However, He will use that suffering we all go through to make us better. It is God's eternal will that we have peace in Him.

He tells us that His children do not belong to this world; however, we will have to deal with the problems of this world until the end of it comes. Jesus and God have prepared the final place for us, and that place includes no suffering, no pain, and no sadness, only the warmness of being home after being gone so very long. Even the animals will be at peace.

Romans 8:18 states:

For I reckon that the **suffer**ings of this present time are not worthy to be compared with the glory which shall be revealed in us.

Again, suffering here on earth is, in many ways, a state of mind. For example, a person who does not get his or her weekly massage could feel he or she is suffering. We all have different suffering points, but let's focus on the suffering that our actions do not control. Examples may include a loving spouse who has been cheated on, a baby who is dying of starvation, or even a child who is being abused as we speak, with no one to protect him. How about the person born blind or deaf, or even born only knowing pain? These are the sufferings that we cry out to God about, pointing a finger, saying, "You are not perfect, for if You were, this would not be."

God says in His truth that we live in a fallen world that is full of sin, and suffering is part of it.

John 12:31 tells us, "Now is the judgment of this **world**: now shall the prince of this **world** be cast out."

God also says the God of this world is Satan, who goes to and fro, looking for whom he can devour. That being said, at the end of the day, nothing can happen to anyone without God's allowing it to happen. God does allow these things to take place—all the atrocities we have seen over history, all the nauseating things that take place every day. Notice I DID NOT say He produces them, but I said He allows them. God has a much bigger plan for us than we have for ourselves. God sees things that we cannot see, and He uses instances and happenings in this life to bring about His plan. However, His plan is for our good, not our demise.

Read the following Scriptures.

Before the LORD: for he cometh, for he cometh to judge the earth: he shall judge the **world** with righteousness, and the people with his truth.

Psalm 96:13

And, behold, there are **last** which **shall** be **first**, and there are **first** which **shall** be **last**.

Luke 13:30

[20]And he lifted up his eyes on his disciples, and said, Blessed be ye poor: for yours is the kingdom of God.
[21]Blessed are ye that hunger now: for ye shall be filled. Blessed are ye that weep now: for ye shall laugh.
[22]Blessed are ye, when men shall hate you, and when they shall separate you from their company, and shall reproach you, and cast out your name as evil, for the Son of man's sake.

Luke 6:20-22

Hath not the potter power over the **clay**, of the same lump to make one vessel unto honour, and another unto dishonour?

Romans 9:21

So why do the innocent suffer, including little children who get cancer and die? The answer to that question is two simple letters: ME.

I have sinned and brought suffering into this world. Each one of us has caused unnecessary sufferings to others. I have caused my spouse, my children, and my friends to suffer. They were all innocent, but because of my choice, their suffering began. Humanity has caused these things to take place. We are to blame for not feeding the child; we are to blame for not helping the sick ones. We are to blame for the state of this world and the reason sin reigns. God could stop it all; yes, He could make it so the little child never got cancer. God says He is the Maker of eternal rewards; He has put the child who suffered in front of the earthly blessed for an eternity. So is He now justified and fair? Does not the reward outweigh the trial gone through? What an awesome God, who takes our sins and our mistakes and, yes, everyone's suffering, and uses them to overcome Satan and bring glory to His kingdom.

We see it as uncaring because God allows anyone to suffer, such as the Jews during the Holocaust, or the baby dying of AIDS. However, God says, "My reward for them who believe in Christ is to come, and is greater than the suffering we have brought into this world." We act as if there should be no suffering for anyone who is blameless in this life. While God does not make that promise anywhere, He does promise, and has accomplished, the ultimate triumph over the end of suffering, which is death itself. He overcame suffering and death, and because of this, so shall we!

As the truth states:

O **death**, where is thy **sting**? O grave, where is thy victory?

1 Corinthians 15:55

15For this we say unto you by the word of the Lord, that we which are alive and remain unto the coming of the Lord shall not prevent them which are asleep.

16For the Lord himself shall descend from heaven with a shout, with the voice of the archangel, and with the trump of God: and the dead in Christ shall rise first:

17Then we which are alive and remain shall be caught up together with them in the clouds, to meet the Lord in the air: and so shall we ever be with the Lord.

1 Thessalonians 4:15-17

The Bible said Jesus suffered, but did He suffer for all, or just some?

Some would say Jesus suffered and died only for His chosen

people; whether it is Jews or Gentiles, He died for them only. On the contrary, the Bible says He died for all mankind. We see this in the following verses.

As thou hast **give**n him power over **all** flesh, that he should **give** eternal **life** to as many as thou hast **give**n him.

John 17:2

[11]For the Son of man is come to save that which was lost.
[12]How think ye? If a man have an hundred sheep, and one of them be gone astray, doth he not leave the ninety and nine, and goeth into the mountains, and seeketh that which is gone astray?
[13]And if so be that he find it, verily I say unto you, he rejoiceth more of that sheep, than of the ninety and nine which went not astray.
[14]Even so it is not the will of your Father which is in heaven, that one of these little ones should perish.

Matthew 18:11-14

For God so loved the world, that he gave his only begotten Son, that whosoever believeth in him should not **perish**, but have everlasting life.

John 3:16

Though this should be obvious enough to us, some still say that when the Bible says *all*, it really means just *all of the chosen*. The truth says that Jesus came to free the world, which means everyone who is overcome by the world can be freed. If someone, anyone, is willing to surrender all and confess with his or her mouth, God is willing to forgive. This cannot happen without the grace of God and the Holy Spirit's intervening. God says if you call on Him, the grace and the Holy Spirit will come.

Second Peter 3:9 says:

The Lord is not slack concerning his promise, as some men count slackness; but is longsuffering to us-ward, not willing that any should **perish**, but that all should come to repentance.

Count yourself blessed if you have been saved and received the Holy Spirit because so many have not. Remember that salvation came for sinners, of whom I am chief, not the riotous.

We are all sinners, and if Christ died for the sinner, He died for all.

First Timothy 1:15 tells us:

This **is** a faithful saying, and worthy of all acceptation, that Christ Jesus **came i**nto the world to save **sinners**; of whom **I** am chief.

Lastly, did God plan all this bad to get to the good? Is my suffering what He intended for me to go through?

Here we go again. Some things are just not meant to be

understood, as our feeble human minds cannot comprehend the ways of God. I know people who truly believe that God would cause a man to rape a child and then allow the parents and the child to go through the anguish of this incident as it is in His eternal plan. To them I say, "Oh, you blind, blind soul."

God has allowed everything that has ever happened to happen, so the buck stops with Him, and He makes no excuses in regards to being in charge. He also says He can overcome our sins and mistakes as well as Satan himself. God says He can bring beautiful things from the vilest of happenings. The question is, Does He cause them to happen to do this? The answer is as simple as this: Absolutely not. Let's see what God has to say about Himself and what He wants for us.

[1]The LORD is my shepherd; I shall not want.

[2]He maketh me to lie down in green pastures: he leadeth me beside the still waters.

[3]He restoreth my soul: he leadeth me in the paths of righteousness for his name's sake.

[4]Yea, though I walk through the valley of the shadow of death, I will fear no evil: for thou art with me; thy rod and thy staff they comfort me.

[5]Thou preparest a table before me in the presence of mine enemies: thou anointest my head with oil; my cup runneth over.

[6]Surely goodness and mercy shall follow me all the days of my life:

and I will dwell in the house of the LORD for ever.

Psalm 23:1-6

Blessed is the man that endureth temptation: for when he is tried, he shall receive the crown of life, which the Lord hath promised to them that love him.

James 1:12

Jesus is a Protector. He is a Father. And He does not have to produce evil to bring good. Evil was not mentioned before Lucifer, the highest of the angels, chose to rebel. Did God cause him to rebel? Evil did not come before Adam and Eve, but only after they rebelled. God did not create evil, but evil happened due to our rebellion against the Father. Evil, in itself, is the absence of God, just as darkness is the absence of light. Light has the measurement, not darkness; darkness is defined as the absence of light.

Read what the truth says about darkness.

John 1:5

And the light shineth in **darkness**; and the **darkness** comprehended it **not**.

John 12:46

I am come a light into the world, that whosoever believeth on me should **not** abide in **darkness**.

1 John 1:5

This then is the **me**ssage which we have heard of him, and declare unto you, that God is light, and in him is **no darkness** at all.

Revelation 21:23

And the city had no need of the sun, neither of the moon, to shine in it: for the glory of God did **light**en it, and the **Lamb is** the **light** thereof.

Though God didn't create evil, He can bring goodness from it. Just as a match can penetrate the darkest of dark, so can God penetrate the hardest of hearts. We serve a powerful God, who sees the past, present, and future all at the same time, so when the battle is being fought, He sees what can be allowed and what will not be allowed. He also chooses who will be in this fight for overall victory in eternal life, not our earthly life. So what I am saying is God can change His mind if He wants about situations in this life. The point is God is not constrained by our actions, only His own.

Story of Moses

[24]And it came to pass by the way in the inn, that the LORD met him, and sought to kill him.

[25]Then Zipporah took a sharp stone, and cut off the foreskin of her son, and cast it at his feet, and said, Surely a bloody husband art thou to me.

²⁶So he let him go: then she said, A bloody husband thou art, because of the circumcision.

Exodus 4:24-26

In this story, Moses had a child and should have circumcised the child. This was part of the covenant God made with Abraham. But Moses had not followed God's orders, and God was going to kill Moses for not doing so. God just as easily could have called another to lead Israel. God decided to kill Moses, but his wife Zipporah did the right thing, and God chose not to kill him. The point is God is not held to our standards of predestation. God does have a plan for us all, and you can choose not to follow that plan, and suffer the consequences, or you can choose to obey and get the blessings. Regardless of your choice or actions, we will not change God and what is to come in His Word.

Jonah and the Whale

We have all heard the story, right? Jonah chose not to follow God's call to go to Nineveh, and even threw himself overboard to end it all, but God provided another way. After a few days in a whale, Jonah finally realized he should go and do as the Lord requested. Jonah repented and went, but the choice was still his, as it is still ours to serve or not to serve. How many whales has God provided for you? As a child of God's, you can choose whether or not to turn from your sins. Either way, no matter what our choice is, we do not change God's plan or His truth. His perfection is not held or changed by our actions; *He changes us* by His actions. The eternal plan God had before the world existed did not include the suffering of man and woman to get to heaven. God's eternal plan is to save us from ourselves. He has fulfilled, and He will continue to fulfill, His plan **through love, not suffering**. Not once did Jesus cause another to suffer, yet He suffered much for us. He only praised His Father and took suffering away while He was on this earth. Never once did Jesus say His Father was the originator of sin and evil. Instead, He is only Goodness and Mercy, Love and Comfort, a Giver to the poor, Mercy to the undeserving, and a Forgiver to the unforgivable.

God's plan was not to originate sin and suffering to bring glory to Him. His only plan was, and still is, that in spite of our sins, He showed us mercy. Through His love, grace, and sacrifice, He is glorified and justified.

Kidney Stone

If you have never had a kidney stone, consider yourself blessed for not having had to go through one of the worst pains known to man. The pain comes from an obstruction in one or both of your kidneys from a stone usually no bigger than a BB that is irregularly shaped and causes your kidney and urinary system to ache horribly. I have had these since I was ten years old. I usually have one a year, around the change of a season, but I never really know when one could strike. The onset is as quick as a breath and will bring any man or woman to his or her knees in an instant. This suffering is one I deal with partly to my own fault, and partly because of the way my kidneys work. If I would drink more water and eat healthier, it would help to not produce them, but my kidneys don't work as a typical person's, so some of this is genetic, it seems. The last stone I had caused excruciating pain, and I was suffering for days with this problem. I prayed, "Lord, please take this away," but He did not. I prayed, "Give me relief, Lord," and though He did, the pain would come again soon enough. I said, "Lord, you promise in Your Word that if I asked in Your name, You would grant my request." I said, "Lord, I will not deny You or curse You for this," and I sang praises to Him while going through this pain. Imagine the site of a man doubled over in pain, singing "Amazing Grace" at the top of his lungs. Yet God did not stop the pain. Was God a liar for not relieving me? Was I doing something to stop the prayer from being answered? The answer is no to both. God did stop the pain, and I did pass the stone eventually, but it was not on my timeline; it was on His. He allowed me to have it, and He allowed me to suffer, but He fulfilled His Word by taking it away in His time. If the pain would have never stopped, and my life would have ended, His Word would have still been true because there is no pain in heaven, and that is where I would have been.

CHAPTER 14

<u>Why God Made Me, and Who Made God?</u>

———— ∽∞∽ ————

Which came first, the chicken or the egg? Because God is the Creator of all things, the question is are: Who created Him? And why did He create me? The answer to the first question: He is the Creator and is creation Himself. He has always been created and will never end. Can something be created without a creator? Yes, one thing only. His name is God, and He is the Creator of all things, including the beginning of something as well as time and matter. When Adam and Eve lived, they had no conception of time; they only knew that they existed and that God had made them. They knew no death, and there was no end to their lives. They knew a beginning, but knew no end. We see our birth as our beginning and death as the end, but what does God tell us? He says the life in this world is only the life before eternal life begins in either heaven or hell.

On the other hand, in this world, we go from our rules on time while alive to death.

Death is when God's timeline begins, so who is this God? Who is this created Creator? Read these passages:

Revelation 21:6

And he said unto me, It is done. I am **Alpha** and **Omega**, the beginning and the end. I will give unto him that is athirst of the fountain of the water of life freely.

Revelation 1:8

I am **Alpha** and **Omega**, the beginning and the ending, saith the Lord, which is, and which was, and which is to come, the Almighty.

1 John 4:8

He that **love**th not knoweth not **God**; for **God is love**.

God tells us He is love and truth, that through His Word He is and was and always will be. This is why God is solid in His foundation and never changes. He defines Himself as the I AM. He tells us He is the Definer of the universe and the world we live in. Most of all, he lets us know life is but a breath, and is gone.

James 4:14 says, "Whereas ye know not what shall be on the morrow. For what **is** your **life**? It **is** even a vapour, that appeareth for a little time, and then vanisheth away."

The story below is about Job, a man of God. He lived a good life serving God, yet God allowed some bad things to happen to Job.

Job had questioned God to the extent of, "Why did You let me be born, if when I serve You, You let bad things happen to me?" Today, the question we ask is the same: Why do bad things happen to good people? God answers by asking Job a question—the same question we should ask ourselves when thinking of God and who He is.

Job 3:1-26

¹After this opened Job his mouth, and cursed his day.

²And Job spake, and said,

³Let the day perish wherein I was born, and the night in which it was said, There is a man child conceived.

⁴Let that day be darkness; let not God regard it from above, neither let the light shine upon it.

⁵Let darkness and the shadow of death stain it; let a cloud dwell upon it; let the blackness of the day terrify it.

⁶As for that night, let darkness seize upon it; let it not be joined unto the days of the year, let it not come into the number of the months.

⁷Lo, let that night be solitary, let no joyful voice come therein.

⁸Let them curse it that curse the day, who are ready to raise up their mourning.

⁹Let the stars of the twilight thereof be dark; let it look for light, but have none; neither let it see the dawning of the day:

¹⁰Because it shut not up the doors of my mother's womb, nor hid sorrow from mine eyes.

¹¹Why died I not from the womb? Why did I not give up the ghost

when I came out of the belly?

¹²Why did the knees prevent me? Or why the breasts that I should suck?

¹³For now should I have lain still and been quiet, I should have slept: then had I been at rest,

¹⁴with kings and counsellors of the earth, which build desolate places for themselves;

¹⁵Or with princes that had gold, who filled their houses with silver:

¹⁶Or as an hidden untimely birth I had not been; as infants which never saw light.

¹⁷There the wicked cease from troubling; and there the weary be at rest.

¹⁸There the prisoners rest together; they hear not the voice of the oppressor.

¹⁹The small and great are there; and the servant is free from his master.

²⁰Wherefore is light given to him that is in misery, and life unto the bitter in soul;

²¹Which long for death, but it cometh not; and dig for it more than for hid treasures;

²²Which rejoice exceedingly, and are glad, when they can find the grave?

²³Why is light given to a man whose way is hid, and whom God hath hedged in?

²⁴For my sighing cometh before I eat, and my roarings are poured

out like the waters.

²⁵For the thing which I greatly feared is come upon me, and that which I was afraid of is come unto me.

²⁶I was not in safety, neither had I rest, neither was I quiet; yet trouble came.

Job 7:1-21

¹Is there not an appointed time to man upon earth? Are not his days also like the days of an hireling?

²As a servant earnestly desireth the shadow, and as an hireling looketh for the reward of his work:

³So am I made to possess months of vanity, and wearisome nights are appointed to me.

⁴When I lie down, I say, When shall I arise, and the night be gone? And I am full of tossings to and fro unto the dawning of the day.

⁵My flesh is clothed with worms and clods of dust; my skin is broken, and become loathsome.

⁶My days are swifter than a weaver's shuttle, and are spent without hope.

⁷O remember that my life is wind: mine eye shall no more see good.

⁸The eye of him that hath seen me shall see me no more: thine eyes are upon me, and I am not.

⁹As the cloud is consumed and vanisheth away: so he that goeth down to the grave shall come up no more.

¹⁰He shall return no more to his house, neither shall his place know

him any more.

[11]Therefore I will not refrain my mouth; I will speak in the anguish of my spirit; I will complain in the bitterness of my soul.

[12]Am I a sea, or a whale, that thou settest a watch over me?

[13]When I say, My bed shall comfort me, my couch shall ease my complaints;

[14]Then thou scarest me with dreams, and terrifiest me through visions:

[15]So that my soul chooseth strangling, and death rather than my life.

[16]I loathe it; I would not live alway: let me alone; for my days are vanity.

[17]What is man, that thou shouldest magnify him? And that thou shouldest set thine heart upon him?

[18]And that thou shouldest visit him every morning, and try him every moment?

[19]How long wilt thou not depart from me, nor let me alone till I swallow down my spittle?

[20]I have sinned; what shall I do unto thee, O thou preserver of men? Why hast thou set me as a mark against thee, so that I am a burden to myself?

[21]And why dost thou not pardon my transgression, and take away my iniquity? For now shall I sleep in the dust; and thou shalt seek me in the morning, but I shall not be.

Job 9:1-35

¹Then Job answered and said,

²I know it is so of a truth: but how should man be just with God?

³If he will contend with him, he cannot answer him one of a thousand.

⁴He is wise in heart, and mighty in strength: who hath hardened himself against him, and hath prospered?

⁵Which removeth the mountains, and they know not: which overturneth them in his anger.

⁶Which shaketh the earth out of her place, and the pillars thereof tremble.

⁷Which commandeth the sun, and it riseth not; and sealeth up the stars.

⁸Which alone spreadeth out the heavens, and treadeth upon the waves of the sea.

⁹Which maketh Arcturus, Orion, and Pleiades, and the chambers of the south.

¹⁰Which doeth great things past finding out; yea, and wonders without number.

¹¹Lo, he goeth by me, and I see him not: he passeth on also, but I perceive him not.

¹²Behold, he taketh away, who can hinder him? Who will say unto him, What doest thou?

¹³If God will not withdraw his anger, the proud helpers do stoop under him.

¹⁴How much less shall I answer him, and choose out my words to

reason with him?

¹⁵Whom, though I were righteous, yet would I not answer, but I would make supplication to my judge.

¹⁶If I had called, and he had answered me; yet would I not believe that he had hearkened unto my voice.

¹⁷For he breaketh me with a tempest, and multiplieth my wounds without cause.

¹⁸He will not suffer me to take my breath, but filleth me with bitterness.

¹⁹If I speak of strength, lo, he is strong: and if of judgment, who shall set me a time to plead?

²⁰If I justify myself, mine own mouth shall condemn me: if I say, I am perfect, it shall also prove me perverse.

²¹Though I were perfect, yet would I not know my soul: I would despise my life.

²²This is one thing, therefore I said it, He destroyeth the perfect and the wicked.

²³If the scourge slay suddenly, he will laugh at the trial of the innocent.

²⁴The earth is given into the hand of the wicked: he covereth the faces of the judges thereof; if not, where, and who is he?

²⁵Now my days are swifter than a post: they flee away, they see no good.

²⁶They are passed away as the swift ships: as the eagle that hasteth to the prey.

²⁷If I say, I will forget my complaint, I will leave off my heaviness, and comfort myself:

²⁸I am afraid of all my sorrows, I know that thou wilt not hold me innocent.

²⁹If I be wicked, why then labour I in vain?

³⁰If I wash myself with snow water, and make my hands never so clean;

³¹Yet shalt thou plunge me in the ditch, and mine own clothes shall abhor me.

³²For he is not a man, as I am, that I should answer him, and we should come together in judgment.

³³Neither is there any daysman betwixt us, that might lay his hand upon us both.

³⁴Let him take his rod away from me, and let not his fear terrify me:

³⁵Then would I speak, and not fear him; but it is not so with me.

What a mouthful. Take a break for a moment, and realize what Job has said. He has not only questioned God's ability to create, but also why He created man in the first place. He wants to know why man can't control his own destiny by following God's laws.

I realize this is a lot of Scripture, but now we get to hear from the Almighty, His reply.

Job 38:1-41

¹**Then the LORD** answered Job out of the whirlwind, and said,

²Who is this that darkeneth counsel by words without knowledge?

³Gird up now thy loins like a man; for I will demand of thee, and answer thou me.

⁴Where wast thou when I laid the foundations of the earth? Declare, if thou hast understanding.

⁵Who hath laid the measures thereof, if thou knowest? Or who hath stretched the line upon it?

⁶Whereupon are the foundations thereof fastened? Or who laid the corner stone thereof;

⁷When the morning stars sang together, and all the sons of God shouted for joy?

⁸Or who shut up the sea with doors, when it brake forth, as if it had issued out of the womb?

⁹When I made the cloud the garment thereof, and thick darkness a swaddlingband for it,

¹⁰and brake up for it my decreed place, and set bars and doors,

¹¹and said, Hitherto shalt thou come, but no further: and here shall thy proud waves be stayed?

¹²Hast thou commanded the morning since thy days; and caused the dayspring to know his place;

¹³That it might take hold of the ends of the earth, that the wicked might be shaken out of it?

¹⁴It is turned as clay to the seal; and they stand as a garment.

¹⁵And from the wicked their light is withholden, and the high arm shall be broken.

¹⁶Hast thou entered into the springs of the sea? Or hast thou walked in the search of the depth?

¹⁷Have the gates of death been opened unto thee? Or hast thou seen the doors of the shadow of death?

¹⁸Hast thou perceived the breadth of the earth? Declare if thou knowest it all.

¹⁹Where is the way where light dwelleth? And as for darkness, where is the place thereof,

²⁰That thou shouldest take it to the bound thereof, and that thou shouldest know the paths to the house thereof?

²¹Knowest thou it, because thou wast then born? Or because the number of thy days is great?

²²Hast thou entered into the treasures of the snow? Or hast thou seen the treasures of the hail,

²³which I have reserved against the time of trouble, against the day of battle and war?

²⁴By what way is the light parted, which scattereth the east wind upon the earth?

²⁵Who hath divided a watercourse for the overflowing of waters, or a way for the lightning of thunder;

²⁶To cause it to rain on the earth, where no man is; on the wilderness, wherein there is no man;

²⁷To satisfy the desolate and waste ground; and to cause the bud of the tender herb to spring forth?

²⁸Hath the rain a father? or who hath begotten the drops of dew?

²⁹Out of whose womb came the ice? And the hoary frost of heaven, who hath gendered it?

³⁰The waters are hid as with a stone, and the face of the deep is frozen.

³¹Canst thou bind the sweet influences of Pleiades, or loose the bands of Orion?

³²Canst thou bring forth Mazzaroth in his season? Or canst thou guide Arcturus with his sons?

³³Knowest thou the ordinances of heaven? Canst thou set the dominion thereof in the earth?

³⁴Canst thou lift up thy voice to the clouds, that abundance of waters may cover thee?

³⁵Canst thou send lightnings, that they may go and say unto thee, Here we are?

³⁶Who hath put wisdom in the inward parts? Or who hath given understanding to the heart?

³⁷Who can number the clouds in wisdom? Or who can stay the bottles of heaven,

³⁸When the dust groweth into hardness, and the clods cleave fast together?

³⁹Wilt thou hunt the prey for the lion? Or fill the appetite of the young lions,

⁴⁰when they couch in their dens, and abide in the covert to lie in wait?

⁴¹Who provideth for the raven his food? When his young ones cry

unto God, they wander for lack of meat.

Job 39:1-30

[1]Knowest thou the time when the wild goats of the rock bring forth? Or canst thou mark when the hinds do calve?

[2]Canst thou number the months that they fulfil? Or knowest thou the time when they bring forth?

[3]They bow themselves, they bring forth their young ones, they cast out their sorrows.

[4]Their young ones are in good liking, they grow up with corn; they go forth, and return not unto them.

[5]Who hath sent out the wild ass free? Or who hath loosed the bands of the wild ass?

[6]Whose house I have made the wilderness, and the barren land his dwellings.

[7]He scorneth the multitude of the city, neither regardeth he the crying of the driver.

[8]The range of the mountains is his pasture, and he searcheth after every green thing.

[9]Will the unicorn be willing to serve thee, or abide by thy crib?

[10]Canst thou bind the unicorn with his band in the furrow? Or will he harrow the valleys after thee?

[11]Wilt thou trust him, because his strength is great? Or wilt thou leave thy labour to him?

[12]Wilt thou believe him, that he will bring home thy seed, and gather

it into thy barn?

¹³Gavest thou the goodly wings unto the peacocks? Or wings and feathers unto the ostrich?

¹⁴Which leaveth her eggs in the earth, and warmeth them in dust,

¹⁵And forgetteth that the foot may crush them, or that the wild beast may break them.

¹⁶She is hardened against her young ones, as though they were not her's: her labour is in vain without fear;

¹⁷Because God hath deprived her of wisdom, neither hath he imparted to her understanding.

¹⁸What time she lifteth up herself on high, she scorneth the horse and his rider.

¹⁹Hast thou given the horse strength? Hast thou clothed his neck with thunder?

²⁰Canst thou make him afraid as a grasshopper? The glory of his nostrils is terrible.

²¹He paweth in the valley, and rejoiceth in his strength: he goeth on to meet the armed men.

²²He mocketh at fear, and is not affrighted; neither turneth he back from the sword.

²³The quiver rattleth against him, the glittering spear and the shield.

²⁴He swalloweth the ground with fierceness and rage: neither believeth he that it is the sound of the trumpet.

²⁵He saith among the trumpets, Ha, ha; and he smelleth the battle afar off, the thunder of the captains, and the shouting.

²⁶Doth the hawk fly by thy wisdom, and stretch her wings toward the south?

²⁷Doth the eagle mount up at thy command, and make her nest on high?

²⁸She dwelleth and abideth on the rock, upon the crag of the rock, and the strong place.

²⁹From thence she seeketh the prey, and her eyes behold afar off.

³⁰Her young ones also suck up blood: and where the slain are, there is she.

Job 40:1-24

¹Moreover the LORD answered Job, and said,

²Shall he that contendeth with the Almighty instruct him? He that reproveth God, let him answer it.

³Then Job answered the LORD, and said,

⁴Behold, I am vile; what shall I answer thee? I will lay mine hand upon my mouth.

⁵Once have I spoken; but I will not answer: yea, twice; but I will proceed no further.

⁶Then answered the LORD unto Job out of the whirlwind, and said,

⁷Gird up thy loins now like a man: I will demand of thee, and declare thou unto me.

⁸Wilt thou also disannul my judgment? Wilt thou condemn me, that thou mayest be righteous?

⁹Hast thou an arm like God? Or canst thou thunder with a voice like

him?

[10]Deck thyself now with majesty and excellency; and array thyself with glory and beauty.

[11]Cast abroad the rage of thy wrath: and behold every one that is proud, and abase him.

[12]Look on every one that is proud, and bring him low; and tread down the wicked in their place.

[13]Hide them in the dust together; and bind their faces in secret.

[14]Then will I also confess unto thee that thine own right hand can save thee.

[15]Behold now behemoth, which I made with thee; he eateth grass as an ox.

[16]Lo now, his strength is in his loins, and his force is in the navel of his belly.

[17]He moveth his tail like a cedar: the sinews of his stones are wrapped together.

[18]His bones are as strong pieces of brass; his bones are like bars of iron.

[19]He is the chief of the ways of God: he that made him can make his sword to approach unto him.

[20]Surely the mountains bring him forth food, where all the beasts of the field play.

[21]He lieth under the shady trees, in the covert of the reed, and fens.

[22]The shady trees cover him with their shadow; the willows of the brook compass him about.

²³Behold, he drinketh up a river, and hasteth not: he trusteth that he can draw up Jordan into his mouth.

²⁴He taketh it with his eyes: his nose pierceth through snares.

Job 41:1-34

¹Canst thou draw out leviathan with an hook? Or his tongue with a cord which thou lettest down?

²Canst thou put an hook into his nose? Or bore his jaw through with a thorn?

³Will he make many supplications unto thee? Will he speak soft words unto thee?

⁴Will he make a covenant with thee? Wilt thou take him for a servant for ever?

⁵Wilt thou play with him as with a bird? Or wilt thou bind him for thy maidens?

⁶Shall the companions make a banquet of him? Shall they part him among the merchants?

⁷Canst thou fill his skin with barbed irons? Or his head with fish spears?

⁸Lay thine hand upon him, remember the battle, do no more.

⁹Behold, the hope of him is in vain: shall not one be cast down even at the sight of him?

¹⁰None is so fierce that dare stir him up: who then is able to stand before me?

¹¹Who hath prevented me, that I should repay him? Whatsoever is

under the whole heaven is mine.

¹²I will not conceal his parts, nor his power, nor his comely proportion.

¹³Who can discover the face of his garment? Or who can come to him with his double bridle?

¹⁴Who can open the doors of his face? His teeth are terrible round about.

¹⁵His scales are his pride, shut up together as with a close seal.

¹⁶One is so near to another, that no air can come between them.

¹⁷They are joined one to another, they stick together, that they cannot be sundered.

¹⁸By his neesings a light doth shine, and his eyes are like the eyelids of the morning.

¹⁹Out of his mouth go burning lamps, and sparks of fire leap out.

²⁰Out of his nostrils goeth smoke, as out of a seething pot or caldron.

²¹His breath kindleth coals, and a flame goeth out of his mouth.

²²In his neck remaineth strength, and sorrow is turned into joy before him.

²³The flakes of his flesh are joined together: they are firm in themselves; they cannot be moved.

²⁴His heart is as firm as a stone; yea, as hard as a piece of the nether millstone.

²⁵When he raiseth up himself, the mighty are afraid: by reason of breakings they purify themselves.

²⁶The sword of him that layeth at him cannot hold: the spear, the dart, nor the habergeon.

²⁷He esteemeth iron as straw, and brass as rotten wood.

²⁸The arrow cannot make him flee: slingstones are turned with him into stubble.

²⁹Darts are counted as stubble: he laugheth at the shaking of a spear.

³⁰Sharp stones are under him: he spreadeth sharp pointed things upon the mire.

³¹He maketh the deep to boil like a pot: he maketh the sea like a pot of ointment.

³²He maketh a path to shine after him; one would think the deep to be hoary.

³³Upon earth there is not his like, who is made without fear.

³⁴He beholdeth all high things: he is a king over all the children of pride.

Now that the answer has been given, the realization of who Job is has taken place. Job now understands the difference in the Creator and the creation.

Job 42:1-13

¹Then Job answered the LORD, and said,

²I know that thou canst do every thing, and that no thought can be withholden from thee.

³Who is he that hideth counsel without knowledge? Therefore have I uttered that I understood not; things too wonderful for me, which I knew not.

⁴Hear, I beseech thee, and I will speak: I will demand of thee, and

declare thou unto me.

[5]I have heard of thee by the hearing of the ear: but now mine eye seeth thee.

[6]Wherefore I abhor myself, and repent in dust and ashes.

[7]And it was so, that after the LORD had spoken these words unto Job, the LORD said to Eliphaz the Temanite, My wrath is kindled against thee, and against thy two friends: for ye have not spoken of me the thing that is right, as my servant Job hath.

[8]Therefore take unto you now seven bullocks and seven rams, and go to my servant Job, and offer up for yourselves a burnt offering; and my servant Job shall pray for you: for him will I accept: lest I deal with you after your folly, in that ye have not spoken of me the thing which is right, like my servant Job.

[9]So Eliphaz the Temanite and Bildad the Shuhite and Zophar the Naamathite went, and did according as the LORD commanded them: the LORD also accepted Job.

[10]And the LORD turned the captivity of Job, when he prayed for his friends: also the LORD gave Job twice as much as he had before.

[11]Then came there unto him all his brethren, and all his sisters, and all they that had been of his acquaintance before, and did eat bread with him in his house: and they bemoaned him, and comforted him over all the evil that the LORD had brought upon him: every man also gave him a piece of money, and every one an earring of gold.

[12]So the LORD blessed the latter end of Job more than his beginning: for he had fourteen thousand sheep, and six thousand camels,

and a thousand yoke of oxen, and a thousand she asses.
[13]He had also seven sons and three daughters.

Now we see what God says He claims to be, but what does He really need with us? God desires us. He wants us to know that His ultimate plan will never be the separation of Him and His children, nor is it for us to live in this world of pain and suffering. God does not want us to be separated from Him. He loves us, and He Himself is love. He also says, "I will give you your needs, but always remember as long as we live on this earth, bad things can, and will, happen." God showed Job that following His ways will bring Job blessings, but it will not keep him from harm's way as long as he is on this earth.

God has made a way to put an end to this, though. He sent His Son, Jesus Christ, to die in our stead so the separation would be no more. God wants you to know He is here for you whenever you call on Him.

Most of all, He has told us that He wants us to love Him, but He gave us the gift of loving us first. When we choose whether or not to love Him, we choose our eternity. As far as following God's rules and laws, if we do truly love Him, our actions will follow by this love.

First we are to love Him, and then a love for one another will grow out of a love for Him. Remember, the only way to love God and one another is by accepting God's love and forgiveness for yourself. When you can do this, His love will live in you, and you will want to share it with someone.

The truth says this about love:

1 John 4:19

We love him, because he **first loved** us.

Luke 10:27

And he answering said, Thou shalt love the Lord thy God with all thy heart, and with all thy soul, and with all thy **strength**, and with all thy mind; and thy neighbour as thyself.

God says we are all brothers and sisters in Christ. When you have accepted the grace of Christ, you become part of His family, a family made up of many different people, nationalities, and races—all in one family, one body, working together across the world and led by the Holy Spirit. And all are united in one Christ, who is our Savior, Father, and Friend.

Matthew 12:50 says, "For whosoever shall do the will of my Father which is in heaven, the same is my **brother**, and sister, and **mother**."

God's love is like our love for one another, but so much more. We love those who love us. While God loves those who love Him, He also loves those who hate Him. God's love is not based on your love for Him, but on His love for you. You may reject what He is and that for which He stands. You may be mad at Him. But those things will never stop Him from loving you.

See the formula of God's love at work below.

Romans 5:5-17

[5]And hope maketh not ashamed; because the love of God is shed abroad in our hearts by the Holy Ghost which is given unto us.

[6]For when we were yet without strength, in due time Christ died for the ungodly.

[7]For scarcely for a righteous man will one die: yet peradventure for a good man some would even dare to die.

[8]But God commendeth his love toward us, in that, while we were yet sinners, Christ died for us.

[9]Much more then, being now justified by his blood, we shall be saved from wrath through him.

[10]For if, when we were enemies, we were reconciled to God by the death of his Son, much more, being reconciled, we shall be saved by his life.

[11]And not only so, but we also joy in God through our Lord Jesus Christ, by whom we have now received the atonement.

[12]Wherefore, as by one man sin entered into the world, and death by sin; and so death passed upon all men, for that all have sinned:

[13](For until the law sin was in the world: but sin is not imputed when there is no law.

[14]Nevertheless death reigned from Adam to Moses, even over them that had not sinned after the similitude of Adam's transgression,

who is the figure of him that was to come.

[15]But not as the offence, so also is the free gift. For if through the offence of one many be dead, much more the grace of God, and the gift by grace, which is by one man, Jesus Christ, hath abounded unto many.

[16]And not as it was by one that sinned, so is the gift: for the judgment was by one to condemnation, but the free gift is of many offences unto justification.

[17]For if by one man's offence death reigned by one; much more they which receive abundance of grace and of the gift of righteousness shall reign in life by one, Jesus Christ.)

Matthew 5:44

But I say unto you, Love your enemies, bless them that curse you, do good to them that hate you, and pray for them which despitefully **use** you, and persecute you.

Matthew 25:34-46

[34]Then shall the King say unto them on his right hand, Come, ye blessed of my Father, inherit the kingdom prepared for you from the foundation of the world:

[35]For I was an hungred, and ye gave me meat: I was thirsty, and ye gave me drink: I was a stranger, and ye took me in:

[36]Naked, and ye clothed me: I was sick, and ye visited me: I was in prison, and ye came unto me.

³⁷Then shall the righteous answer him, saying, Lord, when saw we thee an hungred, and fed thee? or thirsty, and gave thee drink?

³⁸When saw we thee a stranger, and took thee in? Or naked, and clothed thee?

³⁹Or when saw we thee sick, or in prison, and came unto thee?

⁴⁰And the King shall answer and say unto them, Verily I say unto you, Inasmuch as ye have done it unto one of the least of these my brethren, ye have done it unto me.

⁴¹Then shall he say also unto them on the left hand, Depart from me, ye cursed, into everlasting fire, prepared for the devil and his angels:

⁴²For I was an hungred, and ye gave me no meat: I was thirsty, and ye gave me no drink:

⁴³I was a stranger, and ye took me not in: naked, and ye clothed me not: sick, and in prison, and ye visited me not.

⁴⁴Then shall they also answer him, saying, Lord, when saw we thee an hungred, or athirst, or a stranger, or naked, or sick, or in prison, and did not minister unto thee?

⁴⁵Then shall he answer them, saying, Verily I say unto you, Inasmuch as ye did it not to one of the least of these, ye did it not to me.

⁴⁶And these shall go away into everlasting punishment: but the righteous into life eternal.

Not only is God love itself, but He is the beginning of love, and He completes the true definition of "love." This is to put forth love by nature without having to be loved back, like a mother or father who loves her or his child no matter what the child has done to the parent or someone else. The parent may be angry at the child, or may even despise the child, but the love is inherit because the person is his or her child. The love exists because it is a love from something the parents helped create; it is part of who they are. God loves us this way because we were made in His image; we are part of Him in that respect. God's formula is played out in that when He first loved us, and we accepted His love, He sent the Holy Spirit to live inside of us. That Holy Spirit shows us how to love as God loves, to love in any and every situation.

Genesis 9:6 says, "Whoso sheddeth man's blood, by man shall **his** blood be shed: for in the **image** of God **made** he man."

So God has given us this formula for our lives. He is telling us what our foundation should be when it comes to Him and the life we live. He is telling us how to start. You may not want to love Him, but He said, "Come anyway, and see what I will do."

Revelation 3:20 tells us, "Behold, I stand at the **door**, and **knock**: if any man hear my voice, and open the **door**, I will come in to him, and will sup with him, and he with me."

When I was unsaved, I had a love for other people, and I was nice to my friends and to most strangers. Similarly, many people in this world are unsaved and are some of the most pleasant people you could ever meet. Some are even nicer than many people who claim to be saved and some who probably are saved. When I was unsaved and gave to the poor or helped someone, I felt good afterward. I felt good about what I had done, and when I saw the other person feeling good about what had taken place, I felt even better. When I comforted someone and made the person feel better, again, I felt better about who I was. *So what's the problem?* we ask. The problem is I was justifying myself to be good. I was the one receiving the credit; I was the one showing myself how good I was for whatever reason. I justified myself as a human by how good I was. When I was good, I expected the praise and credit, and stored that in my mind to help me have peace with myself in life. When I did bad, I rationalized it, made excuses for what had happened, and looked to see where the real blame lied. Was it my childhood, my parents, or where I was born? Was it due to my wealth or my poverty? I became the judge of good and bad, and I, not God, was the decision-maker as to what truth was. If my good outweighed the bad, then I accepted myself as a decent human being, an acceptable person in society. As I stated before, self-religion is the largest religion in the world. This is the religion of self and pride. *We* decide what is right and wrong, good and bad, based on our surroundings, which continually change. This is where the fault lies. We take pieces of all or some of the religions and ways of the world, we each decide what is right or wrong, and we say it is for the sake of peace. Look at our laws. They were meant to protect the weak and punish those who make bad choices, but we have changed these laws to meet our needs, not to accept the truth, which is the laws of God. Our courts are overrun with manipulation of the truth, built on persuasion and corruption, which are only pieces of the truth. We have made what has always been true into a lie, and what has always been a lie into our own home-grown truth. As I said, the Lord is prepared for our actions, and they do not change who He is. God has told us what will happen to humanity. He has given us the end, and He has used our rebellion and our sins to show us why we need Him. You now get to decide: Do you want it your way or His? The end result will not change Him because He is truth, without a blemish.

Let's not forget those bad things you rationalized—did they hurt someone? Was there ever a deed you committed left undone, left unforgiven, left as a scar for someone to wear as a badge?

Truth statement: We have forgotten more wrong deeds than the good ones we have ever done.

Read the following Scriptures.

1 Peter 4:17

For the time is come that judgment must begin at the house of God: and if it first begin at us, what shall the **end** be of them that obey not the gospel of God?

Revelation 21:6

And he said unto me, It is done. I am Alpha and Omega, the beginning and the **end**. I will give unto him that is athirst of the fountain of the water of life freely.

Philippians 3:19

Whose **end** is destruction, whose God is their belly, and whose glory is in their shame, who mind earthly things.

God said He is the only good and true One, and circumstances do not cause His clarity to waver. Because of this, God wants us all to thrive from Him, and His desire includes every soul toward salvation. If you do not want Him, and you reject Him after long-suffering, He will give you what you really want—and that is yourself. He will give you separation from Him, which is a form of hell.

[1]This second epistle, beloved, I now write unto you; in both which I stir up your pure minds by way of remembrance:

[2]That ye may be mindful of the words which were spoken before by the holy prophets, and of the commandment of us the apostles of the Lord and Saviour:

[3]Knowing this first, that there shall come in the last days scoffers, walking after their own lusts,

[4]And saying, Where is the promise of his coming? for since the fathers fell asleep, all things continue as they were from the beginning of the creation.

[5]For this they willingly are ignorant of, that by the word of God the heavens were of old, and the earth standing out of the water and in the water:

[6]Whereby the world that then was, being overflowed with water,

perished:

[7]But the heavens and the earth, which are now, by the same word are kept in store, reserved unto fire against the day of judgment and perdition of ungodly men.

[8]But, beloved, be not ignorant of this one thing, that one day is with the Lord as a thousand years, and a thousand years as one day.

[9]The Lord is not slack concerning his promise, as some men count slackness; but is longsuffering to us-ward, not willing that any should perish, but that all should come to repentance.

[10]But the day of the Lord will come as a thief in the night; in the which the heavens shall pass away with a great noise, and the elements shall melt with fervent heat, the earth also and the works that are therein shall be burned up.

2 Peter 3:1-10

But **whosoever** drinketh of the water that I shall give him shall never thirst; but the water that I shall give him shall be in him a well of water springing up into everlasting life.

John 4:14

[3]For this is good and acceptable in the sight of God our Saviour;
[4]Who will have all men to be saved, and to come unto the knowledge of the truth.
[5]For there is one God, and one mediator between God and men, the man Christ Jesus;

⁶Who gave himself a ransom for all, to be testified in due time.

1 Timothy 2:3-6

You can see God leaves no one behind, not one person. He has prepared for us the road. Is it the road you will travel? Or will you go the broad way?

Read the following Scriptures.

Matthew 7:13-14

¹³Enter ye in at the strait gate: for wide is the gate, and broad is the way, that leadeth to destruction, and many there be which go in thereat.

¹⁴Because strait is the gate, and narrow is the way, which leadeth unto life, and few there be that find it.

2 Thessalonians 2:8-12

⁸And then shall that Wicked be revealed, whom the Lord shall consume with the spirit of his mouth, and shall destroy with the brightness of his coming:

⁹Even him, whose coming is after the working of Satan with all power and signs and lying wonders,

¹⁰and with all deceivableness of unrighteousness in them that perish; because they received not the love of the truth, that they might be saved.

¹¹And for this cause God shall send them strong delusion, that they

should believe a lie:

[12]That they all might be damned who believed not the truth, but had pleasure in unrighteousness.

God has made you in His image, and He finds pleasure in making you. What you do with what He has given you (life) is up to you. He will use you for His glory if you decide to rebel, and He will use you if you decide to follow. We don't change who God is by what we do; He uses what we do to glorify Him. He does this through servant-hood or rebellion, but either way, He is the Master. He is the Potter, and we are the clay.

Romans 9:10-23

[10]And not only this; but when Rebecca also had conceived by one, even by our father Isaac;

[11](For the children being not yet born, neither having done any good or evil, that the purpose of God according to election might stand, not of works, but of him that calleth;)

[12]It was said unto her, The elder shall serve the younger.

[13]As it is written, Jacob have I loved, but Esau have I hated.

[14]What shall we say then? Is there unrighteousness with God? God forbid.

[15]For he saith to Moses, I will have mercy on whom I will have mercy, and I will have compassion on whom I will have compassion.

[16]So then it is not of him that willeth, nor of him that runneth, but of

God that sheweth mercy.

[17]For the scripture saith unto Pharaoh, Even for this same purpose have I raised thee up, that I might shew my power in thee, and that my name might be declared throughout all the earth.

[18]Therefore hath he mercy on whom he will have mercy, and whom he will he hardeneth.

[19]Thou wilt say then unto me, Why doth he yet find fault? For who hath resisted his will?

[20]Nay but, O man, who art thou that repliest against God? Shall the thing formed say to him that formed it, Why hast thou made me thus?

[21]Hath not the potter power over the clay, of the same lump to make one vessel unto honour, and another unto dishonour?

[22]What if God, willing to shew his wrath, and to make his power known, endured with much **longsuffering** the vessels of wrath fitted to destruction:

[23]And that he might make known the riches of his glory on the vessels of mercy, which he had afore prepared unto glory,

Some people will say because of this, God is a puppet master. However, this is not true. God hates no one person, only the sin into which we are all born. The word "hate" in the previous Scripture means He chooses one over the other. God created us with the ability to choose as well whether or not to follow Him.

God is able to see all things, from the beginning to the end.

Before we are born, before anything is ever done good or bad, He sees and has prepared. Our free will and the decisions we make will only prove to fit in God's plans., not because He made us do them, but because no matter what we do with our free will, He can bring glory from it. When it is all over, His end will not be changed in any way.

My Little Boy

I told my little boy who was running in church that if he did not quit running, he would be predestined for a whipping. While his running in church seemed harmless to him, I could see all the things that could happen if he didn't stop. He could hurt himself and others in many ways by continuing what he was doing, not to mention he should show general respect for the Father's house. I was being sarcastic because someone I know believes we are chosen to go to hell or heaven before we are ever born, and he was there at that time. I explained that if my boy continued to run, I had the ability to give him his punishment in the very near future. He was not guaranteed to receive a punishment; it was only a possibility, if he did not obey the rule. I said if he decides to not run any longer, he will not be punished, and in such, he decided his fate and destiny based on his choices. Regardless of his choice, I said, if he did continue to rebel, there would be consequences, and if he didn't, there would be another set of consequences. But no matter what he chose, I would still love him because he is my child. I would not change due to his actions; I would only follow through with what I said I would do.

This is much like what God has told us to do, and that is to follow His ways, which can only happen by accepting Christ as our Savior and repenting of our sins. If we decide not to, the circumstances will not be in our favor, not because He wants to punish us, but because He wants to protect us as well as those around us. You may think your sins only hurt you, but they hurt so many all around you. Some you may know; some you may not. But God sees the damage in its entirety.

CHAPTER 15

THE HOLLY WOOD LIFE

꧁

When Jesus heard it, he saith unto them, They that are whole have **no need** of the **physician**, but they that are sick: I came not to call the righteous, but sinners to repentance.

Mark 2:17

This chapter is not just for those in Hollywood who are in movies or on TV shows. This chapter is about all those in the public eye, all the lives displayed by what the media want to print or the camera wants to show. This Hollywood life is a perfect example of how the truth can seem to be altered by just a click of a camera or a discussion only half written. In such cases, what we see and hear is not the truth, only what the photographer and writer want us to see.

In many ways, I feel for those in the public eye. They are the dreamers who put the work and action required to make your dreams come true, yet for many of you, you can't even enjoy a walk in the park.

Many times I have heard actors and others say they hate the

paparazzi and all the attention, but it is the price they pay for the fame they possess. I feel even worse for those with this attitude because in many ways, what they're really saying is that this is the cross you must bear because you have popularity. The fame, the money, being looked at as an idol by others—these are the so-called beautiful elements of this world. So because you are able to travel everywhere, you get the limelight, the attention, the beautiful clothes, the big house, and the big parties, with all the important people attending, and think that it is worth losing your privacy for. Let's also remember, this is not only for your privacy, but for your family's privacy as well. Many in this situation struggle with emotions of guilt because they have so much wealth and worldly luxuries, and they assume they don't have the right to feel imprisoned in this high-end lifestyle. Many of these people feel they have everything the world can offer, so who are they to need help? Whether or not it makes you feel better, if you are one of these individuals, you have more right than anyone else to feel this way. You should feel imprisoned; you have strived for this world and received it, only to find it is not what you had hoped it would be. If it is what you hoped it would be, what is it leading you to? Is it leading you to inward satisfaction for your accomplishments? How about peace and joy— where are they? The world only embraces you for as long as you are used by it. When it is done, it will move to another individual. When you fail us and yourself, and you're all used up, and the world has no use for you any longer, it leaves you to yourself. The saying in

Hollywood is "This is the industry that eats its own." How true this seems.

In regards to the regular person, it is so easy for us to judge you based on what we see and hear. We never actually put ourselves in your place or learned what you are truly about. We only see the riches and fame, and when you're not the newest or the best, we just toss you out when we're done. Some of the select few in this industry can keep their husbands or wives and their families out of this public eye, but even then, it is a hard task living this lifestyle. No doubt, this is the reason we see so much divorce, drug addiction, and out-of-control lives played out for the world to see. The truth says that all the fame, fortune, praises, and honor never fully satisfy the inward man or woman. These things only cause us to long for more of the same, something new to inject into the never-ending cavern of our despair.

Ezekiel 7:19 tells us:

They shall cast their silver in the streets, and their gold shall be removed: their silver and their gold shall not be able to deliver them in the day of the wrath of the LORD: they shall not **satisfy** their souls, neither fill their bowels: because it is the stumblingblock of their iniquity.

So you, as a performer, may only be playing a part; you, as a singer, may only be singing a song; you, as a politician, may only be doing a job, but this does not give you or anyone else the right to influence millions by living a lie and telling us it is the truth. What you do is not like everyone else; you directly impact millions, and I hope you realize this every day you do what you do. Be truthful in what you do. At least then, we won't be deceived. I have respect for many politicians, actors, and singers, and I thank God they do what they do. But these are the few who are in Hollywood but not living the Hollywood life.

Read **Luke 12:48**:

But he that knew not, and did commit things worthy of stripes, shall be beaten with few stripes. For unto whomsoever **much is given**, of him shall be **much** required: and to whom men have committed **much**, of him they will ask the more.

In the world, there are essentially three types of people: those who have ever lived, those living today, and those who will ever live in regards to Christ. They are the hot, the cold, and the lukewarm.

This is what the Bible says about this:

Revelation 3:15
I know thy works, that thou art **neither cold nor hot**: I would thou wert **cold** or **hot**.

<u>Revelation 3:16</u>

So then because thou art lukewarm, and **neither cold nor hot**, I will spue thee out of my mouth.

The Cold in Christ

First, let's talk about the cold in Christ. I must say, I have some respect for my brothers and sisters in this Hollywood life, but certainly not exclusively to this life only. I respect these people because they don't profess to believe or adhere to the message of Christ; they are considered cold to Him. These people are honest to their nature. They don't ask for it both ways, and they are men and women enough to have their own ideas about what life is and what it means to them. It doesn't matter that it is the opposite of what the Bible and God say is true; they are at least honest in following their true nature and don't walk the fence. These people embrace their worldly life and will find other means than Christ to make it through. On the Day of Judgment, these will not proclaim they were saved or ever served the Lord. Instead, these will spend their time trying to judge Jesus and God. They will put the Creator on trial by proclaiming, "How could these things be true?" They will say that He made it too difficult, and that He should have done this or that. They will blame others, saying others are responsible for their folly. The one thing that will be clear on that day is these people had no heart for God, and they never accepted Christ. And even if God let them in heaven, they would be out of place. Heaven will not be their home.

Their home is made of earthly things, made by themselves and their works, and no sacrifice was needed. Thus, that is where their heart will be.

Matthew 6:21 says, "For **where your treasure is**, there **will your heart** be also."

God would rather you be this way than the way that follows, which is to claim His name and power, but live and represent the opposite. God appreciates the truth, even when it comes from those who don't believe in Him. At least when someone admits to not having Jesus as his or her Savior, the person may come to realize he or she does need Him one day. The lukewarm that follow have little hope because they play both sides. They are drowning but won't call for help. The reason is because they don't think they need it; they can save themselves.

The Lukewarm in Christ

Once in a while, we hear you say you believe in Christ, but you put out songs and movies that speak the opposite. You play sports and represent us politically, but your real life seems to contradict your belief. I hear many singers write songs about loving the Lord, and the next one they put out is how good it feels to sleep with someone and get drunk. You are destroying your own lives and influencing millions to do the same. You have our children believing you can have it both ways in life, the sin and the righteousness. We need you to stand up for your Christ and portray His things, if that is what you believe. Do what you do because God made you beautifully, but don't sell out to the world and proclaim Christ; they contradict each other, and we see it in your lives. These lukewarm people are the ones who one day will call on the Lord at judgment and say, "Yes, I believed in You, and I proclaimed Your name." Then He will say the following to them.

Matthew 7:13-24

¹³Enter ye in at the strait gate: for wide is the gate, and broad is the way, that leadeth to destruction, and many there be which go in thereat:

¹⁴Because strait is the gate, and narrow is the way, which leadeth unto life, and few there be that find it.

¹⁵Beware of false prophets, which come to you in sheep's clothing, but inwardly they are ravening wolves.

¹⁶Ye shall know them by their fruits. Do men gather grapes of thorns, or figs of thistles?

¹⁷Even so every good tree bringeth forth good fruit; but a corrupt tree bringeth forth evil fruit.

¹⁸A good tree cannot bring forth evil fruit, neither can a corrupt tree bring forth good fruit.

¹⁹Every tree that bringeth not forth good fruit is hewn down, and cast into the fire.

²⁰Wherefore by their fruits ye shall know them.

²¹Not every one that saith unto me, Lord, Lord, shall enter into the

kingdom of heaven; but he that doeth the will of my Father which is in heaven.

[22]Many will say to me in that day, Lord, Lord, have we not prophesied in thy name? And in thy name have cast out devils? And in thy name done many wonderful works?

[23]And then will I profess unto them, I never knew you: depart from me, ye that work iniquity.

[24]Therefore whosoever heareth these sayings of mine, and doeth them, I will liken him unto a wise man, which built his house upon a rock.

There are two points to this. The first point is that our hearts and actions, not what we say, show who we are. The second point is that it is more important that Christ knows us than that we know Him.

Everyone in Hollywood should know what He is saying here. How many of you know who you are and can tell people many things about yourself? I can look up everything about you, from going on vacation, to your family members, to what your favorite color is. I can find out just about anything I want to know about you and could make the claim that I know who you are. I could say I have done great things for you and told many to listen to your songs or watch your movies or vote for you.

However, our relationship is not established because I know you. Instead, it is only established if someone were to ask you if you know me. Then, and only then, would the relationship be real. What the truth is saying is when it comes to Christ, the question is not, "Do you know Me?" but, "Do I know you?" For Jesus to know us, we would have to have given our lives to Him, and He now knows us as His children.

The Bible states:

Matthew 18:3

And said, Verily I say unto you, Except ye be converted, and become as little children, ye shall not enter into the kingdom of heaven.

Luke 20:36

Neither can they die any more: for they are equal unto the angels; and are the children of God, being the children of the resurrection.

We will get to the "hot for Christ" shortly, but I am going to mention a few people here, only because I admire them in many ways and hope to see Christ revealed in their lives one day. I have bought their albums, watched their movies, and paid for tickets to see them play their game. I will not judge them, but I will speak the truth in love because one day the truth will be proclaimed on the house top for all to hear, yours and mine. Also, I am hoping you will someday represent Christ, and I can't wait to see the wonderful things He will do with the gifts you have been given—not for your glory or even your neighbor's, but for His glory alone, as He is the Father, the Provider, and the Creator of all good things.

Romans 8:28 tells us, "And we know that all **things** work together for **good** to them that love God, to them who are the called according to his purpose."

1) Oprah:

I have seen your show many times. I have heard of your past and how you have worked your way to where you are. I see so many of the wonderful works you have done and still do. I see the tabloids' relentlessness to portray your personal life, yet you continue to serve your fellow women and men. I see the respect your peers give you, and no doubt, you are loved, but my question is, Who will get the credit for all your deeds when you are no longer here? Will people say you were a great woman, or will they say because of your relationship with Christ, you were a great woman? I remember an old show in which people were discussing religions, and you said there were other ways to God, not just through Jesus. You made the statement that many people have made, and still make today, and that is that all roads can or may lead to God. I am not sure if this is still what you feel, but as discussed in a previous chapter, we should realize that because religions contradict one another, they can't all be right. So we must decide that either we are all wrong or there is one right. I believe you are a compassionate woman who cares for others and loves to see people overcome and triumph. You have helped so many do just that. So where is the glory going? Is it to you, or to the person involved, maybe to the specialist you brought in to help? One thing is for sure: It certainly doesn't seem to be the one true God.

So the question I have for you is this: Oprah, with all the money you have and all the specialists you have interviewed, with all the famous people whom you have grown to know, which one of them has given you peace that lasts a lifetime? How much money was it that brought complete fulfillment and joy to your life? What specialist gave you the keys to being happy with yourself, knowing you were loved no matter what you looked like? Tell us these things, please, as you must know, because if you don't know after all you have and all you have been with, then the typical person has no chance at all.

During another interview, you said you were in church one time, and the pastor said God is a jealous God, and that did not sit well with you. You did not believe God was jealous and that He would have that emotion, as we do. However, the truth says God is a jealous God.

Deuteronomy 6:15

(For the LORD thy **God** is a **jealous God am**ong you) lest the anger of the LORD thy **God** be kindled against thee, and destroy thee from off the face of the earth.

1 Kings 19:10

And he said, **I** have been very **jealous** for the LORD **God** of hosts: for the children of Israel have forsaken thy covenant, thrown down thine altars, and slain thy prophets with the sword; and **I**, even **I** only, **am** left; and they seek my life, to take it away.

Why is it so hard to believe a father is jealous of who He is to His children? I would not want my children to say another man is their father, and my wife has certainly earned her position as a mother, so should we not expect that as a norm? I do for my children; I sacrifice for them. I am the father, and I am jealous if the credit goes to someone else who has done nothing to deserve it. Thank you, Oprah, for what you do in helping others, but know that if Jesus Christ is not glorified by what you do, you are the one who gets the glory, and that glory dies when you die. Your gifts, as nice as they are, help for a time but soon fade away. If your gifts represent the gift of salvation through Christ, then what you do will honor Him, and He is the only One deserving of honor.

2) **Tom C. and Brad P.:**

I have got to tell ya, guys, you make it hard on us typical fellas out here. Just kidding. I do, however, want you to know I spent many years of my life watching your movies and enjoying your abilities as actors. This is not just about you as much as it is about many of your peers with whom you work as well. You are good-looking, smart, talented men, many not coming from easy backgrounds, who are working your way to the top. You achieved your dreams and probably more than you ever expected. I see you and others now living lives of riches and fame, with beautiful wives, some second or third ones. I admire your abilities on screen, and I wish you more success because in many ways, you have earned it. You work hard and enjoy what you do, so much so that you have lost much of your personal lives by choosing this profession. I see the good things you do with your money in this country and in others, including adopting children in need and giving them the blessings you have been given. You build houses for many, trying to share what you have earned. Your works seem to be good, and no doubt, God will use your success for His glory helping others.

However, for many of you, the success and the wives and the lifestyle will never be enough. No matter how many children you help or have, the peace never lasts, does it? No matter how many movies are made or Oscars are won, the peace only stays long enough to try for another. Your job is great, and your life is good, but you're getting older. What then? Will you always be there for those children you have helped? When you are gone, will the money last forever? Will the fame stay around? You are the elite in what you do, so why not give Jesus Christ the glory for the gifts you have? Why not represent yourself on and off screen as a person concerned not only with what your wealth can offer one child, but what your testimony can do for millions? I am a fan not of who you are, but of your talents. I just hope one day you will proclaim Christ is the reason you do what you do. You both have your own religious beliefs—is either one Christ? If not, will your belief help me in my life? Will your beliefs change who I am as a person to help me to love others? Will your religion forgive me of my wrongdoings? Will your beliefs be the same for the starving as they are for the satisfied? Or is your religion just for you? The thing about death is no ability or talent, no money or fame will stop it from happening, nor will these things go with you. The truth says the only thing you take with you is yourself and the Holy Spirit, if you have it. If you don't have the Spirit, all you have is yourself, and we all know that will never be enough.

3) Miley C.

Now we are getting serious. What an extraordinary young lady she is. She is beautiful, talented, and able to influence all ages, especially children all across the world, with her acting, singing, and general personality. My boys watched her show and enjoyed it. I, myself, watch her works and have been very impressed. *So what's the problem?* we ask. The problem is the change that has occurred. Know I am not looking for perfection from anyone but Christ. I teach my children that all are flawed, and life is about putting your best foot forward. The problem is Miley tells us she believes in God and Christ, that she is saved and will go to heaven when she dies. If this is true, just like any true salvation, the fruit of that salvation comes forth. I have seen the transition that has taken place in her life, at least from the television and news side of it. I've seen the great success she has had as a young child on a clean television show, helping us teach our children good things instead of hurting them. Then the real fame comes when the music takes off. She is a little older and making more of her own decisions, rather than allowing her parents to make them for her. She spreads her wings a little, and the music and the appearance are not so clean any longer. Most of the old fans are still happy, and she is adding new ones who like this sexier, more adult look. Her music is inspiring, to say the least, but showing off her body more and really feeling her way in this new adult freedom is what it seems to be about. And then it happened. I turned on the TV, and there it was—no longer the clean Miley, but the young adult Miley in a video dressed in a seductive way, crawling on her knees with guys all over her.

So my question is, Why the change? I definitely think in this profession, you have to continue to be attractive in some way to continue to be a star. But why give up the truth you say you hold on to, to become something that is the opposite of what you proclaim to be? And what is the reward? What was the reason? Was it your parents or a manager telling you what you must be or do to continue your success? Was it just the idea of following your idols and the idea that this is what you must do to mature in your art? I want you to know, as if you care, I believe you are a Christian, and I do believe you want to represent yourself and your family well. I just want to say, Don't give in to the lies that surround you. Remember, it was the honest and truthful Miley that made you successful, so let that be what leads you to the next segment in your life. Success is only as good as how you got it and what you will do with it next.

4) Kenny C.

I have got to say you are one of the iconic and well-known singers that have made their mark on country music history. You love what you do, and I see the importance you hold in your profession. I look at the artists who are still doing so great today, continuing to excel in their talents after many years— Reba, Dolly, George S., Tim, Faith, ... You are different, and that is what has made you special. But it is hard for me to enjoy you as an artist, or any of the other artists who say how important God is in one song and then go into another that says it is okay to get drunk and sleep around. My children as well as I need to see a Christian who can stand on his or her beliefs and not straddle both sides. The enjoyment my children will find in life will not come from a bottle or a girl who will party with them; it will come from God, a woman, and a family that can have fun without having to give up its morals. As parents, we need you to help us and instill good qualities in our children. Your charities and good works will never do enough good to make up for one hit song that tells my child it is okay to get drunk and sleep around. Again, I hope it is clear, I admire your talents, and I believe God gave you those talents, so if this is true, let the world know for whom and for what you sing.

5) Tiger W.

The name itself proclaims success, professionalism, advertising giant Nike, and, of course, golf at its finest. At one time, Tiger Woods exemplified professional athletics, working hard his entire life, aspiring to his goals, making his friends and family members, especially his father, proud of him. He was married to a beautiful woman, and had millions of dollars, children, fame, and all the glory and prestige of being the best. He had everything the American dream is made of and was on his way to breaking just about every record golf has. But then it happened. We have all seen the downfall of the man called Tiger; he had it all, but it wasn't enough. If this does not show you that this world will never satisfy you, what will? The women he cheated on his wife with were all less attractive than his wife, so what gives? Why the need for other women to sleep with, putting all he has on the line for a moment of lust?

He felt a void that only Christ could ever fill. After making this mistake, as we all would be susceptible to making in his position, with all that money and women throwing themselves at him constantly, I don't judge him for his sins, as we are all sinners and share in the mess we are in. However, I do hope and pray he will one day find what can give him forgiveness of this sin and all others. It is Christ and Christ alone. After apologizing to the world and his family, he said he needed to get back to his roots, which are in Islam. The problem is Muhammad cannot come back and help him because he is dead. His bones show us he was only a man. To the contrary, Christ is alive, not buried. Christ can give him all he ever had back and so much more, if he would only follow Him. Tiger can do all things through Christ, who will strengthen him and turn the mistakes he made into memories of where the Savior brought him from, just as Christ does for the mistakes we make every day.

6) Eminem:

What an artist. This guy not only broke the sound barrier for white rap artists to truly be considered acceptable in an almost exclusive market to black artists, but he also is one of the best. He is respected and, of course, now an icon/idol to hundreds of millions of people. So why did he become so famous? we could ask. It was hard work and talent, of course, loving what he does, and also the ability to relate to the common guy. But the biggest reason his music is so powerful is what this book is about: the truth. It is as simple as this: He tells the truth when he sings, the truth about who he is, his life, his family, all the things people don't talk about themselves. He tells the story of life in his songs, and people want to hear it. I love his style of music. It is almost too good for me to turn from on the radio, but I do, for two reasons. The first reason is he cusses in just about every song he sings. He is one of those artists who feels that has got to be part of his message to make an impact. The second, and the more absolute, reason I don't buy his music is because although he is speaking his truth, which correlates into our truths, his truths are based on the world and not on the truths of God and Christ. His truths tell me and my children the truths of this world, and give no hope for God or Christ to change a man. He sings about the lusts of the world, the power of money, and love of who he is, but that is from a lost soul, not a son of God's. I cannot imagine a more powerful testimony than one day Marshall Bruce Mathers III giving his very life, soul, and talents to his eternal Savior, Jesus Christ. I cannot imagine an artist who could use his talents in his style of music to spread the gospel more across this world than when he realizes he has a Father in heaven who loves him so much and wants to be with him so bad that He gave His only Son's life for him. The hate will go away, and the songs would change, but the talent and the power of who he is would be that much greater in serving Christ.

7) Government:

What a sad place we are in with our politicians at this time in our history. We are going from great, godly men (not perfect, but godly, men) to the men and women who serve our country today. That being said, there are good, godly Christians serving us in Washington, but the problem is they are not able to play under the godly rules there were once. Over the decades, we have taken what our forefathers laid down for us under the Constitution and Bill of Rights, and changed it. We have manipulated it until it is almost the opposite of what it once was. It is like playing cards with my kids—they always win because they make the rules up as they go. Our politicians have set the rules up now as not to serve the public, but to be served by the public; not to provide for, but to be provided for; not to care for, but to be cared for. The rule-makers have gotten the rules all in their favor. That is why they have different health care, salaries that never end, and pensions and raises when everyone else is struggling to keep a job. I want it to get better, but it will never get better until godly men and women start serving the people in godly ways. That will only start when the president, the House, and the Senate lead in that direction. We need leaders and servants to the people in Washington; we need servants first, and leadership second.

The Hot for Christ

Simply, these are people who have given their lives to Christ and received eternal life. Some are rich, and some are poor. Some are famous, and more are not. These men, women, and children bear the mark that Jesus Christ saved their soul, and they received the Holy Spirit. These people aren't perfect, but they seek perfection in Him who is. They believe in trying to forgive their enemies, and trying to love their not-so-lovable selves and their not-so-loveable neighbors. They want to give others what God gave them and see others come to Him, as they did. Most of all, they try to love their Father with all their heart, soul, mind, and strength. They live and thrive on His Word and make mistakes every day, knowing their Father loves them just as much as He did before they made them. The ones of these who have realized the freedom that Christ gave them through His sacrifice flourish with joy and peace. They do not have to have fame and glory to be satisfied, and most of all, they find happiness in others' happiness through the way Christ changes lives. Their purpose is to be used by Him, their Father.**Kirk Cameron, thanks** for staying on the hot side of Christ. He said we will suffer for standing for the truth so know your suffering is not in vain.

Turning the Father Away

I once asked my five-year-old at the time if I could come eat lunch with him at school. He immediately said yes, just as my other boys had said the years before, so I was excited because this had become a tradition for my sons and me. The day before this was to happen, my son told me never mind about having lunch together the next day, and said that he had changed his mind. Needless to say, this had me curious, so I continued to ask him why. But he just blew me off, to say the least. Later, I asked him again, and he would not answer. I decided that because I was going there anyway with the other boys for their lunch, I would just surprise him during his time in the cafeteria. I went to Subway and got everything he liked— a sandwich, chips, a cookie, and chocolate milk. I went off to his school, knowing he would love what I had done. When I walked into the cafeteria, all the kids turned to look, but I couldn't see my son anywhere. I finally saw the teacher and had to ask her where he was. She said, "Right there." My son knew I was there, but kept his back to me so I would not notice him. I said to him, "Hey, buddy, I am here to eat lunch with you," but got no response. The little girl beside him moved over, and I tapped him on the shoulder to get his attention. Then he did what I never would have expected. He turned around in a fit of rage, put his hand out toward me, and said a resounding, "NO." Then he put his head down and started to cry. I had to decide what to do in this moment in time, with only seconds passing. I said: "Son, I am going to leave this here with you and go. I will see you later, okay?" I left that school swirling with emotions of anger (little ingrate), hostility (I should whip his tail), embarrassment (those people think I beat him), and, most of all, sadness and hurt from being rejected by my son, whom I truly loved. Then I went to another restaurant to pick up my other boys' lunch to take back to them.

As I pulled into the parking lot and stopped the car, I was still engulfed in emotions from one end to the other. The Holy Spirit might as well have hit me in the head with a baseball bat. As clear as if Jesus was sitting beside me, saying it Himself, I felt the words, "That is how I feel every time you tell Me no." I didn't expect that; it came from left field. But the point was made clear as a bell. There have been places where I wanted to have the Lord with me, and then there were other times when I did not ask Him to come. To be honest, I didn't really need Him there. Examples include when I was going out with friends or maybe at work or at a party—places where He just wasn't wanted or, I thought, needed. While certain parts of my life were open to Him, others I wanted to keep to myself. Not only did I realize that day that I need to let Christ be in every aspect of my life, but also I learned what it feels like to be rejected by my own son, whom I care for dearly. God showed me the emotion of rejection by a loved one that day, and I will never forget it. He feels that way about each of you, giving you life, giving you a body, and providing for you, only to have a hand and heart put in His face to say, "NO!"

CHAPTER 16

Highway to Hell:
Born to Go, or Going by Choice?

———∞∞———

S ome people believe we are in hell now living on this earth. I almost want to agree at certain moments, but the truth says different.

The truth says hell is a place created for Satan and the other fallen angels. It also says it is the place for all of those who reject God's gift of salvation. Some may say the lake of fire is different from hell, and hell is just the holding place until the end, where all the unsaved will be cast. Regardless of either hell or the lake of fire, the end result is torment and separation from the mercy, grace, and love of our Father, who created us.

Matthew 25:41 states, "Then shall he say also unto them on the left hand, Depart from me, ye cursed, into everlasting fire, prepared for the devil and his angels."

The truth plainly states that, yes, hell exists, and although we have all kinds of ideas of what hell is like, the truth has something to say about this place. The story below is one Jesus spoke about describing this place called hell.

Luke 16:19-31

[19]There was a certain rich man, which was clothed in purple and fine linen, and fared sumptuously every day:

[20]And there was a certain beggar named Lazarus, which was laid at his gate, full of sores,

[21]and desiring to be fed with the crumbs which fell from the rich man's table: moreover the dogs came and licked his sores.

[22]And it came to pass, that the beggar died, and was carried by the angels into Abraham's bosom: the rich man also died, and was buried;

[23]and in hell he lift up his eyes, being in torments, and seeth Abraham afar off, and Lazarus in his bosom.

[24]And he cried and said, Father Abraham, have mercy on me, and send Lazarus, that he may dip the tip of his finger in water, and cool my tongue; for I am tormented in this flame.

[25]But Abraham said, Son, remember that thou in thy lifetime receivedst thy good things, and likewise Lazarus evil things: but now he is comforted, and thou art tormented.

[26]And beside all this, between us and you there is a great gulf fixed: so that they which would pass from hence to you cannot; neither can they pass to us, that would come from thence.

[27]Then he said, I pray thee therefore, father, that thou wouldest send him to my father's house:

²⁸For I have five brethren; that he may testify unto them, lest they also come into this place of torment.

²⁹Abraham saith unto him, They have Moses and the prophets; let them hear them.

³⁰And he said, Nay, father Abraham: but if one went unto them from the dead, they will repent.

³¹And he said unto him, If they hear not Moses and the prophets, neither will they be persuaded, though one rose from the dead.

Jesus told this story and showed us that the reward for living for ourselves is exactly that—ourselves. The rich man in this story needed no Savior and lived his life for himself. He cared for his family, but that was after he realized hell was real, and he had no hope.

Hell is not for good or bad people; hell is for one select group of individuals, all united with one similarity: rebellion against the One who gave them life in the first place. Rebellion transformed to sin, which in turn leads to their final resting place: death. Notice the rich man was buried in his solitude, but Lazarus wasn't. He was carried to heaven with the angels in comfort. We are all born into sin, so without Christ and salvation, our destinies are all the same. Read the following Scripture, and see if this is where you fall.

2 Peter 2:4-22

⁴For if God spared not the angels that sinned, but cast them down to

hell, and delivered them into chains of darkness, to be reserved unto judgment;

⁵and spared not the old world, but saved Noah the eighth person, a preacher of righteousness, bringing in the flood upon the world of the ungodly;

⁶and turning the cities of Sodom and Gomorrha into ashes condemned them with an overthrow, making them an ensample unto those that after should live ungodly;

⁷and delivered just Lot, vexed with the filthy conversation of the wicked:

⁸(For that righteous man dwelling among them, in seeing and hearing, vexed his righteous soul from day to day with their unlawful deeds;)

⁹The Lord knoweth how to deliver the godly out of temptations, and to reserve the unjust unto the day of judgment to be punished:

¹⁰But chiefly them that walk after the flesh in the lust of uncleanness, and despise government. Presumptuous are they, selfwilled, they are not afraid to speak evil of dignities.

¹¹Whereas angels, which are greater in power and might, bring not railing accusation against them before the Lord.

¹²But these, as natural brute beasts, made to be taken and destroyed, speak evil of the things that they understand not; and shall utterly perish in their own corruption;

¹³and shall receive the reward of unrighteousness, as they that count it pleasure to riot in the day time. Spots they are and blemishes, sporting themselves with their own deceivings while they feast with you;

[14]Having eyes full of adultery, and that cannot cease from sin; beguiling unstable souls: an heart they have exercised with covetous practices; cursed children:

[15]Which have forsaken the right way, and are gone astray, following the way of Balaam the son of Bosor, who loved the wages of unrighteousness;

[16]But was rebuked for his iniquity: the dumb ass speaking with man's voice forbad the madness of the prophet.

[17]These are wells without water, clouds that are carried with a tempest; to whom the mist of darkness is reserved for ever.

[18]For when they speak great swelling words of vanity, they allure through the lusts of the flesh, through much wantonness, those that were clean escaped from them who live in error.

[19]While they promise them liberty, they themselves are the servants of corruption: for of whom a man is overcome, of the same is he brought in bondage.

[20]For if after they have escaped the pollutions of the world through the knowledge of the Lord and Saviour Jesus Christ, they are again entangled therein, and overcome, the latter end is worse with them than the beginning.

[21]For it had been better for them not to have known the way of righteousness, than, after they have known it, to turn from the holy commandment delivered unto them.

[22]But it is happened unto them according to the true proverb, The dog is turned to his own vomit again; and the sow that was washed

to her wallowing in the mire.

This is the way we are born; this is our original nature. It may vary in degrees, but the nature itself is corrupt. The only way to obtain the new nature, the nature that is so obvious to someone who has truly been saved, to be born again, is to be forgiven and admonished for these sins. And when you receive this forgiveness, the new nature is the change you and everyone else notice. As an example, let's think of our own laws for a moment. Do we not require a payment for breaking our laws? If I lie to my brother, he may get mad for a while, but the punishment is not so severe. If I do something bad to my wife, it gets a little hairier, right? If I wrong my boss, I could be fired. If I wrong the government, I could go to jail and lose everything I have. In this world, the larger the body that we wrong, the more severe the punishment will be. So why is it so hard to believe that the God who created you and gave you life, the air in your lungs, will provide justice to the wrongs done to Him? God, however, has given much more leniency in regards to His laws that are broken, so much so that He gave us a gift of total admonishment from our sins and offered Another to pay our debt. His name is and was and will always be the one and only Jesus. We get forgiveness, but only because He suffered and paid the penalty for our sins.

Read **1 Corinthians 15:3**:

For I delivered unto you first of all that which I also received, how that Christ **died** for our **sins** according to the scriptures.

So God tells us all throughout the Bible that He does not want us to go to this place called hell. In fact, the whole purpose of the Bible is to speak truth to all people so they know how to live, and more importantly, it prepares us for our real life, which is eternity. However, the most important aspect of the Bible is that it gives us the road map to get to heaven and tells how not to go to hell. The Bible's soul purpose is to give mankind the passage from this life to the next. God provided us with this truth that never changes so that all humanity from the past, present, and future will be able to find salvation. God's reason in creating us is for His pleasure, and God finds no pleasure in His children's going to hell.

Ephesians 1:9 says:

Having **made** known unto us the mystery of his will, according to his good **pleasure** which he hath purposed in himself . . . .

This leads to the final question, which is not, Does hell exist? The Bible plainly says it does. The real question is, Knowing all things, including those people going to hell, before they are ever born, why would God allow them to go there? Because He has the power to create us or destroy us. This is the question asked of me, and I, in turn, asked God, Why not just stop that person from ever being born?

First, let's address, What does God think of me?

Psalm 139:1-18

[1]O lord, thou hast searched me, and known me.

[2]Thou knowest my downsitting and mine uprising, thou under-standest my thought afar off.

[3]Thou compassest my path and my lying down, and art acquainted with all my ways.

[4]For there is not a word in my tongue, but, lo, O LORD, thou knowest it altogether.

[5]Thou hast beset me behind and before, and laid thine hand upon me.

[6]Such knowledge is too wonderful for me; it is high, I cannot attain unto it.

[7]Whither shall I go from thy spirit? Or whither shall I flee from thy presence?

[8]If I ascend up into heaven, thou art there: if I make my bed in hell, behold, thou art there.

[9]If I take the wings of the morning, and dwell in the uttermost parts of the sea;

[10]Even there shall thy hand lead me, and thy right hand shall hold me.

[11]If I say, Surely the darkness shall cover me; even the night shall be light about me.

[12]Yea, the darkness hideth not from thee; but the night shineth as the

day: the darkness and the light are both alike to thee.

[13]For thou hast possessed my reins: thou hast covered me in my mother's womb.

[14]I will praise thee; for I am fearfully and wonderfully made: arvelous are thy works; and that my soul knoweth right well.

[15]My substance was not hid from thee, when I was made in secret, and curiously wrought in the lowest parts of the earth.

[16]Thine eyes did see my substance, yet being unperfect; and in thy book all my members were written, which in continuance were fashioned, when as yet there was none of them.

[17]How precious also are thy thoughts unto me, O God! How great is the sum of them!

[18]If I should count them, they are more in number than the sand: when I awake, I am still with thee.

This passage tells how He loves you and cares for you, and how He knows every part of you.

Did he make me for hell? Does He want me to turn from my ways?

Ezekiel 18:20-32

[20]The soul that sinneth, it shall die. The son shall not bear the iniquity of the father, neither shall the father bear the iniquity of the son: the righteousness of the righteous shall be upon him, and the wickedness of the wicked shall be upon him.

²¹But if the wicked will turn from all his sins that he hath committed, and keep all my statutes, and do that which is lawful and right, he shall surely live, he shall not die.

²²All his transgressions that he hath committed, they shall not be mentioned unto him: in his righteousness that he hath done he shall live.

²³Have I any pleasure at all that the wicked should die? saith the Lord GOD: and not that he should return from his ways, and live?

²⁴But when the righteous turneth away from his righteousness, and committeth iniquity, and doeth according to all the abominations that the wicked man doeth, shall he live? All his righteousness that he hath done shall not be mentioned: in his trespass that he hath trespassed, and in his sin that he hath sinned, in them shall he die.

²⁵**Yet ye say, The way of the LORD is not equal. Hear now, O house of Israel; Is not my way equal? Are not your ways unequal?**

²⁶When a righteous man turneth away from his righteousness, and committeth iniquity, and dieth in them; for his iniquity that he hath done shall he die.

²⁷Again, when the wicked man turneth away from his wickedness that he hath committed, and doeth that which is lawful and right, he shall save his soul alive.

²⁸Because he considereth, and turneth away from all his transgressions that he hath committed, he shall surely live, he shall not die.

²⁹Yet saith the house of Israel, The way of the LORD is not equal. O house of Israel, are not my ways equal? Are not your ways unequal?

³⁰Therefore I will judge you, O house of Israel, every one according to his ways, saith the Lord GOD. Repent, and turn yourselves from all your transgressions; so iniquity shall not be your ruin.

³¹Cast away from you all your transgressions, whereby ye have transgressed; and make you a new heart and a new spirit: for why will ye die, O house of Israel?

³²For I have no pleasure in the death of him that dieth, saith the Lord GOD: wherefore turn yourselves, and live ye.

2 Peter 3:1-14

¹This second epistle, beloved, I now write unto you; in both which I stir up your pure minds by way of remembrance:

²That ye may be mindful of the words which were spoken before by the holy prophets, and of the commandment of us the apostles of the Lord and Saviour:

³Knowing this first, that there shall come in the last days scoffers, walking after their own lusts,

⁴and saying, Where is the promise of his coming? For since the fathers fell asleep, all things continue as they were from the beginning of the creation.

⁵For this they willingly are ignorant of, that by the word of God the heavens were of old, and the earth standing out of the water and in the water:

⁶Whereby the world that then was, being overflowed with water, perished:

[7]But the heavens and the earth, which are now, by the same word are kept in store, reserved unto fire against the day of judgment and perdition of ungodly men.

[8]But, beloved, be not ignorant of this one thing, that one day is with the Lord as a thousand years, and a thousand years as one day.

[9]The Lord is not slack concerning his promise, as some men count slackness; but is longsuffering to us-ward, **not willing that any should perish**, but that all should come to repentance.

[10]But the day of the Lord will come as a thief in the night; in the which the heavens shall pass away with a great noise, and the elements shall melt with fervent heat, the earth also and the works that are therein shall be burned up.

[11]Seeing then that all these things shall be dissolved, what manner of persons ought ye to be in all holy conversation and godliness,

[12]looking for and hasting unto the coming of the day of God, wherein the heavens being on fire shall be dissolved, and the elements shall melt with fervent heat?

[13]Nevertheless we, according to his promise, look for new heavens and a new earth, wherein dwelleth righteousness.

[14]Wherefore, beloved, seeing that ye look for such things, be diligent that ye may be found of him in peace, without spot, and blameless.

God plainly says in this statement He wishes no one would perish and that He is equal in His judgment. We have choices. God is truth and tells us no one is predestined for hell. God's desire is that we all come to the saving knowledge of Him!

1 Timothy 2:1-6

[1]I exhort therefore, that, first of all, supplications, prayers, intercessions, and giving of thanks, be made for all men;

[2]For kings, and for all that are in authority; that we may lead a quiet and peaceable life in all godliness and honesty.

[3]For this is good and acceptable in the sight of God our Saviour;

[4]Who will have all men to be saved, and to come unto the knowledge of the truth.

[5]For there is one God, and one mediator between God and men, the man Christ Jesus;

[6]Who gave himself a ransom for all, to be testified in due time.

Some people cannot imagine a God who is perfect in every way, allowing us to have a hand in what goes on with our salvation. Some people cannot imagine God's not having control over a person's eternity. They can only believe God decides one way or another, and that's just the way it is. What foolishness. God's control and omnipotence is not based on me or my decisions; it is based on His. Whether I choose to surrender to Christ or rebel and deny Him until my death, it does not take away from who He is. God is in control of everything because no matter what happens and how out of control things seem to be, God is prepared and was prepared before it ever happened. God wants me to be saved; He has provided everything for me to be saved, including His hand to guide me every step of the way. Whatever my choice is, whatever happens, as evil as it is here on earth, His desire for me was to be righteous through Him.

God is a God of love, and He, of all people, knows love is only good if it is real. My wife loves me because she has chosen to love me, not because I made her love me. If my children were to choose to rebel and not show me true love, that is better than having them tell me they do love me when they really don't. It would be the worst of all if I had the ability to make them love me, and I used it to do so. Then, I would have only fooled myself because a forced love is no love at all.

We choose hell as our eternal home. This is because that is what we love; we desire the things of hell. People love worldly things, no matter what they may be, from lust, to food, to money. This is where our hearts are and our desires abide. A non-converted person who has never received the Holy Spirit may mentally have chosen heaven over hell, but that is not what his or her heart longs for. The heart of a never-saved sinner loves that person's sin, and he or she will find reasons to keep it in his or her life as much as possible. That sin becomes our God. We worship it, we honor it, we certainly serve it, and, most of all, we dedicate our lives to it.

Let's take a quick peak at the seven deadly sins, and realize, in these seven alone, which we serve. I have served them all, it seems, and by God's grace have been forgiven for each account.

1. Pride. Seeing ourselves as we are and not comparing ourselves to others is humility. Pride and vanity are competitive. If someone else's pride really bothers you, you have a lot of pride.

2. Greed. This is about more than money. Generosity means letting others get the credit or praise. It is giving without having expectations of the other person. Greed wants to get its "fair share," or even a bit more.

3. Envy. "Love is patient, love is kind . . . ." Love actively seeks the good of others for their sake. Envy resents the good others receive or even might receive. Envy is almost indistinguishable from pride at times.

4. Anger. Anger is often our first reaction to the problems of others. Impatience with the faults of others is related to this.

5. Lust. Self-control and self-mastery prevent pleasure from killing the soul by suffocation. Legitimate pleasures are controlled in the same way an athlete's muscles are: for maximum efficiency without damage. Lust is the self-destructive drive for pleasure out of proportion to its worth. Sex, power, or image can be used well, but they tend to get out of control.

6. Gluttony. Temperance accepts the natural limits of pleasures and preserves this natural balance. This does not pertain only to food, but to entertainment and other legitimate goods, and even the company of others.

7. Sloth. Zeal is the energetic response of the heart to God's commands. The other sins work together to deaden the spiritual senses so we first become slow to respond to God, and then drift completely into the sleep of complacency.

All sin can be put into one of these seven, and all lead to the corruption of life. Even more than that, a person who is not saved will continue to desire these sins for all eternity. Heaven would be the last place an unsaved person would want to go. **If a person doesn't want anything to do with God now, why in the world would he or she want to spend eternity with Him?** This would entail their continuously doing the things they ran away from all their lives. No, heaven will not be their home; their home will be themselves and the misery that follows. Of course, the person after death would choose heaven over hell just from the torment and solitude alone, but that will not be a choice of salvation, only one of fear and realization of where their rebellion has left them. That will not be a heart change; instead, that is a mind change, only based on the consequences of actions. For example, a person who has to go to jail for a long time certainly does not want to go there. He may regret what he did and wish he would not have committed the crime, but the jail is the unfortunate end to his choices. So, what if somehow the person going to jail was freed and not held accountable for his crime? If the person's heart was not changed, he will be set free into the world, only to do the same thing over and over again. Some people may have a heart change due to the fear of jail and not commit another crime, but it would have to be a change in their nature, not a change in their minds, for it to last. The truth has plainly showed the first part of this question, Does God predestine people to hell? This is, without a doubt, a resounding NO. God gives us all the opportunity for salvation.

So finally, the second part is, If God knows they will one day be in hell, why does He allow them to be born? Why not make it so they never exist?

God and the Holy Spirit answered this question in one simple way: God says He knew us all before we were born.

Read this Scripture:

Isaiah 44:24

Thus saith the LORD, thy redeemer, and he that **formed** thee from the womb, I am the LORD that maketh all things; that stretcheth forth the heavens alone; that spreadeth abroad the earth by myself.

As the truth states, God knew the end of humanity as much as He did the beginning. He was pleased with His creation of man, and

He knew every man who would ever be born, and when he would die.

Ecclesiastes 3:1-22 tells us:

¹To every thing there is a season, and a time to every purpose under the heaven:

²a time to be born, and a time to die; a time to plant, and a time to pluck up that which is planted;

³a time to kill, and a time to heal; a time to break down, and a time to build up;

⁴a time to weep, and a time to laugh; a time to mourn, and a time to dance;

⁵a time to cast away stones, and a time to gather stones together; a time to embrace, and a time to refrain from embracing;

⁶a time to get, and a time to lose; a time to keep, and a time to cast away;

⁷a time to rend, and a time to sew; a time to keep silence, and a time to speak;

⁸a time to love, and a time to hate; a time of war, and a time of peace.

⁹What profit hath he that worketh in that wherein he laboureth?

¹⁰I have seen the travail, which God hath given to the sons of men to be exercised in it.

¹¹He hath made every thing beautiful in his time: also he hath set the world in their heart, so that no man can find out the work that God maketh from the beginning to the end.

¹²I know that there is no good in them, but for a man to rejoice, and to do good in his life.

¹³And also that every man should eat and drink, and enjoy the good of all his labour, it is the gift of God.

¹⁴I know that, whatsoever God doeth, it shall be for ever: nothing can be put to it, nor any thing taken from it: and God doeth it, that men should fear before him.

¹⁵That which hath been is now; and that which is to be hath already been; and God requireth that which is past.

¹⁶And moreover I saw under the sun the place of judgment, that wickedness was there; and the place of righteousness, that iniquity was there.

¹⁷I said in mine heart, God shall judge the righteous and the wicked: for there is a time there for every purpose and for every work.

¹⁸I said in mine heart concerning the estate of the sons of men, that God might manifest them, and that they might see that they themselves are beasts.

¹⁹For that which befalleth the sons of men befalleth beasts; even one thing befalleth them: as the one dieth, so dieth the other; yea, they have all one breath; so that a man hath no preeminence above a beast: for all is vanity.

²⁰All go unto one place; all are of the dust, and all turn to dust again.

²¹Who knoweth the spirit of man that goeth upward, and the spirit of the beast that goeth downward to the earth?

²²Wherefore I perceive that there is nothing better, than that a man

should rejoice in his own works; for that is his portion: for who shall bring him to see what shall be after him?

So God, knowing all men, creating them in His likeness, wanting them all to come to salvation, saw the lineage of His created people, and I was one of those people. He knew that I would come to Him one day through His grace and His salvation. He had already prepared the way for me to become His child.

As an example, let's use my father and me. I am only using this as an example. If my dad never gave his heart to Christ and lived out his life in is own desires, never repenting of his sins, and then he died, the truth says he would be in hell. God did not want him to be in hell, but that was my father's choice; that path was his own desires. What he really wanted basically was to be his own God. That is what he worshiped, and that is where his heart was. God did not create my father to go to hell, and He finds no pleasure in knowing He is there. But make no mistake, I was to be born. God created me through my mother and father, if any other man was my father, I would be different, different in my genetic makeup, different to scientists in a million ways, I am sure. I am the one God saw as one of His children, and He was not willing to let me go. If my dad were not born, I would not exist, and my father . . . Jesus says He will not leave any behind. In fact, He said He will even leave the ninety-nine that are already His to go get the one lost.

_____**Matthew 18:11-14** states:

¹¹For the Son of man is come to save that which was lost.

¹²How think ye? If a man have an hundred sheep, and one of them be gone astray, doth he not leave the ninety and nine, and goeth into the mountains, and seeketh that which is gone astray?

¹³And if so be that he find it, verily I say unto you, he rejoiceth more of that sheep, than of the ninety and nine which went not astray.

¹⁴Even so it is not the will of your Father which is in heaven, that one of these little ones should perish.

I see so many children of God longing to go to their eternal home with our Father, yet we are left here in this world, waiting, it seems. We're not only waiting, but waiting in a world that wants to slaughter us.

Romans 8:36 says, "As it is written, For thy sake we are killed all the day long; we are accounted as **sheep** for the **slaughter**."

So to you who feel left and abandoned in this world, I hope you realize God's plan will not be cut short. No matter what you are going through, realize that every day more and more brothers and sisters are coming to the same salvation you came to, and God did not leave you behind, nor will He leave them.

To show the truth, God sees all things to come, and He uses this foreknowledge in making decisions.

Let's just look at the Scriptures that show God sees the future and prepares for it in the present.

- Prophecy as a whole shows God has seen all things to come. And He has accounted for everything, and everything has happened as He saw, and his truth never changed in any way.

- Exodus 4:24-26

God says he was going to kill Moses. The fact that He didn't shows us God can change His mind, and the future is not changed in regards to his eternal glory.

- Matthew 21:1-11

Jesus looked ahead and told the disciples what would happen as to their going to get the very donkey He would ride into town on. This shows He knew what would happen, and He accounted for it.

- Matthew 8 - 8

This servant's getting saved without God's going to him shows that God foresees and accounts for it in the present, and can do what needs to be done based on our faith, wherever He is.

- John 4:1-42

Read the story of the woman at the well.

God's foreknowledge shows God knows who will accept Him and who will not. He not only goes to the place to find us, but He also knows the truth about our lives. He allows us to either keep on living as we are and die in our sin, or accept the everlasting water and become a new creature, where all things are new.

John 15:16 tells us:

Ye have not chosen me, but I have chosen you, and ordained you, that ye should go and bring forth fruit, and [that] your fruit should remain: that whatsoever ye shall ask of the Father in my name, he may give it you.

God has chosen you as His child and made the way for you to come to Him. That decision to accept needs to come from you, realizing your sins and believing He sent His Son to pay your debt. Then you must believe Jesus rose again on the third day and overcame death, and because of this, so will you.

His desire is for you to produce for His kingdom, not yours.

So the real question is, What will you do with this life that has been given to you, prepared for you?

CHAPTER 17

HEAVEN IS WHERE THE HEART IS

The truth says there are three heavens: the atmosphere; the universe, including the galaxies and stars; and a place some people will one day call home.

As much as we could talk about the two others, the one most of us want to think about is the one we'll call home.

Let's see what the truth says about this eternal heavenly home.

Genesis 1:1
In the beginning God created the **heaven** and the earth.

So the first question is, Does heaven exist? Answering this would make for a very short chapter, as the truth says a resounding YES. Then the questions become, What is it like? What will I be like there? Will I even be there?

The definition of "heaven" can be summed up in three words: being with them, or being with God. The reason I say *them* is it would include Jesus (the Word) and the Holy Spirit, as well as God,

309

and, of course, you.

First John 5:7 tells us, "For there are three that bear record in **heaven**, the Father, the Word, and the Holy Ghost: and these three are one."

Right now, if you could picture being with God, Jesus, and the Holy Spirit, what would you feel? Would it be fear, friendship, love, closeness, distance, embarrassment, nakedness, or something else?

This question is for you to answer, but if you were to compare it to being with someone else, you know you would truly see if you have, or have ever had, a relationship with our Creator.

If you have a relationship with someone you know or have known in your life, when you see that person, there should be some kind of a connection. When you see God one day, will there be that connection, or will there be just an emptiness from absent memories, memories never made? If I had a relationship with a king or a president, and the day came when I would see him again, I would honor his position and probably be nervous, but the relationship would be known as soon as we were together.

Similarly, one day we will all be in awe of God and no doubt humbled, but the relationship and knowledge of each other from the past memories will be apparent on the day of meeting. This knowledge and relationship starts when we are saved and receive the Holy Spirit.

Read **John 14:16-31**:

¹⁶And I will pray the Father, and he shall give you another Comforter, that he may abide with you for ever;

¹⁷Even the Spirit of truth; whom the world cannot receive, because it seeth him not, neither knoweth him: but ye know him; for he dwelleth with you, and shall be in you.

¹⁸I will not leave you comfortless: I will come to you.

¹⁹Yet a little while, and the world seeth me no more; but ye see me: because I live, ye shall live also.

²⁰At that day ye shall know that I am in my Father, and ye in me, and I in you.

²¹He that hath my commandments, and keepeth them, he it is that loveth me: and he that loveth me shall be loved of my Father, and I will love him, and will manifest myself to him.

²²Judas saith unto him, not Iscariot, Lord, how is it that thou wilt manifest thyself unto us, and not unto the world?

²³Jesus answered and said unto him, If a man love me, he will keep my words: and my Father will love him, and we will come unto him, and make our abode with him.

²⁴He that loveth me not keepeth not my sayings: and the word which ye hear is not mine, but the Father's which sent me.

²⁵These things have I spoken unto you, being yet present with you.

²⁶But the Comforter, which is the Holy Ghost, whom the Father will send in my name, he shall teach you all things, and bring all things to your remembrance, whatsoever I have said unto you.

²⁷Peace I leave with you, my peace I give unto you: not as the world

giveth, give I unto you. Let not your heart be troubled, neither let it be afraid.

²⁸Ye have heard how I said unto you, I go away, and come again unto you. If ye loved me, ye would rejoice, because I said, I go unto the Father: for my Father is greater than I.

²⁹And now I have told you before it come to pass, that, when it is come to pass, ye might believe.

³⁰Hereafter I will not talk much with you: for the prince of this world cometh, and hath nothing in me.

³¹But that the world may know that I love the Father; and as the Father gave me commandment, even so I do. Arise, let us go hence.

The truth says God has given us the Spirit to give us peace and the knowledge that although we must go through this world, He is greater than the world.

You may wonder, *So now that I am assured of heaven through the Holy Spirit, where will I fit into this place?*

The truth says you will be known for who you are, not so much for your job or status as a member of a family in this world, but who you are in your heart. Let's circle back in a moment to your purpose in heaven, and let's see first your purpose in life.

Genesis 9:6

Whoso sheddeth man's blood, by man shall **his** blood be shed: for in the **image** of God **made** he man.

When God made man and woman, He made them to be with Him in perfect harmony.

Genesis 2:21-25

²¹And the LORD God caused a deep sleep to fall upon Adam, and he slept: and he took one of his ribs, and closed up the flesh instead thereof;

²²And the rib, which the LORD God had taken from man, made he a woman, and brought her unto the man.

²³And Adam said, This is now bone of my bones, and flesh of my flesh: she shall be called Woman, because she was taken out of Man.

²⁴Therefore shall a man leave his father and his mother, and shall cleave unto his wife: and they shall be one flesh.

²⁵And they were both naked, the man and his wife, and were not ashamed.

However, when they sinned against God, the harmony was disrupted.

Genesis 3:8

And they heard the voice of the LORD God walking in the garden in the cool of the day: and Adam and his wife hid themselves from the presence of the LORD God amongst the trees of the garden.

So God says He made me for His pleasure and to have a relationship with me. Interestingly, that sounds just like the reason I had my children. In fact, the reason God made us screams at us from every corner of our lives, from our fingerprints to our individuality in every respect. God made you like no other for one reason, and that was because you are special to Him. He takes pleasure in you and wants you to spend eternity with Him. Just like Adam and Eve, we have all sinned and fallen away from the perfect relationship with our Creator. He wants us to come back to Him, and that can only happen through repentance and acceptance of His forgiveness.

The truth also says one day Jesus, who claims to still be alive today, will come back and lead us for a thousand years. A thousand years in heaven's time table, however, could be but a day in ours. No doubt, even I can see how a thousand years compared to eternity is but a grain of sand.

Read the following verses.

2 Peter 3:10

But the day of the Lord will come as a **thief** in the **night**; in the which the heavens shall pass away with a great noise, and the elements shall melt with fervent heat, the earth also and the works that are therein shall be burned up.

1 Corinthians 15:52

In a moment, in the twinkling **of an eye, at the last trump: for the trumpet shall sound, and the dead shall be raised incorruptible, and we shall be changed.**

John 14:1-4

[1]Let not your heart be troubled: ye believe in God, believe also in me.

[2]In my Father's house are many mansions: if it were not so, I would have told you. I go to prepare a place for you.

[3]And if I go and prepare a place for you, I will come again, and receive you unto myself; that where I am, there ye may be also.

[4]And whither I go ye know, and the way ye know.

Revelation 20:4

And I saw thrones, and they sat upon them, and judgment was given unto them: and I saw the souls of them that were beheaded for the witness of Jesus, and for the word of God, and which had not worshipped the beast, neither his image, neither had received his mark upon their foreheads, or in their hands; and they lived and **reign**ed with Christ a **thousand year**s.

2 Peter 3:8

But, beloved, be not ignorant of this **one** thing, that **one day is** with the **Lord** as a **thousand years**, and a **thousand years** as **one day**.

You may wonder, *So, when this time comes and eternity lies ahead for those with God, what will it be like for me once I am there?* Let's take it from the top.

1) Where will I be?

I remember as a child, and even to this day, listening to people, especially the elderly, speak of dying, and they would say, "I am ready to go home." It took me many years to realize what that meant. I realize this only now because I have the same place I call home. The bank may own my home, but that is only until I have defaulted on my payment, and then they take it away. When my home is paid for, and I have the deed from the bank, it can only be taken away if I don't pay taxes. Similarly, heaven is not only prepared, but it is paid for, and we are all joint heirs, with it never to be taken away. This place I call home on earth is where my family is, where I eat my meals and rest. Not only is home a place of privacy, but also it is a place of ownership. In many ways, heaven is going to be like this, but exponentially to the billionth power. Heaven will be a place of peace, knowing you're with the ones you love and the ones who love you. Is that not the definition of a perfect home, surrounded by your loving family?

Hebrews 12:22-24 tells us:

22But ye are come unto mount Sion, and unto the city of the living God, the heavenly Jerusalem, and to an innumerable company of angels,

23To the general assembly and church of the firstborn, which are written in heaven, and to God the Judge of all, and to the spirits of just men made perfect,

²⁴and to Jesus the mediator of the new covenant, and to the blood of sprinkling, that speaketh better things than that of Abel.

When you arrive in heaven, after being delivered by the angels themselves, there will be no Peter at the gate checking the list—only a Savior, a Father, running to you, welcoming you home to the place He has prepared for you. He is ready to celebrate the return of His child. You won't knock on the door as you would a stranger's house; you will walk in because you'll be at home, your home.

Read what it's like to be a child of God's.

1 John 3:1-3

¹Behold, what manner of love the Father hath bestowed upon us, that we should be called the sons of God: therefore the world knoweth us not, because it knew him not.

²Beloved, now are we the sons of God, and it doth not yet appear what we shall be: but we know that, when he shall appear, we shall be like him; for we shall see him as he is.

³And every man that hath this hope in him purifieth himself, even as he is pure.

Romans 8:17

And if children, then **heirs**; **heirs** of God, and **joint**-heirs with Christ; if so be that we suffer with him, that we may be also glorified together.

Now that we see heaven is my eternal home, what will it be like? you ask.

2) What will it be like?

First of all, many of us don't see our earthly home as a peaceful place. Some see it as an unhappy place, a place of conflict or maybe harm. It may be a place of anger or poverty, or even a place of disaster and fear. Or what's worse is many have no home at all. Regardless of people's earthly homes, or lack thereof, one day, the children of God will all be at *home* together. This home is a place of safety, a place of true joy, of equality, and, most of all, a place of peacefulness. This peace will be a peace with yourself, with no more burden of sin or war with our flesh. This will be a peace of comfort being with your Father, a peace of fulfillment knowing and glorifying God for all He is and ever was and ever will be. Heaven is a place of peace that never ends.

We can read about this in **Revelation 21:1-8**:

[1]And I saw a new heaven and a new earth: for the first heaven and the first earth were passed away; and there was no more sea.
[2]And I John saw the holy city, new Jerusalem, coming down from God out of heaven, prepared as a bride adorned for her husband.
[3]And I heard a great voice out of heaven saying, Behold, the tabernacle of God is with men, and he will dwell with them, and they

shall be his people, and God himself shall be with them, and be their God.

[4]And God shall wipe away all tears from their eyes; and there shall be no more death, neither sorrow, nor crying, neither shall there be any more pain: for the former things are passed away.

[5]And he that sat upon the throne said, Behold, I make all things new. And he said unto me, Write: for these words are true and faithful.

[6]And he said unto me, It is done. I am Alpha and Omega, the beginning and the end. I will give unto him that is athirst of the fountain of the water of life freely.

[7]He that overcometh shall inherit all things; and I will be his God, and he shall be my son.

[8]But the fearful, and unbelieving, and the abominable, and murderers, and whoremongers, and sorcerers, and idolaters, and all liars, shall have their part in the lake which burneth with fire and brimstone: which is the second death.

Heaven will be more beautiful than anything that ever was. There will be a city called the new Jerusalem. It will have the gates of pearl, streets of gold, and the crystal sea we hear so much about.

Let's read more from Revelation. .

Revelation 3:12

Him that overcometh will I make a pillar in the temple of my God, and he shall go no more out: and I will write upon him the name of my God, and the name of the city of my God, which is new Jerusalem, which cometh down out of **heaven** from my God: and I will write upon him my new name.

Revelation 21:9-27

[9]And there came unto me one of the seven angels which had the seven vials full of the seven last plagues, and talked with me, saying, Come hither, I will shew thee the bride, the Lamb's wife.

[10]And he carried me away in the spirit to a great and high mountain, and shewed me that great city, the holy Jerusalem, descending out of heaven from God,

[11]having the glory of God: and her light was like unto a stone most precious, even like a jasper stone, clear as crystal;

[12]and had a wall great and high, and had twelve gates, and at the gates twelve angels, and names written thereon, which are the names of the twelve tribes of the children of Israel:

[13]On the east three gates; on the north three gates; on the south three gates; and on the west three gates.

[14]And the wall of the city had twelve foundations, and in them the names of the twelve apostles of the Lamb.

[15]And he that talked with me had a golden reed to measure the city, and the gates thereof, and the wall thereof.

[16]And the city lieth foursquare, and the length is as large as the breadth: and he measured the city with the reed, twelve thousand furlongs. The length and the breadth and the height of it are equal.

¹⁷And he measured the wall thereof, an hundred and forty and four cubits, according to the measure of a man, that is, of the angel.

¹⁸And the building of the wall of it was of jasper: and the city was pure gold, like unto clear glass.

¹⁹And the foundations of the wall of the city were garnished with all manner of precious stones. The first foundation was jasper; the second, sapphire; the third, a chalcedony; the fourth, an emerald;

²⁰the fifth, sardonyx; the sixth, sardius; the seventh, chrysolyte; the eighth, beryl; the ninth, a topaz; the tenth, a chrysoprasus; the eleventh, a jacinth; the twelfth, an amethyst.

²¹And the twelve gates were twelve pearls: every several gate was of one pearl: and the street of the city was pure gold, as it were transparent glass.

²²And I saw no temple therein: for the Lord God Almighty and the Lamb are the temple of it.

²³And the city had no need of the sun, neither of the moon, to shine in it: for the glory of God did lighten it, and the Lamb is the light thereof.

²⁴And the nations of them which are saved shall walk in the light of it: and the kings of the earth do bring their glory and honour into it.

²⁵And the gates of it shall not be shut at all by day: for there shall be no night there.

²⁶And they shall bring the glory and honour of the nations into it.

²⁷And there shall in no wise enter into it any thing that defileth, neither whatsoever worketh abomination, or maketh a lie: but they

which are written in the Lamb's book of life.

I end this portion by saying just this: Think of the most beautiful things you have ever seen in your life, and then let what this Scripture says sink in:

1 Corinthians 2:9

But as it is written, Eye hath not seen, **nor ear heard**, neither have entered into the heart of man, the things which God hath prepared for them that love him.

Heaven also will be a place of family members' knowing us as we were known. However, realize this: Everyone will be in your family. As we are all descendants of Adam, we are all one family. I hear so many people think heaven will be a place of reuniting with mothers and daughters and wives. I say before we bring our earthly families to heaven, let's bring heaven's family to earth.

_____**Matthew 22:24-32** tells us:

24Saying, Master, Moses said, If a man die, having no children, his brother shall marry his wife, and raise up seed unto his brother.
25Now there were with us seven brethren: and the first, when he had married a wife, deceased, and, having no issue, left his wife unto his brother:
26Likewise the second also, and the third, unto the seventh.

²⁷And last of all the woman died also.

²⁸Therefore in the resurrection whose wife shall she be of the seven? For they all had her.

²⁹Jesus answered and said unto them, Ye do err, not knowing the scriptures, nor the power of God.

³⁰For in the resurrection they neither marry, nor are given in marriage, but are as the angels of God in heaven.

³¹But as touching the resurrection of the dead, have ye not read that which was spoken unto you by God, saying,

³²I am the God of Abraham, and the God of Isaac, and the God of Jacob? God is not the God of the dead, but of the living.

There will be no cliques in heaven, and there will be no favorite child, only children. You may have had a large family here on earth, but you will love everyone the same in heaven. This is the way it should be here on earth, as we love one another as ourselves, but alas, it is not. I have known families, especially in a church I attended, that spoke of loving each other as themselves, but their actions and care were really for their own family. If you were not a member of their family, you were not as good, and you were left out, and you knew it.

In heaven, our family will include the little African baby who died of AIDS a week after birth. It will include the man or woman or child who lived in shelters and foster homes, never knowing a real family. Heaven's family will be just as much a reunion for them as it will be for anyone. As you read the Scripture that follows, see what Jesus thinks of His immediate family on earth.

Mark 3:31-35

[31]There came then his brethren and his mother, and, standing without, sent unto him, calling him.

[32]And the multitude sat about him, and they said unto him, Behold, thy mother and thy brethren without seek for thee.

[33]And he answered them, saying, Who is my mother, or my brethren?

[34]And he looked round about on them which sat about him, and said, Behold my mother and my brethren!

[35]For whosoever shall do the will of God, the same is my brother, and my sister, and mother.

Mark 12:29-34

[29]And Jesus answered him, The first of all the commandments is, Hear, O Israel; The Lord our God is one Lord:

[30]And thou shalt love the Lord thy God with all thy heart, and with all thy soul, and with all thy mind, and with all thy strength: this is the first commandment.

[31]And the second is like, namely this, Thou shalt love thy neighbour as thyself. There is none other commandment greater than these.

[32]And the scribe said unto him, Well, Master, thou hast said the truth: for there is one God; and there is none other but he:

[33]And to love him with all the heart, and with all the understanding,

and with all the soul, and with all the strength, and to love his neighbour as himself, is more than all whole burnt offerings and sacrifices. [34]And when Jesus saw that he answered discreetly, he said unto him, Thou art not far from the kingdom of God. And no man after that durst ask him any question.

Don't be deceived and think there will be cliques in heaven, as there are on earth. Heaven will have no Rockefellers or Vanderbilts, no special treatment will be given, and no private reunions will be held. We will experience only the sweetness of all your brothers and sisters coming together in the family of Christ and Him alone.

3) What will I remember, and what will I do?

The truth says when the thousand years is up, you will remember nothing, and all will be new:

Revelation 2:4
And God shall wipe away all tears from their eyes; and there shall be no more death, neither sorrow, nor crying, neither shall there be any more pain: for the former things are passed away.

2 Peter 3:13
Nevertheless we, according to his promise, look for new **heaven**s and a new earth, wherein dwelleth righteousness.

Isaiah 11:1-9

[1]And there shall come forth a rod out of the stem of Jesse, and a Branch shall grow out of his roots:

[2]and the spirit of the LORD shall rest upon him, the spirit of wisdom and understanding, the spirit of counsel and might, the spirit of knowledge and of the fear of the LORD;

[3]and shall make him of quick understanding in the fear of the LORD: and he shall not judge after the sight of his eyes, neither reprove after the hearing of his ears:

[4]But with righteousness shall he judge the poor, and reprove with equity for the meek of the earth: and he shall smite the earth: with the rod of his mouth, and with the breath of his lips shall he slay the wicked.

[5]And righteousness shall be the girdle of his loins, and faithfulness the girdle of his reins.

[6]The wolf also shall dwell with the lamb, and the leopard shall lie down with the kid; and the calf and the young lion and the fatling together; and a little child shall lead them.

[7]And the cow and the bear shall feed; their young ones shall lie down together: and the lion shall eat straw like the ox.

[8]And the sucking child shall play on the hole of the asp, and the weaned child shall put his hand on the cockatrice' den.

[9]They shall not hurt nor destroy in all my holy mountain: for the earth shall be full of the knowledge of the LORD, as the waters cover the sea.

Yes, the truth has spoken, and you will only know what lies ahead for eternity. The vapor of life you will have lived will not be a part of your future with Christ. The lost children, the hurt, the pain . . . it will all be gone. The new family will begin with one father, one being glorified for his works. One family will all be united in one goal, loving the Lord, glorifying Him, serving Him, and through Him serving one another in peace. Yes, we will know no war, only peace among one family, all knowing and accepting the truth, who is Christ alone.

Isaiah 65:16-25

[16]That he who blesseth himself in the earth shall bless himself in the God of truth; and he that sweareth in the earth shall swear by the God of truth; because the former troubles are forgotten, and because they are hid from mine eyes.

[17]For, behold, I create new heavens and a new earth: and the former shall not be remembered, nor come into mind.

[18]But be ye glad and rejoice for ever in that which I create: for, behold, I create Jerusalem a rejoicing, and her people a joy.

[19]And I will rejoice in Jerusalem, and joy in my people: and the voice of weeping shall be no more heard in her, nor the voice of crying.

[20]There shall be no more thence an infant of days, nor an old man that hath not filled his days: for the child shall die an hundred years old; but the sinner being an hundred years old shall be accursed.

[21]And they shall build houses, and inhabit them; and they shall plant

vineyards, and eat the fruit of them.

²²They shall not build, and another inhabit; they shall not plant, and another eat: for as the days of a tree are the days of my people, and mine elect shall long enjoy the work of their hands.

²³They shall not labour in vain, nor bring forth for trouble; for they are the seed of the blessed of the LORD, and their offspring with them.

²⁴And it shall come to pass, that before they call, I will answer; and while they are yet speaking, I will hear.

²⁵The wolf and the lamb shall feed together, and the lion shall eat straw like the bullock: and dust shall be the serpent's meat. They shall not hurt nor destroy in all my holy mountain, saith the LORD.

As the truth states, work will not be a time of trials and tribulation, but a time of fulfillment and joy. It will be a place of refuge, a place of accomplishment. In ending this chapter, I would like to say to all of those who are heaven-bound, "Welcome home."

The Story of J. and His Wife

When my oldest son was about ten, I went on a three-day school trip with him. The trip was to learn about marshlands. As we loaded up the buses and took our seats, the kids were all chattering away as the few adults, I am sure, were pondering the events of the next few days. As we started out on the trip, I started to talk with the other adults, hoping to pass some time. As we grew nearer to our destination, I had a conversation with a man who had lost his wife to cancer. He was about thirty-eight years old, and she had passed away just a year before. He told me about the struggle she had gone through and the emotions, as well as his children's struggles through this devastating time. At that point, we were arriving at the camp, so the conversation ended, but I knew before the trip was over that Jesus had sent me to help this man.

The trip went well, and we all had a great time. We loaded up to return home, and I knew this would be the opportunity to give this man the advice and guidance I had felt led to give. I had been praying for him and what the Lord would have me to say. Now I was ready to do what the Lord had called me to do. As we drove back, all the kids were sleeping, and just as I thought, the conversation was brought back up. As soon as I had the opportunity, I gave him what I thought was the best advice I could give, and that was, "Don't give up on God." I told him to trust in Him no matter what, and though this was a devastating time, allow God to show him what he could do through this. After I gave my best effort to console him and give him the best answers I could, he looked me straight in the eyes and said something I will never forget.

Without blinking one time, he said, "You will never know what it is like to lose someone you love until you sit there with [the person] holding your hand as [she] takes [her] last breath." It took a moment for me to realize the impact of what he had just told me, and at that second, I understood the most amazing thing. The Lord had sent J.

to me, and not the other way around. I am not sure if J. remembers anything I told him, as a hundred others had probably said the same thing, but what he said to me changed my view of life. What God was trying to tell me through J.'s life was to see my life as precious—the time with my children and my wife, the time with family and at work . . . don't take any of it for granted, and as much as you can, live each day as the last.

Jesus has prepared a place for us, and one day J. and his two sons will see their wife and mom again and rejoice, no doubt. But as much as you can, appreciate this home here on earth until the final one comes.

CHAPTER 18

The Not-So-Hidden Wounds

⸺∘∞∘⸺

Jesus said, "I came to heal the sick, help the sinner, and love the unlovable. I came specifically for those who needed my help, whether or not they knew it. I provide healing in every way still today. The question is not, Will I give you help? It is, Will you ask for it and accept it?" So, do you need His help, or are you like so many who say, "I can handle it," while continuously looking for things to stop the pain, but never curing the wound? Jesus also said, "I did not come for those who don't need me—the good, the righteous, the already justified. They have their own holiness, for they have their savior, and that is themselves." The problem with being your own savior and not needing Jesus is you don't have the power He has, the power to heal yourself or anyone else spiritually. The bottom line: The truth says you cannot become spiritually whole without Christ. Yet so many of us keep on trying. We are not willing to give up the former lusts that are making us sick, and we are unwilling to receive a healthy future with Christ. We read about this in the following Scriptures.

1 Peter 1:1-7

[1]Peter, an apostle of Jesus Christ, to the strangers scattered throughout Pontus, Galatia, Cappadocia, Asia, and Bithynia,

[2]elect according to the foreknowledge of God the Father, through sanctification of the Spirit, unto obedience and sprinkling of the blood of Jesus Christ: Grace unto you, and peace, be multiplied.

[3]Blessed be the God and Father of our Lord Jesus Christ, which according to his abundant mercy hath begotten us again unto a lively hope by the resurrection of Jesus Christ from the dead,

[4]To an inheritance incorruptible, and undefiled, and that fadeth not away, reserved in heaven for you,

[5]who are kept by the power of God through faith unto salvation ready to be revealed in the last time.

[6]Wherein ye greatly rejoice, though now for a season, if need be, ye are in heaviness through manifold temptations:

[7]That the trial of your faith, being much more precious than of gold that perisheth, though it be tried with fire, might be found unto praise and honour and glory at the appearing of Jesus Christ.

Mark 8:35

For whosoever **will** save his life shall **lose** it; but whosoever shall **lose** his life for my sake and the gospel's, the same shall save it.

What about those who do seem to have it all together? They seem to be doing fine without Jesus. Do they perhaps not really need this Savior? If Jesus said He only came for these sick sinners, what if I am not sick? Maybe I am not that bad. In fact, I do a lot of good for myself and others, and I am pretty happy, so why rock the boat? Are we all really spiritually sick? Do we all really have to follow this Jesus, or is He just for some of us, maybe even just the weak?

Lastly, many of us feel we are too sick, too far gone with our mistakes in life. We are un-healable by God, Jesus, or anyone else. Is it true that I can be too far gone?

These are valid questions, and all come back to one answer, and that is from the Man who gave the answers: Jesus Himself.

Let's start with Jesus' coming to heal the sick.

Mark 2:15-17

15And it came to pass, that, as Jesus sat at meat in his house, many publicans and sinners sat also together with Jesus and his disciples: for there were many, and they followed him.

16And when the scribes and Pharisees saw him eat with publicans and sinners, they said unto his disciples, How is it that he eateth and drinketh with publicans and sinners?

17When Jesus heard it, he saith unto them, They that are whole have no need of the physician, but they that are sick: I came not to call the righteous, but sinners to repentance.

The question now becomes, Do you need His healing, His spiritual healing, the kind of healing that this world doesn't offer, the kind of spiritual healing that, if given, overcomes any physical wound you may have? Though He may not always take away the physical wound, He does give peace over and above the anguish that wound inflicts on your life. In many cases, He uses that very wound as the foundation to make you in His image.

These questions and opinions are just some of the reasons why we aren't all lined up to go to church on Sundays, but Jesus is being passed over every day as someone who can help us individually and as a whole.

The main reason is we **deny we are sick**, just like these Pharisees. In their case, they thought God is only for the good, the justified. Most of this reasoning comes from viewing God as we view society. Society judges us based on what we can offer society. For instance, are we attractive, skilled, and acceptable to do our part? The better we are, the more skilled we become, the more we are accepted, and the higher we are lifted up. This is a normal evolution that we practice in every aspect of this race called life. Here is the hiccup: The truth says all of us, everyone, the entire human race, before and after, have sinned and fall short of God's acceptance.

1 Timothy 1:15

This is a faithful saying, and worthy of all acceptation, that Christ Jesus came into the world to save **sinner**s; of whom I am chief.

Romans 3:23

For **all** have **sinned**, and come short of the glory of God.

The problem most of us have is we know we are sinners, and we know we mess up, but instead of realizing and accepting the sin as our fault, we justify everything. We tell ourselves: *It is my parents' fault. Friends made me do it. It is because of my circumstances in life.* Rarely is it just ourselves who messed up. We all have these skeletons in the closets. I've never met a person who didn't, just a lot of people who ignore them and hide them better than others. Let's look at an example from the truth.

Mark 10:17-27

[17]And when he was gone forth into the way, there came one running, and kneeled to him, and asked him, Good Master, what shall I do that I may inherit eternal life?

[18]And Jesus said unto him, Why callest thou me good? There is none good but one, that is, God.

[19]Thou knowest the commandments, Do not commit adultery, Do not kill, Do not steal, Do not bear false witness, Defraud not, Honour thy father and mother.

[20]And he answered and said unto him, Master, all these have I observed from my youth.

[21]Then Jesus beholding him loved him, and said unto him, One thing thou lackest: go thy way, sell whatsoever thou hast, and give to the

poor, and thou shalt have treasure in heaven: and come, take up the cross, and follow me.

²²And he was sad at that saying, and went away grieved: for he had great possessions.

²³And Jesus looked round about, and saith unto his disciples, How hardly shall they that have riches enter into the kingdom of God!

²⁴And the disciples were astonished at his words. But Jesus answereth again, and saith unto them, Children, how hard is it for them that trust in riches to enter into the kingdom of God!

²⁵It is easier for a camel to go through the eye of a needle, than for a rich man to enter into the kingdom of God.

²⁶And they were astonished out of measure, saying among themselves, Who then can be saved?

²⁷And Jesus looking upon them saith, With men it is impossible, but not with God: for with God all things are possible.

This man was different from the Pharisees. He didn't judge others or make himself a role model for religious power. His concern was for himself and his path to heaven alone. Was this man not justified in his life for the proper life he had lived? With this man, whom he obviously cared for, Jesus took a different approach and wanted to give him the answers for which he was asking. Jesus told him to follow the law (the Ten Commandments). This man was happy to hear this because just like many of us, he had persuaded himself he had done the right things in life.

He was a good person and had obeyed these laws since he was a child. He had done good to others and was evidently blessed for his good works. He had a well-lived life. This man believed he needed no healing, for he had healed himself and earned his place in heaven. He believed in God and wanted to obey the commandments, and I dare say he probably had a love for God. But God knows everything, including our sins and where we fall short. He knows what we hold on to as the most important aspects of our lives. And though this man wanted heaven and wanted to be good, his heart belonged to his money, not to God and Jesus. Jesus always sees the heart of the person, as well as the heart of the matter. The truth says:

Mark 12:30
And thou shalt love the Lord thy God with all thy heart, and with all thy **soul**, and with all thy **mind**, and with all thy strength: this is the first commandment.

Leviticus 26
Ye shall make you no idols nor graven image, neither rear you up a standing image, neither shall ye set up any image of stone in your land, to bow down unto it: for I am the LORD your God.

This man's satisfaction with his works ended as we read next what Jesus replied to him. Jesus told him to sell everything, give it to the poor, and pick up his cross and follow Him. The story ends by the man walking away sad, unwilling to give up the most important treasure in his heart. Then Jesus told the disciples how hard it is for a rich man to get to heaven. This man's first god was money, and to him this money and his good actions justified his life. Remember, Jesus sees our hearts and sees that every man is a sinner who's in need of His healing. Our problem is we just need to find where the sin is in our lives and take ownership of it. We need to accept that it is we who need His help, and it is our actions that have disobeyed the Lord and put something else above Him. When we do this, then and only then can we find healing through God's forgiveness.

After all, forgiveness is the ointment God provides through Jesus Christ, and no wound can refuse its power. God's forgiveness knows no limits; no wound is so infected, so big, or so old that it can't be cured by God's forgiveness. What we have to do first is accept God's forgiveness because His truth says it is real. Then, for the full healing to be complete, we must forgive ourselves and others. Now that we know the medicine that cures, it's time to figure out where our wounds are so we can apply it.

Romans 5:8

But God commendeth his love toward us, in that, while we were yet **sinner**s, Christ died for us.

Acts 26:18

To open their eyes, and to turn them from darkness to light, and from the power of Satan unto God, that they may receive **forgiveness** of sins, and inheritance among them which are sanctified by faith that is in me.

Psalm 139:1

O lord, thou hast **search**ed **me**, and known **me**.

Psalm 139:23

Search me, O God, and know my heart: try **me**, and know my thoughts.

God will show you where the wounds are, but that comes from your accepting that you need Him and asking for His forgiveness and mercy. When you ask, He says He will give, and when He gives, He is the One who applies it to the areas that need it. God knows the wounds and where to start, for that is His job as the Great Physician, not ours. Read the story below about the woman at the well.

⁶Now Jacob's well was there. Jesus therefore, being wearied with his journey, sat thus on the well: and it was about the sixth hour.
⁷There cometh a woman of Samaria to draw water: Jesus saith unto her, Give me to drink.
⁸(For his disciples were gone away unto the city to buy meat.)
⁹Then saith the woman of Samaria unto him, How is it that thou, being a Jew, askest drink of me, which am a woman of Samaria? For

the Jews have no dealings with the Samaritans.

¹⁰Jesus answered and said unto her, If thou knewest the gift of God, and who it is that saith to thee, Give me to drink; thou wouldest have asked of him, and he would have given thee living water.

¹¹The woman saith unto him, Sir, thou hast nothing to draw with, and the well is deep: from whence then hast thou that living water?

¹²Art thou greater than our father Jacob, which gave us the well, and drank thereof himself, and his children, and his cattle?

¹³Jesus answered and said unto her, Whosoever drinketh of this water shall thirst again:

¹⁴But whosoever drinketh of the water that I shall give him shall never thirst; but the water that I shall give him shall be in him a well of water springing up into everlasting life.

¹⁵The woman saith unto him, Sir, give me this water, that I thirst not, neither come hither to draw.

¹⁶Jesus saith unto her, Go, call thy husband, and come hither.

¹⁷The woman answered and said, I have no husband. Jesus said unto her, Thou hast well said, I have no husband:

¹⁸For thou hast had five husbands; and he whom thou now hast is not thy husband: in that saidst thou truly.

¹⁹The woman saith unto him, Sir, I perceive that thou art a prophet.

²⁰Our fathers worshipped in this mountain; and ye say, that in Jerusalem is the place where men ought to worship.

²¹Jesus saith unto her, Woman, believe me, the hour cometh, when ye shall neither in this mountain, nor yet at Jerusalem, worship the

Father.

²²Ye worship ye know not what: we know what we worship: for salvation is of the Jews.

²³But the hour cometh, and now is, when the true worshippers shall worship the Father in spirit and in truth: for the Father seeketh such to worship him.

²⁴God is a Spirit: and they that worship him must worship him in spirit and in truth.

²⁵The woman saith unto him, I know that Messias cometh, which is called Christ: when he is come, he will tell us all things.

²⁶Jesus saith unto her, I that speak unto thee am he.

John 4:6-26

Jesus shows her where her wound is: She was married many times and living with a man without being married. Notice He does not scold her; He only offers the ointment of never thirsting again. He is showing her that He has come to help her and make her whole again. He came to give her what none of those other men or even the water could give her—healing peace and the ability to never thirst spiritually again. I am glad she accepts this offer. We should all know, this is the same offer He makes to each of us today.

Moving back to the Pharisees, some of them had a sickness of a different matter, and Jesus applied some stronger ointment with a little more sting for their healing needs. Remember, Jesus sees the heart, and for those who have a heart so hardened in themselves and their actions, He provides a dash of alcohol. It may burn when applied, but its purpose is to clean the infection so healing can even start.

Let's look at a few examples of this medicine's being applied:

Matthew 3:1-11

[1]In those days came John the Baptist, preaching in the wilderness of Judaea,

[2]and saying, Repent ye: for the kingdom of heaven is at hand.

[3]For this is he that was spoken of by the prophet Esaias, saying, The voice of one crying in the wilderness, Prepare ye the way of the Lord, make his paths straight.

[4]And the same John had his raiment of camel's hair, and a leathern girdle about his loins; and his meat was locusts and wild honey.

[5]Then went out to him Jerusalem, and all Judaea, and all the region round about Jordan,

[6]and were baptized of him in Jordan, confessing their sins.

[7]But when he saw many of the Pharisees and Sadducees come to his baptism, he said unto them, O generation of vipers, who hath warned you to flee from the wrath to come?

[8]Bring forth therefore fruits meet for repentance:

[9]And think not to say within yourselves, We have Abraham to our father: for I say unto you, that God is able of these stones to raise up children unto Abraham.

[10]And now also the axe is laid unto the root of the trees: therefore

every tree which bringeth not forth good fruit is hewn down, and cast into the fire.

[11]I indeed baptize you with water unto repentance. But he that cometh after me is mightier than I, whose shoes I am not worthy to bear: he shall baptize you with the Holy Ghost, and with fire.

Luke 11:35-44

[35]Take heed therefore that the light which is in thee be not darkness. [36]If thy whole body therefore be full of light, having no part dark, the whole shall be full of light, as when the bright shining of a candle doth give thee light.

[37]And as he spake, a certain Pharisee besought him to dine with him: and he went in, and sat down to meat.

[38]And when the Pharisee saw it, he marvelled that he had not first washed before dinner.

[39]And the Lord said unto him, Now do ye Pharisees make clean the outside of the cup and the platter; but your inward part is full of ravening and wickedness.

[40]Ye fools, did not he that made that which is without make that which is within also?

[41]But rather give alms of such things as ye have; and, behold, all things are clean unto you.

[42]But woe unto you, Pharisees! For ye tithe mint and rue and all manner of herbs, and pass over judgment and the love of God: these ought ye to have done, and not to leave the other undone.

⁴³Woe unto you, Pharisees! For ye love the uppermost seats in the synagogues, and greetings in the markets.

⁴⁴Woe unto you, scribes and Pharisees, hypocrites! For ye are as graves which appear not, and the men that walk over them are not aware of them.

These Pharisees had their holiness not only wrapped up in their own actions, but by their positions as religious authority. God says, "Your outside is clean, but your inside is dirty." Many religious leaders today still hold themselves in high authority, above others, justifying themselves with their own holiness. We have seen so many instances of religious leaders' falling down, whether it is due to money, sex scandals, or molestation or other abuse of children. This is not the leadership of which the truth spoke. The truth says if you want to be a leader for Christ, you must serve as Christ.

John 13:3-16

³Jesus knowing that the Father had given all things into his hands, and that he was come from God, and went to God;

⁴He riseth from supper, and laid aside his garments; and took a towel, and girded himself.

⁵After that he poureth water into a bason, and began to wash the disciples' feet, and to wipe them with the towel wherewith he was girded.

⁶Then cometh he to Simon Peter: and Peter saith unto him, Lord,

dost thou wash my feet?

[7]Jesus answered and said unto him, What I do thou knowest not now; but thou shalt know hereafter.

[8]Peter saith unto him, Thou shalt never wash my feet. Jesus answered him, If I wash thee not, thou hast no part with me.

[9]Simon Peter saith unto him, Lord, not my feet only, but also my hands and my head.

[10]Jesus saith to him, He that is washed needeth not save to wash his feet, but is clean every whit: and ye are clean, but not all.

[11]For he knew who should betray him; therefore said he, Ye are not all clean.

[12]So after he had washed their feet, and had taken his garments, and was set down again, he said unto them, Know ye what I have done to you?

[13]Ye call me Master and Lord: and ye say well; for so I am.

[14]If I then, your Lord and Master, have washed your feet; ye also ought to wash one another's feet.

[15]For I have given you an example, that ye should do as I have done to you.

[16]Verily, verily, I say unto you, The servant is not greater than his lord; neither he that is sent greater than he that sent him.

These Pharisees, as many leaders today, had an outward action, but they lacked the inward meaning, and that is to love. They lacked a love for God's truth and not their own, a love for everyone and not just who they feel earned it.

Now, let's finally prove this whole sick sinner versus good person wrong. Let's look at those who have it right without Jesus, and then we can say the truth is a lie. Who are these people who seem to have it all without Christ? Let's view their daily lives and decide if it's true.

Ted Turner

All I can say is read his life story; it is filled with sickness, divorce, suicide, and, most of all, wealth and success. He is a man honored by many for his accomplishments and no doubt does many good things for our world. But he is said to have said this in a 1990 speech to the American Humanist Association at an atheist conference: "Christianity is a religion for losers." Though he apologized later for the statement, he still believes it.

My heart goes out to Ted Turner, and I pray God will show him that the real winners in life will be the ones who have a life in Christ. What I find the saddest about his life is it seems he thinks he could not have gotten the wealth and accomplished all those things being a Christian. I just wonder what greater things he would have accomplished being in Christ.

Hugh Hefner

A name that carries its own connotations, Hugh Marston Hefner, born April 9, 1926, not only founded the billion-dollar Playboy

Enterprises, but also did much to spearhead the "sexual revolution," first by publishing *Playboy* magazine in 1953, and then by expanding his girlie magazine into supper clubs, cable networks, book publishing, apparel, adult-entertainment home videos, and scores of other arenas. *Playboy* magazine itself began with a well-known business coup.

These are two of the most powerful men known to this world. They are rich both in money and in lusts, but neither believes he sins, only that he's a product of this world, and the strongest survive. The problem with this is the truth says we are all sick in sin; some of us just hide it better than others.

So have these men or anyone else hidden their sins well enough that God cannot see them? The first commandment is that you will have no other God except Him. Have you another God, whether it is money or a person? Have you justified spiritual healing through physical pleasure? Are these men's good works in the world enough to please God over the obvious wound we can all see?

Do they, and *all* of us, really need Jesus? The truth says yes, over and over again. And do you know what? Deep down, we all know we need Him.

We are all sick. We have these open wounds we keep trying to heal with stuff, yet this stuff doesn't help; it only makes the pain subside. The pain of divorce, death, rebellion, mistakes, and betrayal are all painful gashes we try to hide and make subside, never getting true healing. The wounds are there, but we hide them so well. Why?

Because we know if others see our wounds, we will be counted as weak, and our world does not respect the weak, only the strong.

Let's look at this example. You go to a doctor or a hospital to seek attention for a wound. One of the first things they try to do there is establish where the wound is. Next they determine the cause of it, and then what it will take to fix it. During this time of evaluation, the patient's biggest concern is to stop the pain, so the docs use drugs and techniques to not necessarily heal anything, but just to numb the pain.

This is what we want spiritually from our wounds. We want them to be fixed, and we want to be healthy, but more than anything, we wish to numb the pain. The truth says Jesus is the only Way to be healed from spiritual death, and because many of us don't want to choose Him or His ways, we just want to numb the pain. Our "Novocain" becomes drugs, alcohol, sex, pornography, money, and power . . . whatever it takes to dull the pain. At first, these worldly Novocains seem to work, but just like real pain meds, when they're taken over and over again, our bodies need more and more to get the same effect as before. The thing about Novocain is that it eventually wears off, and the pain is still there. Spiritually, this means more drugs, more sex, and more power, until we are consumed by the addiction, all because we are dealing with the pain and not the injury. Contrary to us, Jesus is not interested in numbing the pain as much as He is in healing the wound. When the wound is healed, the pain needs no numbing, for it has stopped, and the patient is healed.

Lastly, to those who ask, "Am I too sick? Have I gone too far?

Have I sinned too much? Is there really hope for me?" let's see what the truth says:

1 Timothy 1:15
This is a faithful saying, and worthy of all acceptation, that Christ Jesus came into the world to save **sinner**s; of whom I am chief.

John 10:28
And I give unto them eternal life; and they shall never perish, neither shall any man pluck them out of my **hand**.

Whatever your healing need is, wherever you fall short, give it to Christ. Admit your sinfulness, and know that strength in Christ means you will be weak to the world. Ask for the healing of your soul and your life; ask for His hands to do the work that so needs to be done. God says no sin is so great that it cannot be forgiven by His mercy and grace. Even though the wound may look devastating, and the sin may be the worst of all, the ointment of grace will repair and forgive any wound or life. No matter where you are or where you've been, no matter the devastation left in your tracks, Jesus said, "I came for you, and I can give you a new beginning."

2 Corinthians 5:17
Therefore if any man be in Christ, he is a **new** creature: **old things** are passed away; behold, **all things** are become **new**.

349

The Two Pastor Mikes

There are two pastors I love dearly who are both named Mike. The first Mike told me once, while lying in an assisted-living facility, recovering from the amputation of his second leg due to a life of suffering from diabetes, that people in the home were coming to talk to him about Christ. He told me one lady asked him if she could ever lose her salvation. Mike told her at times in his life when he felt far away from God and felt he had gone too far, he would close one hand and speak to it. He would say, "Lord, have I gone too far? Have You left me for good?" He would then take the same hand, put it up to his ear, and listen. He said the hand always said the same thing. The Lord would reply, "I will never leave you nor forsake you. I am closer than a brother." Read what the truth says:

Proverbs 18:24
A man that hath friends must shew himself friendly: and there is a friend that sticketh **closer than** a **brother**.

Hebrews 13:5
Let your conversation be without covetousness; and be content with such things as ye have: for he hath said, I will **never** leave thee, nor **forsake** thee.

This Mike lived a hard life, especially in the later years, fighting many health problems. His wounds are real. Some were caused from his lifestyle, and some were caused from the world, but despite his physical wounds, he is whole spiritually. He sings praises to God and is always looking for a person to encourage. He loves to tell others about his Father God and what He has done in his life. I thank God so much for bringing him into my life.

Though I have only known the second Mike for a short time, he has completely renewed my faith in pastors. He not only preaches the truth, but he also lives it the best he can. He said once during a sermon that our church should be a hospital to the spiritually sick, a beacon of light welcoming them, just as the hospital does for the physically sick. A hospital does not accept only certain types of sickness, but all those who are sick in any way. This means our spiritual hospital should be open twenty-four-seven to the sickest of the sin sick—the prostitutes, the beggars, the addicts, the lost, the betrayed, the struggling, wounded sinners we all once were, and still seem to be at times. This does not mean we accept the sin and agree with it; it means the opposite: We denounce the sin and give the cure. **This is why Jesus hates the sin, but loves the sinner.**

CHAPTER 19

Is It a Sin to Be Gay if I was Born This Way?

—∞∞—

To most Christians and non-Christians, this should be a simple chapter and a question with a short answer. In some ways, I guess it is, but the understanding of who this affects is not simple at all.

Homosexuality is something that has been part of our world's culture for a long time. It is engrained into our history from before Sodom and Gomorrah and the Roman Empire to the present day. Same-sex partners have been argued and debated through this time, and who am I to say it is right or wrong? My judgment on this would only be my opinion, and as I have said, it's not worth much. The question is, What does the truth say? Furthermore, let's look at what nature itself has to say on this topic. Lastly, I was asked, "What do I do if I feel I am attracted to someone who's the same sex?"

Let's see what the truth says.

We'll start this discussion by talking about nature briefly. Nature proclaims that homosexuality is the opposite and is a contradiction to its intentions, does it not? Natural reproduction and the mating system were made for a female and a male. Not mentioning the Bible, nature alone shows us the correct way to produce an offspring is through the joining of a male and a female. The human body, specifically the woman's, is made, in a way, to accept the man's body. The man's body produces the excretions the woman needs to fertilize her eggs. This is not rocket science in any way, and we all know that this is nature's intention for us. God says He created man, woman, and nature, and just like the truth, they were created in a way that served a purpose. We read about this in the book of Genesis.

Genesis 1:27

So God **created** man in his own image, in the image of God **created** he him; **male** and **female created** he them.

Genesis 5:2

Male and **female created** he them; and blessed them, and called their name Adam, in the day when they were **created**.

Genesis 1:19-28

[19]And the evening and the morning were the fourth day.

[20]And God said, Let the waters bring forth abundantly the moving creature that hath life, and fowl that may fly above the earth in the open firmament of heaven.

[21]And God created great whales, and every living creature that moveth, which the waters brought forth abundantly, after their kind, and every winged fowl after his kind: and God saw that it was good.

[22]And God blessed them, saying, Be fruitful, and multiply, and fill the waters in the seas, and let fowl multiply in the earth.

[23]And the evening and the morning were the fifth day.

[24]And God said, Let the earth bring forth the living creature after his kind, cattle, and creeping thing, and beast of the earth after his kind: and it was so.

[25]And God made the beast of the earth after his kind, and cattle after their kind, and every thing that creepeth upon the earth after his kind: and God saw that it was good.

[26]And God said, Let us make man in our image, after our likeness: and let them have dominion over the fish of the sea, and over the fowl of the air, and over the cattle, and over all the earth, and over every creeping thing that creepeth upon the earth.

[27]So God created man in his own image, in the image of God created he him; male and female created he them.

[28]And God blessed them, and God said unto them, Be fruitful, and multiply, and replenish the earth, and subdue it: and have dominion over the fish of the sea, and over the fowl of the air, and over every living thing that moveth upon the earth.

So now that we see God created man and woman to reproduce, and He created the animals, male and female, to mate and be together, what does He say about creating nature?

Genesis 1:9-13

[9]And God said, Let the waters under the heaven be gathered together unto one place, and let the dry land appear: and it was so.

[10]And God called the dry land Earth; and the gathering together of the waters called he Seas: and God saw that it was good.

[11]And God said, Let the earth bring forth grass, the herb yielding seed, and the fruit tree yielding fruit after his kind, whose seed is in itself, upon the earth: and it was so.

[12]And the earth brought forth grass, and herb yielding seed after his kind, and the tree yielding fruit, whose seed was in itself, after his kind: and God saw that it was good.

[13]And the evening and the morning were the third day.

God's intentions as shown in nature prove that male and female, specifically in mammals, were made to be joined for many reasons, one being to produce offspring. Nature is the obvious proof that what I am saying is truth. God's Word is the reason for nature, so this should be enough for us to obey this commandment. As we have seen in the past, and will continue to see, these two truths will not be enough because we want it our way, not His.

The truth is clear on same-sex partners, and my opinion and your opinion do not change God or make Him right or wrong. We like to judge God based on what we have done and what our friends and family members have done. We try to change His original design for our lives and others' because we want to fill our wishes, not His. If a person is attracted to someone of the same sex, we say the person was born this way, or even that God made the person this way. God has made each and every one of us in His image, with our own talents and uniqueness, but He never says He has made us to contradict His truth. God also says He made us, He loves each of us, and He knows everything about us.

Matthew 10:28-32 says:

[28]And fear not them which kill the body, but are not able to kill the soul: but rather fear him which is able to destroy both soul and body in hell.

[29]Are not two sparrows sold for a farthing? And one of them shall not fall on the ground without your Father.

[30]But the very hairs of your head are all numbered.

[31]Fear ye not therefore, ye are of more value than many sparrows.

[32]Whosoever therefore shall confess me before men, him will I confess also before my Father which is in heaven.

Also, **Luke 12:6-7** says:

[6]Are not five sparrows sold for two farthings, and not one of them is forgotten before God?

[7]But even the very hairs of your head are all numbered. Fear not

therefore: ye are of more value than many sparrows.

Furthermore, God tells us He loves us and wants us to have joy in Him first, and then He will show us the joy in a partner. He has made a way for us to follow His truth and laws. That way was and still is today Jesus Christ. Jesus came and died and rose again to overcome death so that we may overcome death through Him. He also came to follow everything His Father, God, commanded, and He never sinned, but He allowed Himself to die for our sins.

Now that this is complete, I follow God's laws and commandments out of love for what He has done for me in salvation. I follow this in my life through His Son, Jesus, and the Holy Spirit, not because He told me to. This is why those of us who are saved are not under the law anymore; we are under grace. When it is truly received, grace changes a person for life. The person's actions moving forward, although never perfect, are done out of love. When love is the reason you obey, that is of more value to God than any commandment obeyed without love. God does not approve of homosexuality, so that alone should be enough, but He has made a way for you to follow His ways, and do it with joy, never wanting to turn back.

Katy Perry has a song called "Firework." The video shows different people with different issues in their lives, wanting, but unable or unwilling, to be free from them. One is an overweight girl not swimming at a party, and another is a teenage boy who is gay and attracted to another boy, but doesn't have the courage to let the other know. The song encourages all of us to come out of our shells and be ourselves and explode like fireworks across the sky—to be beautiful, no matter what. I have to admit, the lyrics to this song are great, and in many ways, the message is encouraging. But in so many ways, it leads to destruction and misguidance. Without the video, you would never see what it is encouraging, but when you watch the video, it shows the guy finally walking straight up to the other and kissing him on his lips. What a statement that made then; the statement to God and us is, "I am going to be free in my ways, and if I have a feeling that I want to be gay, I am going to act on it and let it out. This will make me free because that's who I am." I ask myself, Well if this works for gay people, what about married people? If my wife and I are not getting along, and I see a beautiful woman across the room, I just want to get this love and emotion for her released so I can feel free from it, so what should I do? Should I just get up, go across the room, and kiss her? What if I just want to live my life without my kids anymore, if there is just too much responsibility being a father of four. What if I just want to leave and be free and let my fireworks be shown to the world? The message to "be beautiful because that's who I am, and that's how God made me" is a destroying message, and it comes in such a beautiful wrapping.

God has not made you to be gay, nor has He made you to be imprisoned. But God does want you to be free and allow His beauty to shine through you, which will make those fireworks look like duds. His purpose for you is to do just that, live free, not under a bunch of laws and commandments, but under grace, a grace given to you by a loving Father who wants to see exciting things happen in your life. He sent us the Holy Spirit to help us in this journey. Read the following verses.

John 14:26

But the **Comforter**, which is the Holy Ghost, whom the Father will **send** in my name, he shall teach you all things, and bring all things to your remembrance, whatsoever I have said unto you.

Luke 11:13

If ye then, being evil, know how to give good gifts unto your children: how much more shall your heavenly Father give the **Holy Spirit** to them that ask him?

Galatians 5:16-26

[16]This I say then, Walk in the Spirit, and ye shall not fulfil the lust of the flesh.

[17]For the flesh lusteth against the Spirit, and the Spirit against the flesh: and these are contrary the one to the other: so that ye cannot do the things that ye would.

[18]But if ye be led of the Spirit, ye are not under the law.

[19]Now the works of the flesh are manifest, which are these; Adultery, fornication, uncleanness, lasciviousness,

[20]idolatry, witchcraft, hatred, variance, emulations, wrath, strife,

seditions, heresies,

21envyings, murders, drunkenness, revellings, and such like: of the which I tell you before, as I have also told you in time past, that they which do such things shall not inherit the kingdom of God.

22But the fruit of the Spirit is love, joy, peace, longsuffering, gentleness, goodness, faith,

23meekness, temperance: against such there is no law.

24And they that are Christ's have crucified the flesh with the affections and lusts.

25If we live in the Spirit, let us also walk in the Spirit.

26Let us not be desirous of vain glory, provoking one another, envying one another.

We see the truth says that this song is works of the flesh. The works of the flesh feel great, especially in the beginning. They look great and are very attractive sometimes, but when you act on them, the result is always the same: destruction. I have stopped smoking for about ten years now. If I were to listen to the world, in many ways, it would encourage me to smoke. It would remind me of the flavor and the buzz I get. It would give me that flick of the hand I so enjoyed, not to mention the smoke passing through my lips. Yes, I am free to smoke and come out of my closet and let my fireworks blaze for all to see. I am a smoker and proud of it. What the world would not remind me of that the Spirit does is that it is killing me! The Spirit reminds me that smoking makes my breath stink and my clothes smell, that by my smoking, my boys are more likely to follow in these same footsteps, that if I don't get cancer, I will most definitely get some type of health problem, and I certainly won't feel like working out. No, these issues are of no concern to the flesh, which only says, "Feed me, feed me, and feed me more." The coming out and being gay is not a statement of who a person is, but a statement of who a person is in the flesh. The problem is if we continue to live in our flesh, it only leads to one thing: death, not eternal life, but eternal damnation. God does not want this for you! After all, you are His creation. He wants wonderful things for you, but the question now becomes, What do you want for yourself?

Now let's get to the million-dollar question: What if I do feel like I am attracted to another person who is of the same sex? What do I do then?

What you do with this question, as well as any other you have, no matter how big or small, is first seek Jesus for His answers. Seek God and His Word to bring this to light for you. When you seek God's Word, it will lead you to Jesus, and when you see Jesus, you will find the answers and the freedom He will bring to your life.

The Bible tells us:

Romans 8:2
For the law of the Spirit of life in Christ Jesus hath **made** me **free** from the law of sin and death.

Galatians 5:1

Stand fast therefore in the liberty wherewith Christ hath **made** us **free**, and be not entangled again with the yoke of bondage.

Jesus wants to be first in your life because He knows the true joy and freedom He can bring that the flesh will never accomplish. Jesus desires for you to be joyful and have peace, and He knows that will never come from feeding the flesh in any way.

The next step in the formula is to decide, Is your action, whether it is becoming gay or acting on any other emotion, really going to make you free, or is it something that you just desire to do? I personally don't have a desire for men, but I can admit that I have met good-looking men. There are men, especially on TV and in movies, who are there for their looks. Male models are hired because they represent whatever they are modeling in a positive way. I acknowledge their beauty, just as I acknowledge the beauty of a woman, but I realize God does not want me to marry or have intimate thoughts about either one, only my wife. I see beautiful women every day at work, and I have to get to know them because I am in sales. I feel the desires and the flesh calling sometimes, but to give in to these would not proclaim I have come out of my closet, and I am who God made me to be; it would only proclaim I have given in to my fleshly desires. In this case, only my desire would have been fulfilled, not God's, not my wife's, and not my children's. It all goes back to this: Who is your God, and who is your truth—is it the One who wrote it and proclaimed it through His Son, or is it all about YOU? You have become your own God with your own rules—who needs another?

One might ask, So if God did not make me to be gay, why am I so feminine as a male, and why am I so masculine as a female? The answer is God made us all to be special and unique. He wants to work in our lives, but we have to realize that what God made us to be is not what we have become. If I am fifty pounds overweight, God did not make me to be unhealthy; I chose to be. Maybe it was because I was given sweets as a child and am now addicted to them. Maybe I use food as a suppressant to problems in my life. The point is God did not make me to be overweight, and He does not want me to be unhealthy, so I must make some changes, with God's help, or I can live with what I have sown.

Galatians 6:7 says, "Be not deceived; God is not mocked: for **what**soever a man **sow**eth, that shall he also **reap**."

Being gay is no different from this. My characteristics are made by God, my parents, and my past; these things make up who I am. The God characteristics are true to your beauty, and His pieces of you were never made to contradict His ways. What we have to do, each and every one of us, is understand that we have to make the right decisions about the things we need to change and accept the things we can't. Either way, we don't get to give in to the flesh every time it wants something and say that is how God made us. On the contrary, that is how the world, not the Father, has made you. In ending, so there is no confusion, God does not like sin, and being gay is a contradiction to

Him, the truth, and nature, so it is a sin. But He does love you, and you are His child. Likewise, if my child rebels against my wishes, I did not want him to rebel, I certainly didn't make him rebel, and my hope is that he will not continue to rebel. My love for him, which is still there every day, is not based on his actions, but on his being a part of me. These are Scriptures that show being gay has never been okay in the eyes of our Father. It is not always easy to follow the truth; sometimes the first step is just accepting it.

1 Corinthians 6:9-10

[9]Know ye not that the unrighteous shall not inherit the kingdom of God? Be not deceived: neither fornicators, nor idolaters, nor adulterers, nor effeminate, nor abusers of themselves with mankind,

[10]nor thieves, nor covetous, nor drunkards, nor revilers, nor extortioners, shall inherit the kingdom of God.

Romans 1:27

And likewise also the men, leaving the natural use of the woman, burned in their lust one toward another; men with men working that which is unseemly, and receiving in themselves that recompence of their error which was meet.

Leviticus 18:22

Thou shalt not lie with mankind, as with womankind: it is abomination.

CHAPTER 20

<u>What's It Going to Take?</u>

———∽∽∽———

What does it take for someone to really turn his or her life over to Christ and receive this salvation the Bible talks about? And what does it take to receive not just the salvation and the assurance of life after death, but the change that is supposed to occur while the person is still living, a change the Bible says will bring me peace, strength, love, and joy? How do I receive this adoption to a family where I belong, and where I won't be forgotten, where I will grow and become something beautiful, where I am forgiven? What's it going to take? How many things must happen before I surrender my life to the Father so these things can happen? How much can I take before I am willing to give up my life for a life in Christ? How long will Christ continue to try and reach me? Will it ever be too late? Will He ever give up?

Lastly, once I am saved and have given my life to Him, can or will it be taken away for any reason, especially as a result of my actions in the future?

Luke 17:33 says, "Whosoever shall seek to save his life shall lose it; and whosoever shall lose his life shall preserve it."

For some people, salvation will never take place. The reason some will never receive this salvation is because no matter what, some people will never give up their lives to follow Christ. No matter how many times God touches their hearts, no matter what is taken away or given to them in their lives, they will always be just that: their lives. These people are in control. God may help when needed, but not as the captain, only an advisor. These souls are not lost because they were not wanted or desired by God; they are lost because the people did not desire or want the things of God. They denied the call to salvation and chose the call to themselves.

2 Timothy 3:1-17

[1]This know also, that in the last days perilous times shall come.

[2]For men shall be lovers of their own selves, covetous, boasters, proud, blasphemers, disobedient to parents, unthankful, unholy,

[3]without natural affection, trucebreakers, false accusers, incontinent, fierce, despisers of those that are good,

[4]traitors, heady, highminded, lovers of pleasures more than lovers of God;

[5]having a form of godliness, but denying the power thereof: from such turn away.

[6]For of this sort are they which creep into houses, and lead captive silly women laden with sins, led away with divers lusts,

[7]ever learning, and never able to come to the knowledge of the truth.

[8]Now as Jannes and Jambres withstood Moses, so do these also resist the truth: men of corrupt minds, reprobate concerning the faith.

[9]But they shall proceed no further: for their folly shall be manifest unto all men, as their's also was.

[10]But thou hast fully known my doctrine, manner of life, purpose, faith, longsuffering, charity, patience,

[11]persecutions, afflictions, which came unto me at Antioch, at Iconium, at Lystra; what persecutions I endured: but out of them all the Lord delivered me.

[12]Yea, and all that will live godly in Christ Jesus shall suffer persecution.

[13]But evil men and seducers shall wax worse and worse, deceiving, and being deceived.

[14]But continue thou in the things which thou hast learned and hast been assured of, knowing of whom thou hast learned them;

[15]and that from a child thou hast known the holy scriptures, which are able to make thee wise unto salvation through faith which is in Christ Jesus.

[16]All scripture is given by inspiration of God, and is profitable for doctrine, for reproof, for correction, for instruction in righteousness: [17]That the man of God may be perfect, thoroughly furnished unto all good works.

So if you are still alive, and I assume you are if you're reading this, what is it going to take to reach you? Will it be money? Is that your first love? Or how about good looks? Maybe it is power you desire. What does God have to do to prove He exists? The fact that He created the world is not enough, but He gave you His Word to follow and set you free. What more must God sacrifice to win your soul? He gave you His perfect Son, Jesus Christ, not only as a gift to salvation and a freedom to walk with God Himself, but also so that your sin is forgiven and overcome. What we must realize is there's nothing left for Him to give, for it has all been given. The ultimate Gift, the All in All, has been submitted, and for some, it is not enough; it will *never* be enough. For many, Jesus was not enough. That is why we have other religions, because we are not satisfied with what Jesus did; we think there must be more. We must continue to find new ways of satisfying our desires and lusts to fit our ways and not God's.

Maybe it will take a life-or-death instance to bring you to Him. Maybe the loss of a child or a bout with cancer is what it will take. So does God cause these things to happen to reach us? God does not have to dish these atrocities out to us, for sin does that abundantly. However, God will use these atrocities to bring many to Him.

Romans 8:28-31

[28]And we know that all things work together for good to them that love God, to them who are the called according to his purpose.

[29]For whom he did foreknow, he also did predestinate to be conformed to the image of his Son, that he might be the firstborn among many brethren.

³⁰Moreover whom he did predestinate, them he also called: and whom he called, them he also justified: and whom he justified, them he also glorified.

³¹What shall we then say to these things? If God be for us, who can be against us?

This Scripture does not mean God will send a bad thing into your life, for the world and mankind have brought these things to us from the beginning. We not only bring these things on ourselves, but we, in turn, pass them down to our children. What this Scripture does mean is God can use all these things, and He will allow these things to happen many times to reach the lost and glorify His name. God has and still does chastise and punish us; He allows us to go through many horrible things in this world, but these things are due to our sins, our parents' sins, and the world's sin. His plan was never to keep us in this world, but only for us to travel through it until the final days have come. So evaluate the events that happen in your life, and first take ownership of your actions. When an action is not something you have brought on yourself, or even if it is, get things right with yourself and the Lord, and realize there is nothing He cannot overcome, and He will overcome abundantly!

John 16:28-33 tells us:

²⁸I came forth from the Father, and am come into the world: again, I leave the world, and go to the Father.

²⁹His disciples said unto him, Lo, now speakest thou plainly, and speakest no proverb.

³⁰Now are we sure that thou knowest all things, and needest not that any man should ask thee: by this we believe that thou camest forth from God.

³¹Jesus answered them, Do ye now believe?

³²Behold, the hour cometh, yea, is now come, that ye shall be scattered, every man to his own, and shall leave me alone: and yet I am not alone, because the Father is with me.

³³These things I have spoken unto you, that in me ye might have peace. In the world ye shall have tribulation: but be of good cheer; I have overcome the world.

After it is all said and done, God has not only made a way back to Him through His Son, Jesus, but He also has freed us from our sins. He has promised us goodness and mercy all the days of our lives if we follow His ways. He has given us peace through the Holy Spirit to change our lives and walk with us daily. He has showed us He has not left us, but is coming back to bring us home to be with Him eternally.

Despite all of this, it is not enough for some, for many, for millions, because they will always choose themselves over Him.

So if God knows I will never choose Him—I will never give up my life or accept Jesus or any other sacrifice He has made—will He keep trying to reach me? **The answer is God never stops being**

God. He continues to send His children out into a world that rejects them to tell others of Him, as **Matthew 10:16** states: "Behold, I send you forth as sheep in the midst of wolves: be ye therefore wise as serpents, and harmless as doves."

He doesn't give up on us; instead, we give up on ourselves and Him. We come to an acceptance of ourselves, so much so that God gives us what we ask for: ourselves. He gives us the life we are striving for, a life filled with independence and self-serving ideals. He gives us our own lusts and our own direction. He even allows us to commit unthinkable deeds because no matter what we do, it will never change who He is. Our actions don't change God's will; they change our future.

Romans 1:18-32 tells us:

[18]For the wrath of God is revealed from heaven against all ungodliness and unrighteousness of men, who hold the truth in unrighteousness; [19]Because that which may be known of God is manifest in them; for God hath shewed it unto them.

[20]For the invisible things of him from the creation of the world are clearly seen, being understood by the things that are made, even his eternal power and Godhead; so that they are without excuse:

[21]Because that, when they knew God, they glorified him not as God, neither were thankful; but became vain in their imaginations, and their foolish heart was darkened.

[22]Professing themselves to be wise, they became fools,

²³and changed the glory of the uncorruptible God into an image made like to corruptible man, and to birds, and fourfooted beasts, and creeping things.

²⁴Wherefore God also gave them up to uncleanness through the lusts of their own hearts, to dishonour their own bodies between themselves:

²⁵Who changed the truth of God into a lie, and worshipped and served the creature more than the Creator, who is blessed for ever. Amen.

²⁶For this cause God gave them up unto vile affections: for even their women did change the natural use into that which is against nature:

²⁷And likewise also the men, leaving the natural use of the woman, burned in their lust one toward another; men with men working that which is unseemly, and receiving in themselves that recompence of their error which was meet.

²⁸And even as they did not like to retain God in their knowledge, God gave them over to a reprobate mind, to do those things which are not convenient;

²⁹Being filled with all unrighteousness, fornication, wickedness, covetousness, maliciousness; full of envy, murder, debate, deceit, malignity; whisperers,

³⁰backbiters, haters of God, despiteful, proud, boasters, inventors of evil things, disobedient to parents,

³¹without understanding, covenantbreakers, without natural affection, implacable, unmerciful:

³²Who knowing the judgment of God, that they which commit such things are worthy of death, not only do the same, but have pleasure in them that do them.

This is why God gave us grace. God realizes we are not sinless; that is why we needed a sacrifice for our sins, someone willing to pay our debt, so if that debt is paid for those living in Christ, we are under His grace. God uses this grace to forgive us and continue to care for us as we live in this world. He uses this grace to pick us back up when we have failed Him and ourselves. He uses this grace to help us overcome the things that keep us down in life. The sacrifice, plus the grace, plus the Holy Spirit's living in us equals unity with Christ.

Read **John 17:13-23:**

¹³And now come I to thee; and these things I speak in the world, that they might have my joy fulfilled in themselves.

¹⁴I have given them thy word; and the world hath hated them, because they are not of the world, even as I am not of the world.

¹⁵I pray not that thou shouldest take them out of the world, but that thou shouldest keep them from the evil.

¹⁶They are not of the world, even as I am not of the world.

¹⁷Sanctify them through thy truth: thy word is truth.

¹⁸As thou hast sent me into the world, even so have I also sent them into the world.

¹⁹And for their sakes I sanctify myself, that they also might be

sanctified through the truth.

[20]Neither pray I for these alone, but for them also which shall believe on me through their word;

[21]That they all may be one; as thou, Father, art in me, and I in thee, that they also may be one in us: that the world may believe that thou hast sent me.

[22]And the glory which thou gavest me I have given them; that they may be one, even as we are one:

[23]I in them, and thou in me, that they may be made perfect in one; and that the world may know that thou hast sent me, and hast loved them, as thou hast loved me.

This was one of the last prayers Jesus prayed before His death—and when Jesus asked, God gave. So when you're saved by Christ, He is always there. He says, "I will never leave you or forsake you." We read this in Hebrews 13:5: "Let your conversation be without covetousness; and be content with such things as ye have: for he hath said, I will **never leave** thee, nor **forsake** thee."

Again, the problem is with those who never receive this adoption, those who may believe, but never receive. Will God give up on you? No. The question is, Will *you* give up on *Him*? Will you give up to the point that nothing will allow His Word to penetrate your heart? Though you have heard His Word, and have felt the Spirit move, you hold on to your life, even though that life has betrayed you in many ways. It is full of death, vanity, and riches, but there is no peace. You are healthy at times, but getting older every day. Every day you are getting closer to death, a death that is certain for all, but only looked forward to by some.

You ask, Once I have given Him my all, could He or would He ever give me back?

Can I lose this salvation by my actions, now or in the future, even up to the point of suicide?

The joyous answer to that: No way, no how, absolutely, unquestionably NO. He would not and could not, as He has never been, nor will He ever be, a liar.

How can I be so sure of this? That is by one reason and one reason alone, because He tells me so.

Read **Romans 8:35-39**:

[35]Who shall separate us from the love of Christ? Shall tribulation, or distress, or persecution, or famine, or nakedness, or peril, or sword? [36]As it is written, For thy sake we are killed all the day long; we are accounted as sheep for the slaughter.
[37]Nay, in all these things we are more than conquerors through him that loved us.
[38]For I am persuaded, that neither death, nor life, nor angels, nor principalities, nor powers, nor things present, nor things to come,
[39]nor height, nor depth, nor any other creature, shall be able to separate us from the love of God, which is in Christ Jesus our Lord.

As powerful as this Scripture is, what happens is after salvation, all of us mess up in life. We make mistakes; we don't listen to everything God is telling us to do. When we start to slip, many of us repent to God, acknowledging we have messed up and accepting the fact that we need to do better. When we do this, God is faithful to forgive.

Sometimes He allows us to fall after our mistakes and suffer the consequences. The important thing to note is He is involved. He is now not only our God, but also our Father. He has a responsibility to us as His children, and unlike us in many ways, He is not slack when it comes to taking care of His family. The point is the gift God gave through His Son, Jesus Christ, is an unreturnable item. He did not need us to give this gift, and nothing we ever did or ever will do is deserving of such a gift. The salvation gift was His to give, and Jesus accepted the cross to give it. Then if we accept this gift wholeheartedly and receive salvation, nothing we ever do can take it away. God does not give back His children; He only molds them into the vessels of His desire. We are vessels of meekness and love, changed by an ever-loving Father and a mighty Holy Spirit.

So the question then becomes, Why not have the best of both worlds—sin and salvation? The question has already been asked and answered. Look to Romans 6:1-7:

[1]What shall we say then? Shall we continue in sin, that grace may abound?

²God forbid. How shall we, that are dead to sin, live any longer therein?

³Know ye not, that so many of us as were baptized into Jesus Christ were baptized into his death?

⁴Therefore we are buried with him by baptism into death: that like as Christ was raised up from the dead by the glory of the Father, even so we also should walk in newness of life.

⁵For if we have been planted together in the likeness of his death, we shall be also in the likeness of his resurrection:

⁶Knowing this, that our old man is crucified with him, that the body of sin might be destroyed, that henceforth we should not serve sin.

⁷For he that is dead is freed from sin.

Paul made the claim, and the answer is evident. When you have truly been saved, you are no longer who you were spiritually. Though you are the same person in the same body, now the Holy Spirit lives in you, and so your nature has changed. You are dead to the old man, and all things are new. You may sin, but you will not love sin, as you did before. You may desire it, but it has lost its internal savor. True salvation has changed everyone who has ever received it, and once changed, you are His child, never to be given away.

You may ask, Is suicide unforgivable? While it is awful, cowardly, and unfaithful, it is not unforgivable. Suicide is a sin, but God says when you are saved, all your sins are forgiven as far as the east is from the west. What suicide is, however, is giving up. Speaking of giving up (spiritually speaking, that is), that is exactly what you did when you gave your life to Christ (or will do when you do so); it is "spiritual suicide."

If you want to give up on life, and you are tired of this world and of living in it, commit "spiritual suicide." This entails dying to yourself. After all, that's what you're tired of anyway. Die to the world, as that's where your problems are. Die to your fleshly desires, for they are the cancer destroying your life a little every day. Die to all of this, and find your new life in Christ. Remember, death on earth with Christ is life eternally in joy, but death on earth without Christ is death eternally, with no escape, only pain. Christ will never ask anyone to give up joy, peace, love, confidence, strength, beauty, or freedom; these are the things that come with salvation. But we would rather believe the lie Satan tells. He says to hold on to what we think is happiness, while chasing our tails the whole time and never finding our desires fulfilled, but only finding emptiness.

The Story of G.

This story is about a personal struggle a family I care about is going through, and how the mistake of one impacts many. I have a friend who has several children, who all grew up going to church together. He was a great father and showed his children love and compassion, as well as guided them in the right direction. He was a stern father when it came to behavior, but he taught his children the way of Jesus and salvation. This father and his wife lived near us years ago. We were all close socially, and we even attended church together. Our children played together, we worshiped together, and this father was a leader in the church. They had to move away due to his job, but we stayed in touch by phone and saw one another once in a while when they would visit. Over the last years, this couple has seen three of their children get married, while the youngest two are still at home. All seemed well with this family, until I found out the father had been cheating on his wife with prostitutes as well as engaging in online relationships and pornography. So what happened? Was it all a lie? I am sure if I was their child, I would be asking the same question of my father. I would ask whether all the stuff he had taught me was a lie. After all, why would he do this to us if he is saved? The answer: Saved or not, we all struggle with the flesh. The lie Satan tells us is to go just so far, and no one gets hurt. Before you know it, the line gets further and further away, and when you turn around, you can't find your way back. The actions of this man's sin have caused a lot of problems for the people he loves, but does it mean he is not saved? It just means that although he gave in to this desire, he will never get inner peace from it. He realizes it was a mistake to do it, but the flesh is calling out for it. The flesh is calling out for it to fill a void in his life at a time when his marriage needed help. This father will always be God's child and will need that relationship now more than ever. God did not plan for him to do this, and He did not want him to do this, but He will never abandon him because he did it.

CHAPTER 21

Churches, Clubs, Whatever—They're All the Same

———⟨∞⟩———

When I say the word "church," what do you think of? For many, it's a place you remember as a child, maybe a small country building with close family and friends, and kids running around and having Sunday dinners with the preacher. For others, it is a big cathedral with solemn music and properly dressed attendees, and everyone trying to act his or her best for the time allotted. For others, church is a small shack barely standing, with people hoping for God to send help. The people may be hungry for food and thirsty for water, in need of medical attention, and looking for help in any way they can get it. Still for others, church is a place of healing, a place of security, where they feel at home. Lastly, for many, church is a place of fakes and lies, a place where people, from the preacher to the people sitting in the pews, put on the act, and the act is never good enough. At this so-called "club," I mean church, everyone is saying what not to do and how to live. Most are doing what they shouldn't and living how they want, justifying their actions every step of the way. So what is your church? Is it a place at all? Have you ever even been to one? Is it a place you have decided is not for you, maybe because the hypocrites all go there? You see them outside of church, and you see how they really live. Do you want to go but feel you need to make some changes first, and need to be a better person before you start?

The question at hand is, Is church a place for everyone, or just for some? Do you really have to go to church to please God or at least stay in His good graces? Do you really feel you belong there?

Let's start with the definition of this place called church.

First of all, "church" is a pretty wide and dynamic word. Everybody seems to be going to a church, but the question is, What is church?

Defining "Church"

The definition of "church" at its basic root is: a building for public and especially Christian worship.

Jesus, being of Jewish heritage, along with all the other Jewish people, worshiped in temples or synagogues. A **temple** (from the Latin word *templum*) is a Roman structure reserved for religious or spiritual activities, such as prayer and sacrifice, or analogous rites, according to Merriam-Webster.

Jesus went to the temple and taught when He was very young. Read **Luke 2:42-49**:

⁴²And when he was twelve years old, they went up to Jerusalem after the custom of the feast.

⁴³And when they had fulfilled the days, as they returned, the child Jesus tarried behind in Jerusalem; and Joseph and his mother knew not of it.

⁴⁴But they, supposing him to have been in the company, went a day's journey; and they sought him among their kinsfolk and acquaintance.

⁴⁵And when they found him not, they turned back again to Jerusalem, seeking him.

⁴⁶And it came to pass, that after three days they found him in the temple, sitting in the midst of the doctors, both hearing them, and asking them questions.

⁴⁷And all that heard him were astonished at his understanding and answers.

⁴⁸And when they saw him, they were amazed: and his mother said unto him, Son, why hast thou thus dealt with us? Behold, thy father and I have sought thee sorrowing.

⁴⁹And he said unto them, How is it that ye sought me? Wist ye not that I must be about my Father's business?

So the history of church is very old, and places of worship have been around since the beginning of man. Adam and Eve needed noplace to worship, for their very existence was worship to God. They walked with Him and were with Him every day, but as soon as they chose to rebel, the consequences came. The rebellion caused a separation between them and God, and sacrifice was needed; an offering was needed as penance for man's sin. The first church was just an altar. Read **Genesis 4:1-7**:

[1]And Adam knew Eve his wife; and she conceived, and bare Cain, and said, I have gotten a man from the LORD.

[2]And she again bare his brother Abel. And Abel was a keeper of sheep, but Cain was a tiller of the ground.

[3]And in process of time it came to pass, that Cain brought of the fruit of the ground an offering unto the LORD.

[4]And Abel, he also brought of the firstlings of his flock and of the fat thereof. And the LORD had respect unto Abel and to his offering:

[5]But unto Cain and to his offering he had not respect. And Cain was very wroth, and his countenance fell.

[6]And the LORD said unto Cain, Why art thou wroth? And why is thy countenance fallen?

[7]If thou doest well, shalt thou not be accepted? And if thou doest not well, sin lieth at the door. And unto thee shall be his desire, and thou shalt rule over him.

So the altar was the first church, a place to come and acknowledge and worship God as well as give Him your time and first fruits. This showed God was the priority in your life, and helped one get the forgiveness needed for sins and rebellion. Since the rebellion, God has always required these things to be done. They have never been an option, but a commandment. In the previous story, notice that even in the very first church, there was one who attended for the right reason, and another, for the wrong. Abel gave the better offering because it came from his heart; it came from his best. Many say his gift was better because it was a living animal and was needed as a sacrifice. Look at what God said to Cain about his gift's being accepted.

While Abel gave the best of what he had and gave in love, Cain gave out of abundance of what he had and because he knew he was supposed to. Notice God still loved both men, but He was not going to compliment one for doing something for the wrong reasons.

Why does God expect this from us? Why make God the priority in your life? Well, let's see, do you expect to be a priority in your child's life? You created your child, and have clothed him, fed him, loved him, and cared for him the best you've been able. Is it wrong to expect to be considered important to him? Would it not be an insult if he disregarded all these things and paid you no attention? We even expect our pets to appreciate what we do for them. If my dog never acknowledged me as her master, I wouldn't consider her a very good dog. Yet we want to live our lives in a way that doesn't include God or show any appreciation for Him at all. What if your child did what you said all the time, but only because you said to? And then what if another child did the same jobs in a way that said, "I love you, and that is why I am doing this, not just because you told me to"? We all know which we would honor more. Both did the job, but only one did it for the right reason. God sees the intentions of your gift and honor to Him; He knows what your treasure is.

Matthew 6:21 states, "For where your treasure is, there will your heart be also."

What about the sin—why is forgiveness needed? We have laws every day that we abide by, and even though some people do not follow these laws, they are there for a reason. We need people to follow these laws for many reasons. When the laws are broken, we have consequences for this because a law without consequence is not a law; it is a request. There would be no value in keeping it, nor would it protect anyone if it had no consequences. This is a staple in our history and world in every form of society that ever was, or ever will be. There are rules and laws, and they are set up for many reasons, mainly to keep order in some way or another. Forgiveness for these broken rules or laws is required by God because without forgiveness, without a debt being paid for the broken law, there is no law, only chaos and anarchy.

Read **Leviticus 26:3-12**:

[3]If ye walk in my statutes, and keep my commandments, and do them;

[4]Then I will give you rain in due season, and the land shall yield her increase, and the trees of the field shall yield their fruit.

[5]And your threshing shall reach unto the vintage, and the vintage shall reach unto the sowing time: and ye shall eat your bread to the

full, and dwell in your land safely.

[6]And I will give peace in the land, and ye shall lie down, and none shall make you afraid: and I will rid evil beasts out of the land, neither shall the sword go through your land.

[7]And ye shall chase your enemies, and they shall fall before you by the sword.

[8]And five of you shall chase an hundred, and an hundred of you shall put ten thousand to flight: and your enemies shall fall before you by the sword.

[9]For I will have respect unto you, and make you fruitful, and multiply you, and establish my covenant with you.

[10]And ye shall eat old store, and bring forth the old because of the new.

[11]And I set my tabernacle among you: and my soul shall not abhor you.

[12]And I will walk among you, and will be your God, and ye shall be my people.

We did not do these things; we still don't today. And God said if we do not obey, this will happen:

[14]But if ye will not hearken unto me, and will not do all these commandments;

[15]and if ye shall despise my statutes, or if your soul abhor my judgments, so that ye will not do all my commandments, but that ye

break my covenant:

[16]I also will do this unto you; I will even appoint over you terror, consumption, and the burning ague, that shall consume the eyes, and cause sorrow of heart: and ye shall sow your seed in vain, for your enemies shall eat it.

[17]And I will set my face against you, and ye shall be slain before your enemies: they that hate you shall reign over you; and ye shall flee when none pursueth you.

[18]And if ye will not yet for all this hearken unto me, then I will punish you seven times more for your sins.

Leviticus 26:14-18

So the first church, even as an altar, was a place for direction, a place for redemption and refuge. It was a place to start anew, a place of freshness. This redemption and refuge and starting over was an ongoing event because we could not and would not follow the law of God. Then God provided a permanent way to keep His laws in place. This way did not come at a small price. Just as we have consequences for our laws and a debt needs to be paid, so it is with God's law. This is why animal sacrifices were made before Jesus, and that is why Jesus gave His life on the cross, so we could have a constant renewal of God's grace. We would be able to walk in His ways out of love and not duty.

We read in **John 14:12-18**:

¹²Verily, verily, I say unto you, He that believeth on me, the works that I do shall he do also; and greater works than these shall he do; because I go unto my Father.

¹³And whatsoever ye shall ask in my name, that will I do, that the Father may be glorified in the Son.

¹⁴If ye shall ask any thing in my name, I will do it.

¹⁵If ye love me, keep my commandments.

¹⁶And I will pray the Father, and he shall give you another Comforter, that he may abide with you for ever;

¹⁷Even the Spirit of truth; whom the world cannot receive, because it seeth him not, neither knoweth him: but ye know him; for he dwelleth with you, and shall be in you.

¹⁸I will not leave you comfortless: I will come to you.

Jesus knows the heart, and He desires that our giving and forgiveness be done out of love, not duty. The only way we can have this love is by receiving and believing upon Him. At that time, He sends the Holy Spirit, which gives us the ability to have this heart.

So what about today's church, God's intended church? The rules are not much different than they were before. It is supposed to be a place for broken and rebellious people who need redemption and a new beginning. Church does not begin in a building; it begins in your heart. That is the only temple God will accept. When you have given Him this place, He will reside there, and church begins and never ends. After this church has taken root in your heart, the next church God is looking to start is in your home, whether it is a cardboard box, a park bench, or a mansion on the hill. Wherever you wake up in the morning and go to sleep at night, where you eat, work, and play—that is the church God requires you to attend. The name of that church is ALL MY LIFE CHURCH.

This church is a place that can never be burned down and never dies. It's a place you are always in and where you can worship God freely. This church is where you meet God face to face every day, and you can walk with Him continuously. This is what **1 Thessalonians 5:8-18** says about it:

⁸But let us, who are of the day, be sober, putting on the breastplate of faith and love; and for an helmet, the hope of salvation.

⁹For God hath not appointed us to wrath, but to obtain salvation by our Lord Jesus Christ,

¹⁰Who died for us, that, whether we wake or sleep, we should live together with him.

¹¹Wherefore comfort yourselves together, and edify one another, even as also ye do.

¹²And we beseech you, brethren, to know them which labour among you, and are over you in the Lord, and admonish you;

¹³and to esteem them very highly in love for their work's sake. And be at peace among yourselves.

¹⁴Now we exhort you, brethren, warn them that are unruly, comfort the feebleminded, support the weak, be patient toward all men.

¹⁵See that none render evil for evil unto any man; but ever follow that which is good, both among yourselves, and to all men.

¹⁶Rejoice evermore.

¹⁷Pray without ceasing.

¹⁸In every thing give thanks: for this is the will of God in Christ Jesus concerning you.

When you find this church in your life, it will be a wonderful place for you! No one will have to ask you to go or remind you to be there. This church will give you an everlasting refuge, and no matter what anyone does, he or she cannot take it away. This is the church of your heart and soul. The problem with this church is many people have to go to the next church we will discuss to find where this one is. The woman discussed in the following story was not looking for a public church to go to, as she knew she was not good enough. Her sins and mistakes showed this. However, she was looking for help, and that is when Jesus invited her to His church.

⁶Now Jacob's well was there. Jesus therefore, being wearied with his journey, sat thus on the well: and it was about the sixth hour.

⁷There cometh a woman of Samaria to draw water: Jesus saith unto her, Give me to drink.

⁸(For his disciples were gone away unto the city to buy meat.)

⁹Then saith the woman of Samaria unto him, How is it that thou, being a Jew, askest drink of me, which am a woman of Samaria? For

the Jews have no dealings with the Samaritans.

[10]Jesus answered and said unto her, If thou knewest the gift of God, and who it is that saith to thee, Give me to drink; thou wouldest have asked of him, and he would have given thee living water.

[11]The woman saith unto him, Sir, thou hast nothing to draw with, and the well is deep: from whence then hast thou that living water?

[12]Art thou greater than our father Jacob, which gave us the well, and drank thereof himself, and his children, and his cattle?

[13]Jesus answered and said unto her, Whosoever drinketh of this water shall thirst again:

[14]But whosoever drinketh of the water that I shall give him shall never thirst; but the water that I shall give him shall be in him a well of water springing up into everlasting life.

[15]The woman saith unto him, Sir, give me this water, that I thirst not, neither come hither to draw.

[16]Jesus saith unto her, Go, call thy husband, and come hither.

[17]The woman answered and said, I have no husband. Jesus said unto her, Thou hast well said, I have no husband:

[18]For thou hast had five husbands; and he whom thou now hast is not thy husband: in that saidst thou truly.

[19]The woman saith unto him, Sir, I perceive that thou art a prophet.

[20]Our fathers worshipped in this mountain; and ye say, that in Jerusalem is the place where men ought to worship.

[21]Jesus saith unto her, Woman, believe me, the hour cometh, when ye shall neither in this mountain, nor yet at Jerusalem, worship the

Father.

[22]Ye worship ye know not what: we know what we worship: for salvation is of the Jews.

[23]But the hour cometh, and now is, when the true worshippers shall worship the Father in spirit and in truth: for the Father seeketh such to worship him.

[24]God is a Spirit: and they that worship him must worship him in spirit and in truth.

[25]The woman saith unto him, I know that Messias cometh, which is called Christ: when he is come, he will tell us all things.

[26]Jesus saith unto her, I that speak unto thee am he.

John 4:6-26

Lastly, I guess the church we think of mostly is a place God expects us to attend. It is a place with others, some like us and some not, where all are in need of comfort, refuge, and direction. It is a place where we gather to celebrate our Father, a place of renewing our strength and learning from one another. This church is a place where we come together as many, yet become one as we gather and worship our Father, our Creator, or Savior, and our Friend. This is a place that God expects you to attend. Let me say it again: YES, God does expect you to go to this place of gathering with others, some of whom are saved, and some of whom are not. But why? you ask. The real reason God wants us at this place is for worshiping, renewed strengthening, conditioning, and training. God's church is supposed to be a place for renewal of the spirit, where we can help ourselves and, more importantly, help others. It is a place to care for the widows and orphans. It is a place to prepare for one thing and one thing only: TO TAKE HIS WORD OUT INTO A LOST AND DYING WORLD, not just to preach and speak His Word, but to live it, always being ready to give an answer to why you have peace.

[8]Finally, be ye all of one mind, having compassion one of another, love as brethren, be pitiful, be courteous:

[9]Not rendering evil for evil, or railing for railing: but contrariwise blessing; knowing that ye are thereunto called, that ye should inherit a blessing.

[10]For he that will love life, and see good days, let him refrain his tongue from evil, and his lips that they speak no guile:

[11]Let him eschew evil, and do good; let him seek peace, and ensue it.

[12]For the eyes of the Lord are over the righteous, and his ears are open unto their prayers: but the face of the Lord is against them that do evil.

[13]And who is he that will harm you, if ye be followers of that which is good?

[14]But and if ye suffer for righteousness' sake, happy are ye: and be not afraid of their terror, neither be troubled;

[15]But sanctify the Lord God in your hearts: and be ready always to give an answer to every man that asketh you a reason of the hope that is in you with meekness and fear:

[16]Having a good conscience; that, whereas they speak evil of you, as of evildoers, they may be ashamed that falsely accuse your good conversation in Christ.

[17]For it is better, if the will of God be so, that ye suffer for well doing, than for evil doing.

1 Peter 3:8-17

This is where the difference between God's church and our clubs comes in. Let's break these both down, and I think then we will see where we have gone wrong. Furthermore, we will see if we attend a real church, or just another club.

Psalm 26:1-3 tells us:

[1]Judge me, O LORD; for I have walked in mine integrity: I have trusted also in the LORD; therefore I shall not slide.

[2]Examine me, O LORD, and prove me; try my reins and my heart.

[3]For thy lovingkindness is before mine eyes: and I have walked in thy truth.

The club (man's church) prepares us to come to it, whereas God's church prepares us to go out *from* it into the world. Think about it. Is your church a place you have to be dressed up to attend, or be looked upon as lesser than others? Is it a place that welcomes you in, even if you're not one of the major families that have attended the church for a long period? Is it a place that is preparing its members to go out into the world to tell people about and show them the love of Christ, or is it focused on what is always happening within its own walls? Is it a place giving to missions and taking care of the widows and orphans, or is it a place focused on making the pastor rich? Is your church a place of refuge, or is it a place of strife and discontentment? Is it a place that is more worried about who attends than about who is going out and attending the lost? Is this place focused on the preaching of the Word and what to do with it, or is it about a man who preaches great whom people want to hear again next week? Does this place cause you to want to help others in need, or focus on helping it get better? Does your church care what color you are when you come there, or if you're rich or poor? Is it a place of warmth, or a place of bitterness?

God's true church can be defined as simply as this: It is a place for salvation and forgiveness. It is a place where people gather to worship and prepare, and then go forth from. Everything else is fluff—the parties, the buildings, the amusements, the ceremonies . . . . These are good things for many reasons, but are not required. The church is one unit working together as the hands, feet, eyes, and ears of God. Today, we are working on that method, trying to make that apparent, but the problem is we keep dividing over differences instead of becoming one body of Christ. Instead, we become little bodies of Christ spread out all over. One day, though, God says we will all be one body, not divided, but united. Believe it or not, we will be His bride. We read this in the following verses.

Revelation 21:2

And I John saw the holy city, new Jerusalem, coming down from God out of heaven, prepared as a **bride** adorned for her husband.

Revelation 21:9

And there came unto me one of the seven angels which had the seven vials full of the seven last plagues, and talked with me, saying, Come hither, I will shew thee the **bride**, the Lamb's wife.

Revelation 22:17

And the Spirit and the **bride** say, Come. And let him that heareth say, Come. And let him that is athirst come. And whosoever will, let him take the water of life freely.

Who gets the blame for messing our churches up? Who can we string up and punish for this deed? Who is responsible for the church and the state it is in? If we can find the responsible parties, maybe we can fix it. The answer is almost assuredly the same as with almost any other organization that is not working right. It is the leaders of our church today and in the past. We are the examples of what a Christian should be. We are the role models, and what have we done with this great calling? We have molested children and hidden it. We have murdered our neighbor with our thoughts. We come up with our own ideas instead of using God's Word. We have made church a place of volume and membership, a place of wealth and not service. At worst, we have made God good and evil. His happiness with us is based on how good we can follow His rules, man's rules, somebody's rules. We are the responsible party, changing from looking after others to looking after ourselves. We became the masters instead of the servants. We split the people with our legalism and personal beliefs, and start all over again in a new place. I can say positive things about our churches also. There are good leaders, not perfect ones, but leaders who listen to God and live the way He desires. These are the men and women who keep a hope alive for the next generation.

Most sick people want a doctor, and most people who are sin sick want a spiritual leader. If a patient comes in and needs medicine to save his life, and the doctor starts telling the patient about all his symptoms instead of curing them, what use is the doctor? Maybe the doctor decides to tell the patient what he did wrong before he helps him. What use is that? What about the doctor who gives the patient the cure, but doesn't lead him in the direction that'll keep him from coming back? In the church, leadership is our failure, and the only way to change this course is to stop leading and start serving. If we serve, the leadership will come. The people will follow and serve as well. Do it at a higher level than ever expected, a righteous, joyful, godly level. Then we will have a real church, God's church.

Truth statement: A church's success is measured on its missions and the reason for those missions—both the missions of the leaders to the people, and the missions of the people to the world.

CHAPTER 22

Where Does Sin Begin and the Truth End?

⸻ ⊗⊗⊗ ⸻

After all the chapters discussed previously, this question still comes up: Where does sin begin and the truth end? Who decides what sin is and what it is not? What should I stop doing, if anything? What can I depend on to be the truth, especially in today's world? Does following the truth mean I won't have any fun anymore? And is there too much truth?

First, where does sin begin? The truth says it begins as soon as you are born. It may not immediately be your sin, but is definitely by your parents. They certainly aren't perfect, and they sure make mistakes. Some are worse than others, but they all bring their sins upon their children's table. These sins range from the constant bad attitudes and yelling at you or around you, to a mother who smokes, affecting her child's breathing, to a mother who is eating bad foods or even taking drugs while breast-feeding. Let's not leave the dad out of all this. Many of us either leave or work so much that the child doesn't feel the presence of a male holding him or her. I may be a great dad, who does pretty good most of the time, but I do get angry sometimes and take it out on the child. No matter how good your parents are, their sins overflow onto you as soon as you are born. You are also born into a world full of imperfect people who do a lot of very bad things. Depending on the day you arrive, their garbage is dumped on you as well. It does not take long for us to take over our surroundings and commit our own sins, but it is not just learned; we are born with this as our nature. We have to teach children to do good; they do bad all on their own.

So if sin is all around me from the time I am born, who defines the word "sin"? Who decides what is right and wrong for me in my life?

James 4:1-17 says:

[1]From whence come wars and fightings among you? Come they not hence, even of your lusts that war in your members?
[2]Ye lust, and have not: ye kill, and desire to have, and cannot obtain: ye fight and war, yet ye have not, because ye ask not.
[3]Ye ask, and receive not, because ye ask amiss, that ye may consume it upon your lusts.
[4]Ye adulterers and adulteresses, know ye not that the friendship of the world is enmity with God? Whosoever therefore will be a friend of the world is the enemy of God.
[5]Do ye think that the scripture saith in vain, The spirit that dwelleth in us lusteth to envy?

⁶But he giveth more grace. Wherefore he saith, God resisteth the proud, but giveth grace unto the humble.

⁷Submit yourselves therefore to God. Resist the devil, and he will flee from you.

⁸Draw nigh to God, and he will draw nigh to you. Cleanse your hands, ye sinners; and purify your hearts, ye double minded.

⁹Be afflicted, and mourn, and weep: let your laughter be turned to mourning, and your joy to heaviness.

¹⁰Humble yourselves in the sight of the Lord, and he shall lift you up.

¹¹Speak not evil one of another, brethren. He that speaketh evil of his brother, and judgeth his brother, speaketh evil of the law, and judgeth the law: but if thou judge the law, thou art not a doer of the law, but a judge.

¹²There is one lawgiver, who is able to save and to destroy: who art thou that judgest another?

¹³Go to now, ye that say, To day or to morrow we will go into such a city, and continue there a year, and buy and sell, and get gain:

¹⁴Whereas ye know not what shall be on the morrow. For what is your life? It is even a vapour, that appeareth for a little time, and then vanisheth away.

¹⁵For that ye ought to say, If the Lord will, we shall live, and do this, or that.

¹⁶But now ye rejoice in your boastings: all such rejoicing is evil.

¹⁷Therefore to him that knoweth to do good, and doeth it not, to him it is sin.

God says He wrote the line for what is right and wrong, what should be done and what should not be done, in His original laws, after the Fall of man. It was called the Ten Commandments. They are worth mentioning.

- Thou shalt have no other gods before me. (Other "gods" can include possessions, power, or prominence.)

- Thou shalt not make unto thee any graven image. (Worship no idols.)

- Thou shalt not take the name of the Lord thy God in vain.

- Remember the Sabbath day, to keep it holy.

- Honour thy father and thy mother.

- Thou shalt not kill.

- Thou shalt not commit adultery.

- Thou shalt not steal.

- Thou shalt not bear false witness against thy neighbour.

- Thou shalt not covet thy neighbour's house, thou shalt not covet thy neighbour's wife, nor his manservant, nor his maidservant, nor his ox, nor his ass, nor any thing that is thy neighbour's.

How many of these have you broken in your life, or should I say, how many times have you broken these? Our ancestors could not follow these rules/laws, and neither can we. God made a way for us to follow these rules by writing them in our hearts and minds. This only happened because Jesus gave His life willingly and died on a cross for the sins of the world. Because of this, we are forgiven and able to receive this gift of grace. When we receive this gift, the truth says the entire Word of God, right and wrong, is written and placed in our minds and hearts. This takes place because the Holy Spirit is the Word of God and makes His home in us.

Hebrews 10:16

This is the covenant that I will make with them after those days, saith the Lord, I will put my laws into their **heart**s, and in their **mind**s will I write them.

John 14:26

But the Comforter, which is the Holy Ghost, whom the Father will send in my name, he shall teach you all things, and bring all things to your remembrance, whatsoever I have said unto you.

John 15:26-27

²⁶But when the Comforter is come, whom I will send unto you from the Father, even the Spirit of truth, which proceedeth from the Father, he shall testify of me:

²⁷And ye also shall bear witness, because ye have been with me from the beginning.

John 16:13-15

¹³Howbeit when he, the Spirit of truth, is come, he will guide you into all truth: for he shall not speak of himself; but whatsoever he shall hear, that shall he speak: and he will show you things to come.

¹⁴He shall glorify me: for he shall receive of mine, and shall show it unto you.

¹⁵All things that the Father hath are mine: therefore said I, that he shall take of mine, and shall shew it unto you.

The disciples were having a hard time understanding what Jesus was saying and why He was leaving. When you study the Gospels, you will see how confused the disciples were at times when Jesus spoke to them.

Now we see the reason for the Holy Spirit is not only to change our nature, but also to have an entity, an actual spiritual person, in us, one in the Trinity residing in our bodies after salvation has taken place. This Spirit changes our nature so instead of running from God's laws, we chase His laws. We want to follow them because of a desire He has placed in us. This is not a desire we have placed in ourselves, so all the yoga and self-help books will never bring this type of change to your life. This is the reason why when a person gets truly saved, you will see a real, unexplainable difference in them. It is not a change they could ever bring to themselves; it can only come from God. Also note chapter 15; as you live and when you die, it is the Spirit that is a witness to your salvation being real or of self.

Back to the laws and rules, I want to know why God made laws we could not possibly follow. He says He made the laws to be followed, with each one being part of the formula of perfection. When God walked with Adam and Eve, the points/laws were all obeyed, and God and man were together in one accord. When the sin entered, the formula was broken, and God separated His union with them due to this. God's laws (formula) have been around since before they were ever spoken or broken; they were just not needed until we had sinned. God did not give us the law because we could follow it; He gave it to show us what the requirements (formula) are to walk and be with Him with no sin. The laws are signs, which show us where we are going wrong. They show what we have done to rebel against the One who created us. God gave us these rights and wrongs, and we could not follow them in our actions. As if that was not enough, Jesus taught and said it is just as sinful to simply think of adultery or hate your brother. Even if there are no actions behind your thoughts, Jesus said even thinking these things is a sin.

Let's read **1 John 3:1-24**:

¹Behold, what manner of love the Father hath bestowed upon us, that we should be called the sons of God: therefore the world knoweth us not, because it knew him not.

²Beloved, now are we the sons of God, and it doth not yet appear what we shall be: but we know that, when he shall appear, we shall be like him; for we shall see him as he is.

³And every man that hath this hope in him purifieth himself, even as he is pure.

⁴Whosoever committeth sin transgresseth also the law: for sin is the transgression of the law.

⁵And ye know that he was manifested to take away our sins; and in him is no sin.

⁶Whosoever abideth in him sinneth not: whosoever sinneth hath not seen him, neither known him.

⁷Little children, let no man deceive you: he that doeth righteousness is righteous, even as he is righteous.

⁸He that committeth sin is of the devil; for the devil sinneth from the beginning. For this purpose the Son of God was manifested, that he might destroy the works of the devil.

⁹Whosoever is born of God doth not commit sin; for his seed remaineth in him: and he cannot sin, because he is born of God.

¹⁰In this the children of God are manifest, and the children of the devil: whosoever doeth not righteousness is not of God, neither he

that loveth not his brother.

¹¹For this is the message that ye heard from the beginning, that we should love one another.

¹²Not as Cain, who was of that wicked one, and slew his brother. And wherefore slew he him? Because his own works were evil, and his brother's righteous.

¹³Marvel not, my brethren, if the world hate you.

¹⁴We know that we have passed from death unto life, because we love the brethren. He that loveth not his brother abideth in death.

¹⁵Whosoever hateth his brother is a murderer: and ye know that no murderer hath eternal life abiding in him.

¹⁶Hereby perceive we the love of God, because he laid down his life for us: and we ought to lay down our lives for the brethren.

¹⁷But whoso hath this world's good, and seeth his brother have need, and shutteth up his bowels of compassion from him, how dwelleth the love of God in him?

¹⁸My little children, let us not love in word, neither in tongue; but in deed and in truth.

¹⁹And hereby we know that we are of the truth, and shall assure our hearts before him.

²⁰For if our heart condemn us, God is greater than our heart, and knoweth all things.

²¹Beloved, if our heart condemn us not, then have we confidence toward God.

²²And whatsoever we ask, we receive of him, because we keep his

commandments, and do those things that are pleasing in his sight.

²³And this is his commandment, That we should believe on the name of his Son Jesus Christ, and love one another, as he gave us commandment.

²⁴And he that keepeth his commandments dwelleth in him, and he in him. And hereby we know that he abideth in us, by the Spirit which he hath given us.

So why did Jesus go to that level, especially if we couldn't even obey with our actions? The reason is God wants our hearts. Jesus sees the meaning behind the actions, and He requires our hearts. If a man's wife never cheats on him physically, but mentally she has love for another, does it make it okay that she never physically cheated on him? No, the man wants his wife's heart; he wants her to love him, for that is what matters the most.

God showed we can never be perfect in all of our actions. Only His Son, Jesus, fulfilled these requirements. Jesus did fulfill the law with His actions and thoughts. This shows us it is what is in our minds and hearts that needs changing. This is where God is looking. God's measurements are based on the heart of a matter, *why* you are really doing whatever it is you are doing.

The truth says in **Matthew 15:7-20**:

⁷Ye hypocrites, well did Esaias prophesy of you, saying,

⁸This people draweth nigh unto me with their mouth, and honoureth

me with their lips; but their heart is far from me.

⁹But in vain they do worship me, teaching for doctrines the commandments of men.

¹⁰And he called the multitude, and said unto them, Hear, and understand:

¹¹Not that which goeth into the mouth defileth a man; but that which cometh out of the mouth, this defileth a man.

¹²Then came his disciples, and said unto him, Knowest thou that the Pharisees were offended, after they heard this saying?

¹³But he answered and said, Every plant, which my heavenly Father hath not planted, shall be rooted up.

¹⁴Let them alone: they be blind leaders of the blind. And if the blind lead the blind, both shall fall into the ditch.

¹⁵Then answered Peter and said unto him, Declare unto us this parable.

¹⁶And Jesus said, Are ye also yet without understanding?

¹⁷Do not ye yet understand, that whatsoever entereth in at the mouth goeth into the belly, and is cast out into the draught?

¹⁸But those things which proceed out of the mouth come forth from the heart; and they defile the man.

¹⁹For out of the heart proceed evil thoughts, murders, adulteries, fornications, thefts, false witness, blasphemies:

²⁰These are the things which defile a man: but to eat with unwashen hands defileth not a man.

I hope you can now see the truth about the state in which we are born. We are born in a state of sin, and that is the starting point. The truth begins and ends in one Person, and His name is Jesus. Jesus said that not only when you break the law of adultery have you committed a sin, but also when you lust after another in your heart and mind, it is the same. As an example, I may never cheat on my wife physically, but if I were to lust after another in my mind and heart, does that make it better or less serious to my wife? I want my wife to love me, think of me, desire me, not another. If she never physically touched another, but daily thought of being with another and desired to be with another, it is worse because the other has what I need the most: her heart. Jesus sees sin as it is. It is defined as anything that separates you mentally or physically from a perfect Father, who created you. Jesus came for a purpose; He gave His life by His own choice, not because we took it. Read the following passages.

Matthew 26:39

And he went a little farther, and fell on his face, and prayed, saying, O my Father, if it be possible, **let** this **cup pass** from me: nevertheless not as I will, but as thou wilt.

John 10:7-18

[7]Then said Jesus unto them again, Verily, verily, I say unto you, I am the door of the sheep.

[8]All that ever came before me are thieves and robbers: but the sheep

did not hear them.

⁹I am the door: by me if any man enter in, he shall be saved, and shall go in and out, and find pasture.

¹⁰The thief cometh not, but for to steal, and to kill, and to destroy: I am come that they might have life, and that they might have it more abundantly.

¹¹I am the good shepherd: the good shepherd giveth his life for the sheep.

¹²But he that is an hireling, and not the shepherd, whose own the sheep are not, seeth the wolf coming, and leaveth the sheep, and fleeth: and the wolf catcheth them, and scattereth the sheep.

¹³The hireling fleeth, because he is an hireling, and careth not for the sheep.

¹⁴I am the good shepherd, and know my sheep, and am known of mine.

¹⁵As the Father knoweth me, even so know I the Father: and I lay down my life for the sheep.

¹⁶And other sheep I have, which are not of this fold: them also I must bring, and they shall hear my voice; and there shall be one fold, and one shepherd.

¹⁷Therefore doth my Father love me, because I lay down my life, that I might take it again.

¹⁸No man taketh it from me, but I lay it down of myself. I have power to lay it down, and I have power to take it again. This commandment have I received of my Father.

So He gave it up. Even though He said, "If there is any other way, let it not be this way," he also said, "no matter what, I will do as you say, Father." In giving up His very life, He took on all the sin of the world, all the sin that ever was and ever will be, to make the slate clean for us all. This completed the formula back to its original state.

[17]Think not that I am come to destroy the law, or the prophets: I am not come to destroy, but to fulfil.

[18]For verily I say unto you, Till heaven and earth pass, one jot or one tittle shall in no wise pass from the law, till all be fulfilled.

[19]Whosoever therefore shall break one of these least commandments, and shall teach men so, he shall be called the least in the kingdom of heaven: but whosoever shall do and teach them, the same shall be called great in the kingdom of heaven.

Matthew 5:17-19

He did this, and on the third day, He rose, conquering death itself. He conquered death Himself and for us, and now the formula is complete. The Holy Spirit now becomes the truth in your life, the truth you never had before. Whose truth? Only God's truth, and nothing but the truth, so help Himself.

So if I believe and give all that I am over to Christ and receive the Holy Spirit, what do I need to start or stop doing?

Do I stop having fun and just try and be good? What are the definitions of "good" and "bad"?

This is a gigantic problem we have as both unsaved people and saved Christians. We have some idea that if we walk the imaginary good line, then everything is okay, and if we step on the bad, we are in trouble. What makes it worse is people try to place value on themselves and others based on how successfully they or others can walk these two lines. These are the lines our parents and society have defined for us. To make it even worse, we realize it is impossible to stay on the good line all the time, and the bad line is kind of fun sometimes. Why not just say, "There are no lines, and I will make up my own lines; the heck with the rest." The "no lines" sounds pretty good, but make no mistake, there is a line that is to be followed by all. That line is set by God, and it's His line; He made it. It is the line He walks, and if you are to ever be at peace with God or yourself, you must walk on His line. God knows his line is not easy to walk on, but if you follow the formula, it is filled with blessings and peace, happiness and joy. It is filled with strength, honor, and truth. It never bends and never fades. It never compromises. God's line is a line of safety, rest, love, and passion. His line is a light that leads us through all the problems this world can bring, even unto death. We see His line, and we know it seems good, but it looks too far off to obtain and too hard to keep on. I know His line is the one to walk, but I like my line better. Even if I don't have those things, I am comfortable with my line because it is all I know. Herein lies the answer to this question. It is not your job to make God happy; it is not your job to make God's line and then try to walk on it. His line was made before you were born, and it is not on you to perform or meet any expectations. The only requirement God wants from us is this: REST IN HIM. You see, when you rest in Him and have given Him your life, surrendered to His salvation, He begins the work in you to walk His line. You see, it is His job, not yours, to put you on His line.

Philippians 1:6 says, "Being confident of this very thing, that he which hath begun a good work in you will perform it until the day of Jesus Christ."

If we could only continue to remember it was His work that made us, and it was His work that freed us. It is also His works that will raise us from our tombs to everlasting life. As far as doing good or bad, defining either one, when I have received the Holy Spirit upon salvation, it is His job to do this moving forward. The Holy Spirit will then allow me to enjoy walking God's line, and the line is not a burden any longer, but a relief. Is the line still difficult at times? Absolutely, but only because I am trying to walk it in a world that is against me. The flesh desires all the lusts of this world, but the nature, my internal man, has changed. This is done through the work He has done in me through the giving of this Holy Spirit. In the following passage, Paul describes this battle that we, as the truly saved, go through every day.

[14]For we know that the law is spiritual: but I am carnal, sold under sin.

[15]For that which I do I allow not: for what I would, that do I not; but what I hate, that do I.

[16]If then I do that which I would not, I consent unto the law that it is good.

[17]Now then it is no more I that do it, but sin that dwelleth in me.

[18]For I know that in me (that is, in my flesh,) dwelleth no good thing: for to will is present with me; but how to perform that which is good I find not.

[19]For the good that I would I do not: but the evil which I would not, that I do.

[20]Now if I do that I would not, it is no more I that do it, but sin that dwelleth in me.

[21]I find then a law, that, when I would do good, evil is present with me.

[22]For I delight in the law of God after the inward man:

[23]But I see another law in my members, warring against the law of my mind, and bringing me into captivity to the law of sin which is in my members.

[24]O wretched man that I am! Who shall deliver me from the body of this death?

[25]I thank God through Jesus Christ our Lord. So then with the mind I myself serve the law of God; but with the flesh the law of sin.

Romans 7:14-25

So how much truth is enough? Truth is never a bad thing. Yes, it may hurt, but there is no bad amount of truth that can be given. The more truth is given, the more God's light shines. The problem with us is the truth hurts, and we don't want it, even if it may make us better. It's like when a child needs medicine or a shot. The parent knows the medicine or shot will make the child well, and it is necessary. Without it, death may occur. But the child is only focused on the pain of the shot, not the cure to the disease. We are the same; we would rather allow the sin in our lives to kill us from the inside out than take a shot of truth and allow it to heal the deadly disease of sin eating at us every day. We are so worried about the shot we need, we may even go so far as to decide there must be another way besides the doctor and the shot. Maybe there is another way.

This is why there are so many religions and cults in this world. We are looking for a solution other than the shot of truth. However, the truth is what cures us, the truth will make us whole, and the truth will cleanse us. But remember, it is God's, not man's, truth. What we need to do is keep our eyes on God's and no one else's truth. Knowing you are getting truth from God is a great thing! Our problem is we realize man is sinful and untrustworthy, so when people are the ones giving the truth, it is a lot easier not to accept it. We feel judged by others, put down, and beat up on by preachers, leaders, and others. They say they are giving out God's truth when most of what they are saying consists of their own opinions. Let's stop listening to man and start listening to God. How is this going to happen? One way, and one way only, and that is by our opening the Bible and letting godly men and women who love the Lord help us find the one and only real truth. That truth will surely hurt when given, but the medicine will soon take effect, and healing will begin. That is what you are looking for; that is what we are all looking for.

CHAPTER 23

The X Factor

⸺◦◦◦◦⸺

An old saying goes, "Be careful what you ask for because you just might get it." We have heard this line many times, especially when it comes to wishing for things in life, such as a perfect person to be with, a winning lottery ticket, or fame. The reason you have to be careful what you ask for is because many times when we get what we want, it turns out not to be what we wanted at all.

As stated in the chapters before, when you are truly saved and have received salvation from your sins, the truth says the Holy Spirit indwells you. The Holy Spirit takes up shop in your body and becomes your Guide in a new life, one focused not on the things of this world, but on the things to come.

Second Corinthians 5:17 reads, "Therefore if any man be in Christ, he is a new creature: old things are passed away; behold, all things are become new. And First Corinthians 3:16 says, "Know ye not that ye are the temple of God, and that the Spirit of God dwelleth in you."

This Holy Spirit has a job to do in you and through you. No matter who you are or what circumstances you have faced, are facing, or face in the future, the Holy Spirit job is the same for everyone. The job is to teach you the things of God, to show you the love of God, and even to speak to God for you. Eventually, it will stand with you before God and acknowledge your salvation in heaven, as you have acknowledged your salvation here on earth.

Romans 8:26 reads:

Likewise the Spirit also helpeth our infirmities: for we know not what we should pray for as we ought: but the Spirit itself maketh intercession for us with groanings which cannot be uttered.

You see, the Holy Spirit, God, and Jesus are the one Holy Trinity. Before Jesus was born, the Bible says He was with God and was God.

[1]In the beginning was the Word, and the Word was with God, and the Word was God.

[2]The same was in the beginning with God.

[3]All things were made by him; and without him was not any thing made that was made.

[4]In him was life; and the life was the light of men.

[5]And the light shineth in darkness; and the darkness comprehended it not.

[6]There was a man sent from God, whose name was John.

⁷The same came for a witness, to bear witness of the Light, that all men through him might believe.

⁸He was not that Light, but was sent to bear witness of that Light.

⁹That was the true Light, which lighteth every man that cometh into the world.

¹⁰He was in the world, and the world was made by him, and the world knew him not.

¹¹He came unto his own, and his own received him not.

¹²But as many as received him, to them gave he power to become the sons of God, even to them that believe on his name:

¹³Which were born, not of blood, nor of the will of the flesh, nor of the will of man, but of God.

¹⁴And the Word was made flesh, and dwelt among us, (and we beheld his glory, the glory as of the only begotten of the Father,) full of grace and truth.

John 1:1-14

Note: The Word of God is the power in all things. When God created the universe and the earth, He did what? He spoke them into existence: "Let there be light . . ., let there be land . . . ."

¹In the beginning God created the heaven and the earth.

²And the earth was without form, and void; and darkness was upon the face of the deep. And the Spirit of God moved upon the face of the waters.

³And God said, Let there be light: and there was light.

Genesis 1:1-3

Jesus was that word before He was ever born. You might think, *How could anything be spoken and then take on a form of its own?* Oh, I don't know, is there anything we could compare this to in our own world? Let's see, maybe ultrasounds. Have you seen the new ultrasound machines that show 4-D images of a baby before he or she is born? The machine and the software are man-made, but the images are formed by sound waves bouncing off the body to produce a form. If we can produce something with sound, just imagine what God can do.

Moving on to Jesus, in His life, He spoke of having to leave so He could send the Comforter. This is the Holy Spirit, sent to change all of mankind, not just the few He encountered in his thirty or so years on earth. God's purpose was to send Jesus to show us three essential things. The first was that He loves us, His creation, you and me, so much that He would sacrifice His only Son, Himself in flesh, so that we could be together one day. The second was that the truth incarnate, His truth, is the opposite of the world's truth. Lastly, Jesus was sent to show us He knows what it is like to be a man, and to endure the trials and tribulations this life brings. We talk about the first two all the time, but let's think about the third one. God knows what it is like to suffer, to have no home, to be hungry, to be broke, to be tempted, to be ridiculed, to be tortured, to be shamed, and finally, to be killed as an innocent Man. So what will you say at judgment? What you will *not* say is that you had it worse than He did, that He did not put on your shoes and walk in your path. God has seen our predicament, and He sees the end result, which is an eternity with Him in peace. For now, we are here suffering, but He said, "I will not leave you stranded, but I will send a Helper, a Comforter."

Let's take a look at **John 14:12-31.**

[12]Verily, verily, I say unto you, He that believeth on me, the works that I do shall he do also; and greater works than these shall he do; because I go unto my Father.

[13]And whatsoever ye shall ask in my name, that will I do, that the Father may be glorified in the Son.

[14]If ye shall ask any thing in my name, I will do it.

[15]If ye love me, keep my commandments.

[16]And I will pray the Father, and he shall give you another Comforter, that he may abide with you for ever;

[17]Even the Spirit of truth; whom the world cannot receive, because it seeth him not, neither knoweth him: but ye know him; for he dwelleth with you, and shall be in you.

[18]I will not leave you comfortless: I will come to you.

[19]Yet a little while, and the world seeth me no more; but ye see me: because I live, ye shall live also.

[20]At that day ye shall know that I am in my Father, and ye in me, and I in you.

²¹He that hath my commandments, and keepeth them, he it is that loveth me: and he that loveth me shall be loved of my Father, and I will love him, and will manifest myself to him.

²²Judas saith unto him, not Iscariot, Lord, how is it that thou wilt manifest thyself unto us, and not unto the world?

²³Jesus answered and said unto him, If a man love me, he will keep my words: and my Father will love him, and we will come unto him, and make our abode with him.

²⁴He that loveth me not keepeth not my sayings: and the word which ye hear is not mine, but the Father's which sent me.

²⁵These things have I spoken unto you, being yet present with you.

²⁶But the Comforter, which is the Holy Ghost, whom the Father will send in my name, he shall teach you all things, and bring all things to your remembrance, whatsoever I have said unto you.

²⁷Peace I leave with you, my peace I give unto you: not as the world giveth, give I unto you. Let not your heart be troubled, neither let it be afraid.

²⁸Ye have heard how I said unto you, I go away, and come again unto you. If ye loved me, ye would rejoice, because I said, I go unto the Father: for my Father is greater than I.

²⁹And now I have told you before it come to pass, that, when it is come to pass, ye might believe.

³⁰Hereafter I will not talk much with you: for the prince of this world cometh, and hath nothing in me.

³¹But that the world may know that I love the Father; and as the

Father gave me commandment, even so I do. Arise, let us go hence.

The Holy Spirit came and indwelt man, and now man not only has the ability to communicate with God directly, but also has the power of God through two things: God's Word and the faith that His word is true.

First, let's look at faith.

[1]Now faith is the substance of things hoped for, the evidence of things not seen.

[2]For by it the elders obtained a good report.

[3]Through faith we understand that the worlds were framed by the word of God, so that things which are seen were not made of things which do appear.

[4]By faith Abel offered unto God a more excellent sacrifice than Cain, by which he obtained witness that he was righteous, God testifying of his gifts: and by it he being dead yet speaketh.

[5]By faith Enoch was translated that he should not see death; and was not found, because God had translated him: for before his translation he had this testimony, that he pleased God.

[6]But without faith it is impossible to please him: for he that cometh to God must believe that he is, and that he is a rewarder of them that diligently seek him.

[7]By faith Noah, being warned of God of things not seen as yet, moved with fear, prepared an ark to the saving of his house; by the

which he condemned the world, and became heir of the righteousness which is by faith.

[8]By faith Abraham, when he was called to go out into a place which he should after receive for an inheritance, obeyed; and he went out, not knowing whither he went.

[9]By faith he sojourned in the land of promise, as in a strange country, dwelling in tabernacles with Isaac and Jacob, the heirs with him of the same promise:

[10]For he looked for a city which hath foundations, whose builder and maker is God.

[11]Through faith also Sara herself received strength to conceive seed, and was delivered of a child when she was past age, because she judged him faithful who had promised.

[12]Therefore sprang there even of one, and him as good as dead, so many as the stars of the sky in multitude, and as the sand which is by the sea shore innumerable.

[13]These all died in faith, not having received the promises, but having seen them afar off, and were persuaded of them, and embraced them, and confessed that they were strangers and pilgrims on the earth.

[14]For they that say such things declare plainly that they seek a country.

[15]And truly, if they had been mindful of that country from whence they came out, they might have had opportunity to have returned.

[16]But now they desire a better country, that is, an heavenly: wherefore God is not ashamed to be called their God: for he hath prepared

for them a city.

¹⁷By faith Abraham, when he was tried, offered up Isaac: and he that had received the promises offered up his only begotten son,

¹⁸of whom it was said, That in Isaac shall thy seed be called:

¹⁹Accounting that God was able to raise him up, even from the dead; from whence also he received him in a figure.

²⁰By faith Isaac blessed Jacob and Esau concerning things to come.

²¹By faith Jacob, when he was a dying, blessed both the sons of Joseph; and worshipped, leaning upon the top of his staff.

²²By faith Joseph, when he died, made mention of the departing of the children of Israel; and gave commandment concerning his bones.

²³By faith Moses, when he was born, was hid three months of his parents, because they saw he was a proper child; and they were not afraid of the king's commandment.

²⁴By faith Moses, when he was come to years, refused to be called the son of Pharaoh's daughter;

²⁵Choosing rather to suffer affliction with the people of God, than to enjoy the pleasures of sin for a season;

²⁶Esteeming the reproach of Christ greater riches than the treasures in Egypt: for he had respect unto the recompence of the reward.

²⁷By faith he forsook Egypt, not fearing the wrath of the king: for he endured, as seeing him who is invisible.

²⁸Through faith he kept the passover, and the sprinkling of blood, lest he that destroyed the firstborn should touch them.

²⁹By faith they passed through the Red sea as by dry land: which the

Egyptians assaying to do were drowned.

[30]By faith the walls of Jericho fell down, after they were compassed about seven days.

[31]By faith the harlot Rahab perished not with them that believed not, when she had received the spies with peace.

[32]And what shall I more say? for the time would fail me to tell of Gedeon, and of Barak, and of Samson, and of Jephthae; of David also, and Samuel, and of the prophets:

[33]Who through faith subdued kingdoms, wrought righteousness, obtained promises, stopped the mouths of lions.

[34]Quenched the violence of fire, escaped the edge of the sword, out of weakness were made strong, waxed valiant in fight, turned to flight the armies of the aliens.

[35]Women received their dead raised to life again: and others were tortured, not accepting deliverance; that they might obtain a better resurrection:

[36]And others had trial of cruel mockings and scourgings, yea, moreover of bonds and imprisonment:

[37]They were stoned, they were sawn asunder, were tempted, were slain with the sword: they wandered about in sheepskins and goatskins; being destitute, afflicted, tormented;

[38](Of whom the world was not worthy:) they wandered in deserts, and in mountains, and in dens and caves of the earth.

[39]And these all, having obtained a good report through faith, received not the promise:

[40]God having provided some better thing for us, that they without us should not be made perfect.

Hebrews 11:1-40

By faith all things can be done because faith is the X factor in God's formula.

Man also has power through the Word of God. As we said, Jesus is the Word made flesh. God created the world by His word. God gave us His Word not just to read and study, but to live in us, to be placed in our hearts and minds, so that no man can steal it. God gave us His Word to be used and to protect us as we live here on this earth of desolation. When you need God, when you're looking for healing and protection, when you are weak and weary, His Word is your strength, the power to bring these things to reality for you. Let's read what the truth says:

Luke 4:1-13

[1]And Jesus being full of the Holy Ghost returned from Jordan, and was led by the Spirit into the wilderness,

[2]being forty days tempted of the devil. And in those days he did eat nothing: and when they were ended, he afterward hungered.

[3]And the devil said unto him, If thou be the Son of God, command this stone that it be made bread.

[4]And Jesus answered him, saying, It is written, That man shall not live by bread alone, but by every word of God.

[5]And the devil, taking him up into an high mountain, shewed unto him all the kingdoms of the world in a moment of time.

[6]And the devil said unto him, All this power will I give thee, and the glory of them: for that is delivered unto me; and to whomsoever I will I give it.

[7]If thou therefore wilt worship me, all shall be thine.

[8]And Jesus answered and said unto him, Get thee behind me, Satan: for it is written, Thou shalt worship the Lord thy God, and him only shalt thou serve.

[9]And he brought him to Jerusalem, and set him on a pinnacle of the temple, and said unto him, If thou be the Son of God, cast thyself down from hence:

[10]For it is written, He shall give his angels charge over thee, to keep thee:

[11]And in their hands they shall bear thee up, lest at any time thou dash thy foot against a stone.

[12]And Jesus answering said unto him, It is said, Thou shalt not tempt the Lord thy God.

[13]And when the devil had ended all the temptation, he departed from him for a season.

Note: Jesus only used the Word of God against Satan.

James 4:1-10

[1]From whence come wars and fightings among you? Come they not

hence, even of your lusts that war in your members?

²Ye lust, and have not: ye kill, and desire to have, and cannot obtain: ye fight and war, yet ye have not, because ye ask not.

³Ye ask, and receive not, because ye ask amiss, that ye may consume it upon your lusts.

⁴Ye adulterers and adulteresses, know ye not that the friendship of the world is enmity with God? Whosoever therefore will be a friend of the world is the enemy of God.

⁵Do ye think that the scripture saith in vain, The spirit that dwelleth in us lusteth to envy?

⁶But he giveth more grace. Wherefore he saith, God resisteth the proud, but giveth grace unto the humble.

⁷Submit yourselves therefore to God. Resist the devil, and he will flee from you.

⁸Draw nigh to God, and he will draw nigh to you. Cleanse your hands, ye sinners; and purify your hearts, ye double minded.

⁹Be afflicted, and mourn, and weep: let your laughter be turned to mourning, and your joy to heaviness.

¹⁰Humble yourselves in the sight of the Lord, and he shall lift you up.

Revelation 19:14-17

¹⁴And the armies which were in heaven followed him upon white horses, clothed in fine linen, white and clean.

¹⁵And out of his mouth goeth a sharp sword, that with it he should smite the nations: and he shall rule them with a rod of iron: and he

treadeth the winepress of the fierceness and wrath of Almighty God. [16]And he hath on his vesture and on his thigh a name written, KING OF KINGS, AND LORD OF LORDS.

[17]And I saw an angel standing in the sun; and he cried with a loud voice, saying to all the fowls that fly in the midst of heaven, Come and gather yourselves together unto the supper of the great God.

It is the Word that we must use to help us. So start speaking these words when you are facing trials in this life. Read the Scriptures, not to tempt God to do your every whim, but to be with Him as one. God gave us His Word for a reason, to be used as a resource for our protection as well as our needs.

Since we are talking about my needs, I need a lot; I want a lot. Will this Holy Spirit, this X factor, give me whatever I want? The Word says if you ask anything in His name, He will give it to you.

Since I was a little boy, there was something that told me money was the key to making things happen in this world. Money could bring me happiness, peace, power, health, friends, confidence, and nice things. To tell the truth, in this world, money does a pretty good job at being god. In fact, money is the closet thing to God that you can have without God. In this world, if I have money, I can get the best health care, the best houses, and nice cars. I can have the finest clothes, and I can even alter my appearance if I have enough money. It will give me power over others and confidence to meet my goals. Money can buy me comfort and happiness. So if I have money, why do I need God? Let's look at this story:

[18]And a certain ruler asked him, saying, Good Master, what shall I do to inherit eternal life?

[19]And Jesus said unto him, Why callest thou me good? None is good, save one, that is, God.

[20]Thou knowest the commandments, Do not commit adultery, Do not kill, Do not steal, Do not bear false witness, Honour thy father and thy mother.

[21]And he said, All these have I kept from my youth up.

[22]Now when Jesus heard these things, he said unto him, Yet lackest thou one thing: sell all that thou hast, and distribute unto the poor, and thou shalt have treasure in heaven: and come, follow me.

[23]And when he heard this, he was very sorrowful: for he was very rich.

Luke 18:18-23

The god of this world is money, but this money has a problem. While it may replicate many godly things, it can never do what God can do. God has eternal value, whereas money is only an empty source. It is only as good as how much is available. Money runs out, but God doesn't.

When you choose God over money, He gives you life after death. He gives you true peace, not Novocain peace. He loves you, and we all know money can't buy that. He can cure cancer; money can't do that either. He gives you value as His child, and money can't buy value; it can only give you acceptance. God gives you a peace that only He can give. Ask Tiger Woods, Oscar De La Hoya, or Bill Gates if their money brings them peace in their lives. Money is only as good as how it is being used in your life, how it is being used in others' lives. It is only righteous if it is being used for God's purpose, not our own.

I have heard all my life that God will give you what you ask if it is in His name. Let's look at some other verses about giving.

John 14:13

And whatsoever ye shall ask in my name, that will I do, that the Father may be glorified in the Son.

Luke 11:9

And I say unto you, Ask, and it shall be given you; seek, and ye shall find; knock, and it shall be opened unto you.

God is the ultimate Gift Giver, and His Word says He will give you whatever you ask. We do need to be clear on this: You must first be His child before you can use this part of the formula, as these are promises to the saved of God, not the unsaved. These are promises to the ones with the Holy Spirit, the ones who accepted Christ. God has saved this for His children, not the children of wrath. So if you're truly saved, and you want something from God, He says He will give it to you. But be careful what you ask for because you will get it. Notice one thing, though: God never promised *when* you will get it, just that He will give it to you. That changes things a bit from our perspective. God is letting us know that all the things we dream of and desire are not bad things. He wants us to know He gives wonderful gifts to His children, even greater gifts than those for which we are asking. Don't limit your requests, but don't put Him on your timetable, either.

The following verses shed more light.

[7]Ask, and it shall be given you; seek, and ye shall find; knock, and it shall be opened unto you:

[8]For every one that asketh receiveth; and he that seeketh findeth; and to him that knocketh it shall be opened.

[9]Or what man is there of you, whom if his son ask bread, will he give him a stone?

[10]Or if he ask a fish, will he give him a serpent?

[11]If ye then, being evil, know how to give good gifts unto your children, how much more shall your Father which is in heaven give good things to them that ask him?

Matthew 7:7-11

[9]But as it is written, Eye hath not seen, nor ear heard, neither have entered into the heart of man, the things which God hath prepared for them that love him.

¹⁰But God hath revealed them unto us by his Spirit: for the Spirit searcheth all things, yea, the deep things of God.

¹¹For what man knoweth the things of a man, save the spirit of man which is in him? Even so the things of God knoweth no man, but the Spirit of God.

¹²Now we have received, not the spirit of the world, but the spirit which is of God; that we might know the things that are freely given to us of God.

¹³Which things also we speak, not in the words which man's wisdom teacheth, but which the Holy Ghost teacheth; comparing spiritual things with spiritual.

¹⁴But the natural man receiveth not the things of the Spirit of God: for they are foolishness unto him: neither can he know them, because they are spiritually discerned.

¹⁵But he that is spiritual judgeth all things, yet he himself is judged of no man.

¹⁶For who hath known the mind of the Lord, that he may instruct him? But we have the mind of Christ.

1 Corinthians 2

Nowhere in the Bible does God say, "I will give you what you request when you want it." It is only stated that He will give it.

My child may want a car at the age of ten, I want to help him get a car, but I will not put him or the world at danger by giving him a car at that age. When asking God for things, you can be specific, but also let it be God's will and not your own. Anyway, His plans and gifts are better than anything you could dream up.

Lastly, understand the Holy Spirit that is in you. You need to recognize who He is and what He means in your life. The Holy Spirit is just as important as Jesus and God, not to mention they are one and the same. Even being one, though, you should acknowledge the power the Holy Spirit has. Recognize the use of it during your life here on earth.

The Spirit is in us for many reasons. One main reason is to change our nature. Before I was saved, I loved my sin, I made excuses for what I did, and I desired my sins more than anything else. I loved smoking and doing drugs, I loved sleeping around, and I looked for ways to have sinful fun. I also loved the fact that so many others joined me. I had decided that was what life was about, having fun and living for my flesh. I realize this was all just a way of escaping, a way of getting away from the truth with which I didn't want to deal. But the truth was I didn't like what all of this sin was doing to me or my friends—the deaths, the addictions, the pain it was causing to those who loved me the most. I just wanted to escape the truth and hide out in the world. As I had some money, some drugs, and parties, life was bearable.

Let's look at this Katy Perry's song "Last Friday Night":

It talks about a stranger in my bed, and a pounding in her head
It says there is Glitter all over the room, and Pink flamingos in the

pool

she smells like a minibar, someone is passed out in the yard

She is trying to see if she has a a hickie or a bruise

Pictures of the night, Ended up online

She says she is screwed, Oh well, It's just a black top blur, But I'm

pretty sure it ruled and I had a great time.

Last Friday night, they all danced on tabletops, And took too many

shots, Think she kissed someonw but forgot,

Shemaxed our credit cards, And got kicked out of the bar

She says she hit the boulevard, and went streaking in the park

She went Skinny dipping in the dark, Then had a menage a trois

she thinks she broke the law. She says they Always say we're gonna

stop, but they do it all again.

To a teenager, and sadly enough, even some adults, this is what life is about, being carefree with our sin and looking for ways to exercise these addictions that bring us self-fulfillment and ways of escape from reality.

I wonder why Katy doesn't put the results of this night in her song—the going to jail for breaking the law, the online pictures that will embarrass those who really love her. How about the pregnancy from the one or two guys she slept with? Where is that in the song? I understand why it's not there; it's kind of a downer, and I agree. What do we do, though? We, especially our young people, hear that song, and we turn it up because we like the beat. She sings great, and we want to be free of the day we had. We want to be free of our bosses and crappy lives, and this is the only freedom we can find. For a while, it helps, but like she said, when the credit card is maxed out and the money goes away, so do the friends and the parties. Let's not forget how ridiculous a forty-year-old looks at a twenty-five-year-olds party trying to act like this. My point is there is another way to be free, a way to enjoy your life without wasting it. Find this freedom in giving your life to Christ, receive the Holy Spirit, and know His freedom leads to success. His freedom is not boring; it is passionate. His freedom doesn't break any laws, but instead his freedom fulfills them.

The Story of B.C.

I did love all those things, and I would have done, and did do, anything I could to live that lifestyle. The funny thing is if that lifestyle would have kept me happy, I would still be living it today. It didn't, just like it doesn't keep you happy. That lifestyle is like Chinese food—it tastes great, and we love to eat it, but you never get full, and not too long afterward, you're looking for something else. The reason I loved the things of the world and of Satan was because that was my nature. I was a good person compared to most, and I loved my family and wanted love from others, but what I really wanted was peace, a peace I could not have, so I settled for escaping. My nature cried out for all those things, for that was the only peace I could find.

When I finally gave up this fight, I was in a hotel room by myself, and I begged Christ into my life. I didn't know the Bible, only that somebody told me if I asked Jesus into my heart, He would come and give me peace. I remember that one moment in time when I got up, and then laid my head on the pillow, and for the first time in my life, there it was—peace. Peace came, and when it came, I took it, and when I took it, I accepted it, and when I accepted it, I wanted to tell others what He had done for me so they could have it to. That is what happens when you find true peace; you want to share it with someone. You want to see others get it, and most of all you want to live in it. What I didn't know at the time was that when I received that peace, my nature changed. I still had sinful desires because I had lived that way for so long, and my flesh called out for it still. The kicker was that the peace that came to me changed my nature. I didn't love that lifestyle any longer. All I seemed to love were the things of the Spirit.

I love that peace that is the Holy Spirit, able to come through Christ, and His giving His life for ours. Why did He give His life? Because it was His Father's will to give it. That Father is God, the One who created us all and loves us all.

The End

To end on the truth, I would like to state the final truth: We are the ones who have always changed, not God. We want the truth to adapt to us and our way of life, but instead, what we must realize is we must adapt to the truth, and that is the Word of God.

Read Daniel 12:1-2.

[1]And at that time shall Michael stand up, the great prince which standeth for the children of thy people: and there shall be a time of trouble, such as never was since there was a nation even to that same time: and at that time thy people shall be delivered, every one that shall be found written in the book.

[2]And many of them that sleep in the dust of the earth shall awake, some to everlasting life, and some to shame and everlasting contempt.

Some people will denounce this book and go back to their own opinions based on themselves. The truth will always remain the truth, no matter how much we change or how much we would like to change GOD. He will forever be wonderfully unchangeable!

For all that **is** in the world, the lust of the flesh, and the lust of the eyes, and the pride of **life**, **is** not of the Father, but **is** of the world.

1 John 2:16